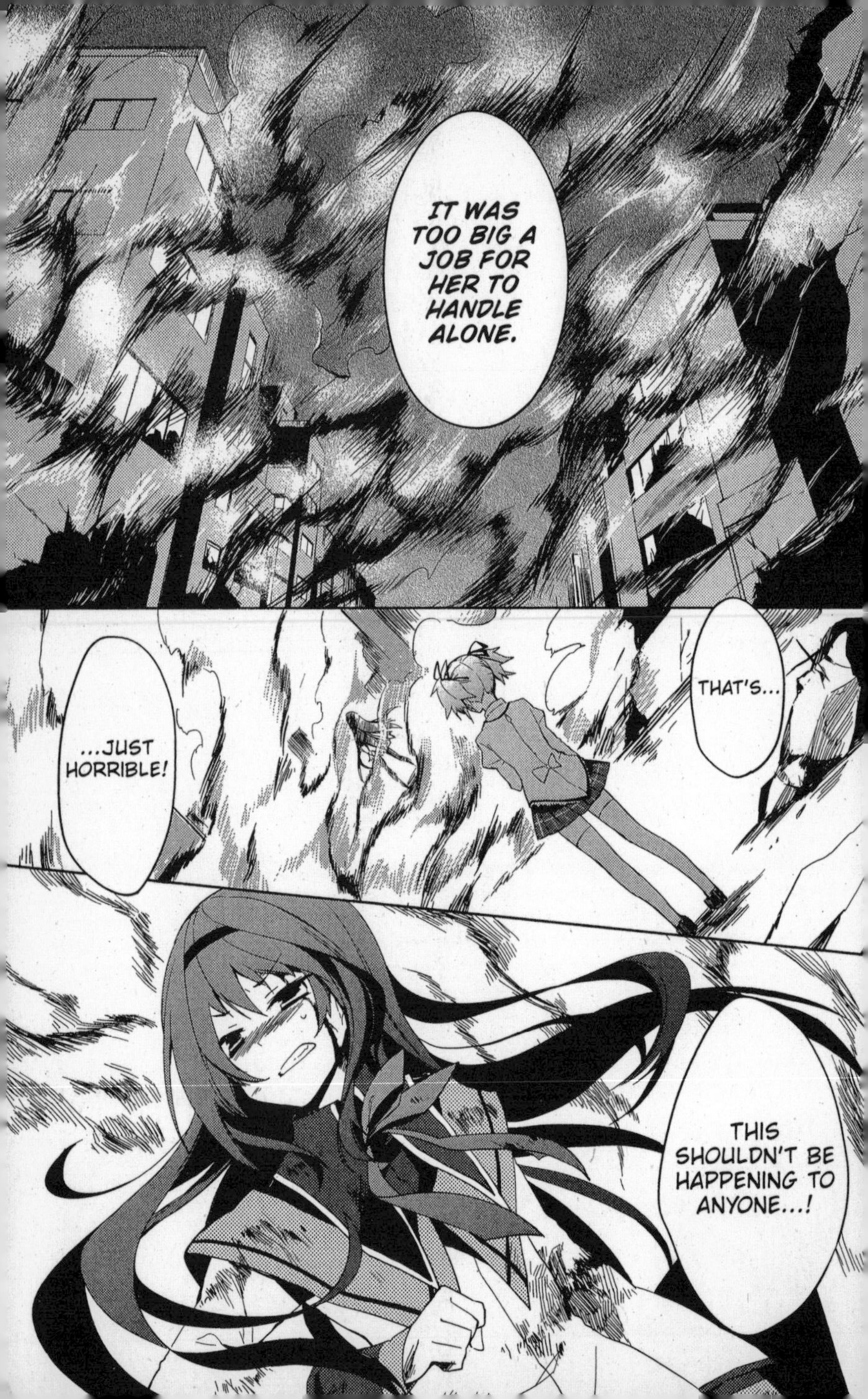
IT WAS TOO BIG A JOB FOR HER TO HANDLE ALONE.
THAT'S...
...JUST HORRIBLE!
THIS SHOULDN'T BE HAPPENING TO ANYONE...!

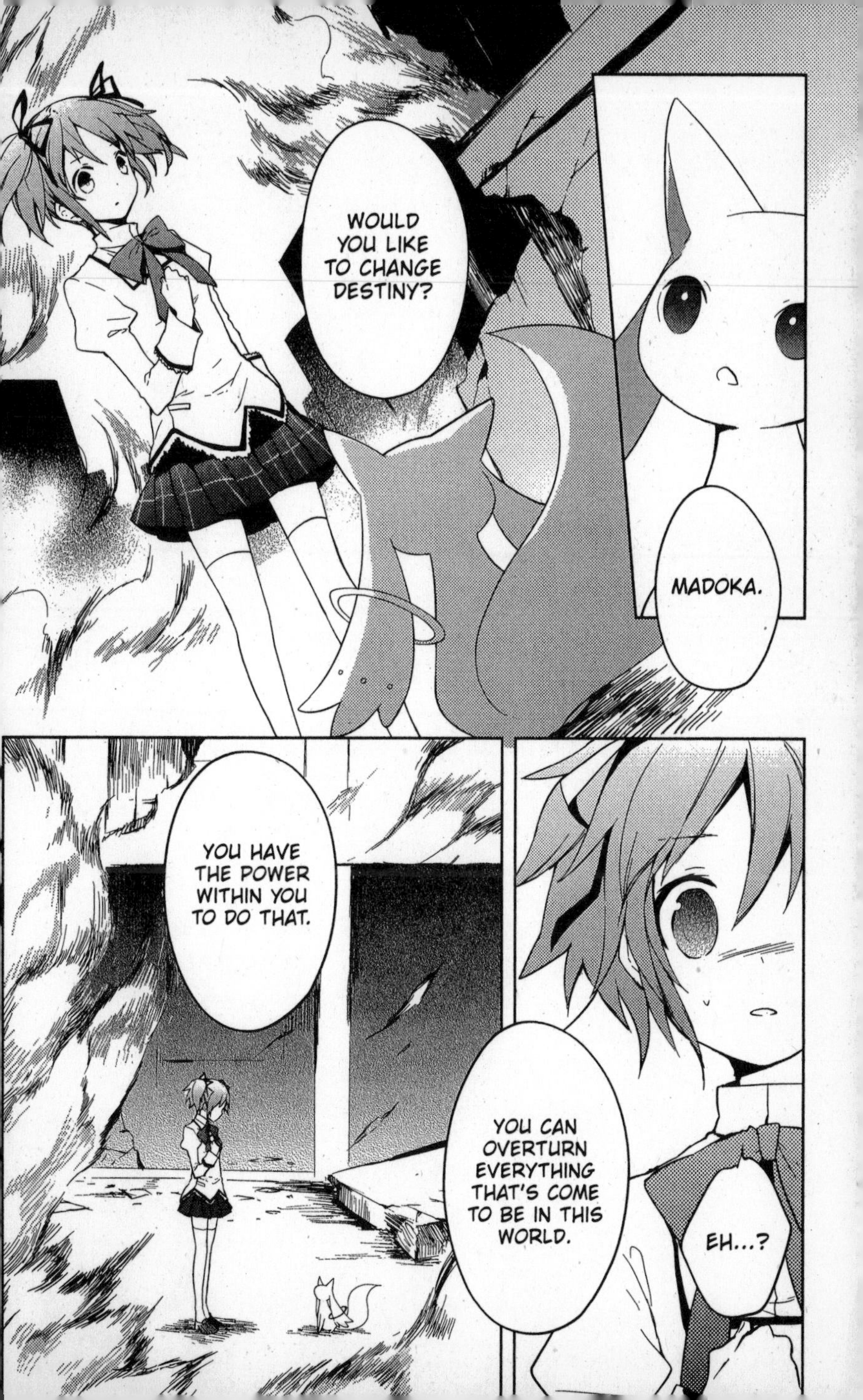
MADOKA.
WOULD YOU LIKE TO CHANGE DESTINY?
EH...?
YOU CAN OVERTURN EVERYTHING THAT'S COME TO BE IN THIS WORLD.
YOU HAVE THE POWER WITHIN YOU TO DO THAT.

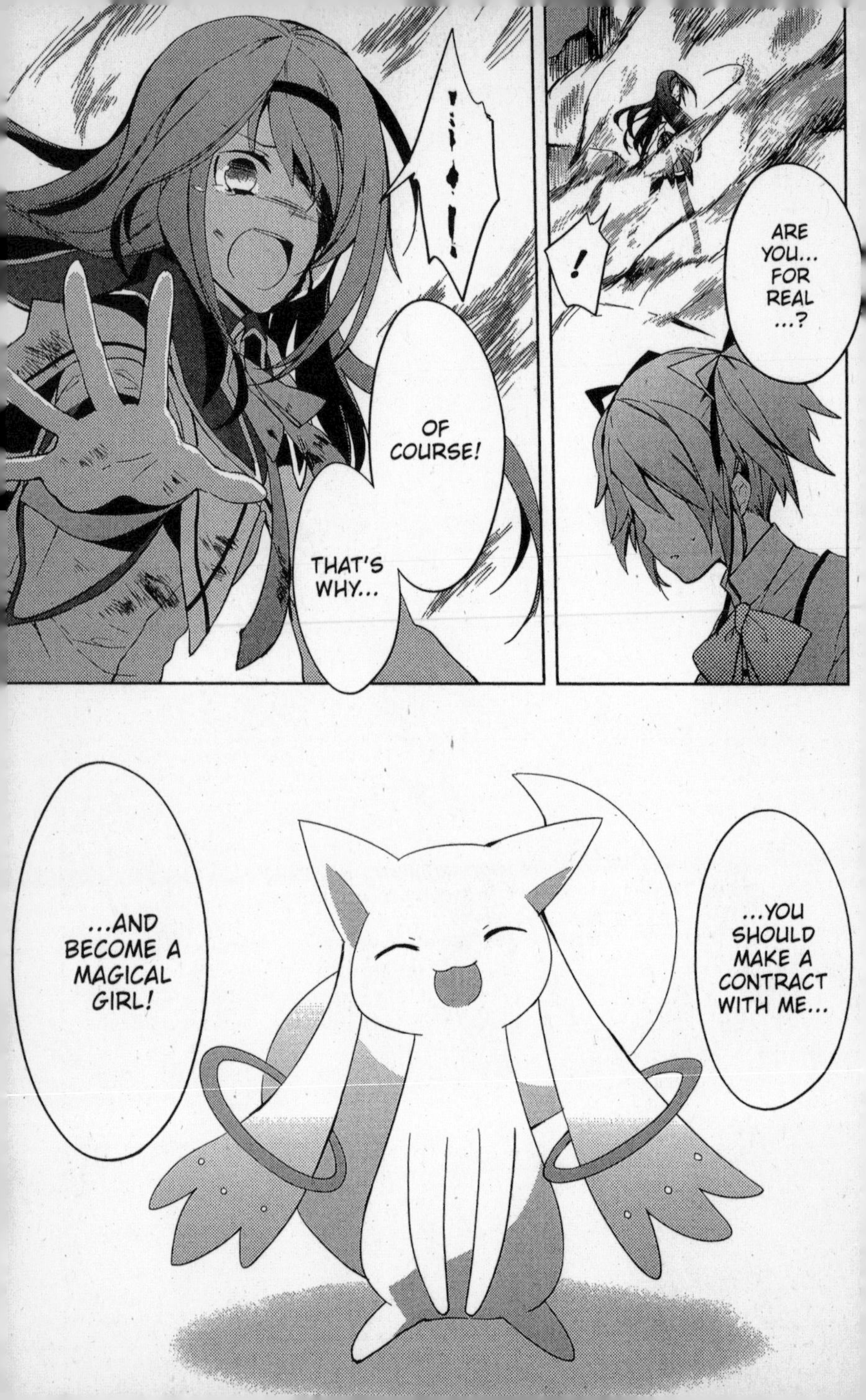
!
ARE YOU... FOR REAL ...?
OF COURSE!
THAT'S WHY...
...YOU SHOULD MAKE A CONTRACT WITH ME...
...AND BECOME A MAGICAL GIRL!

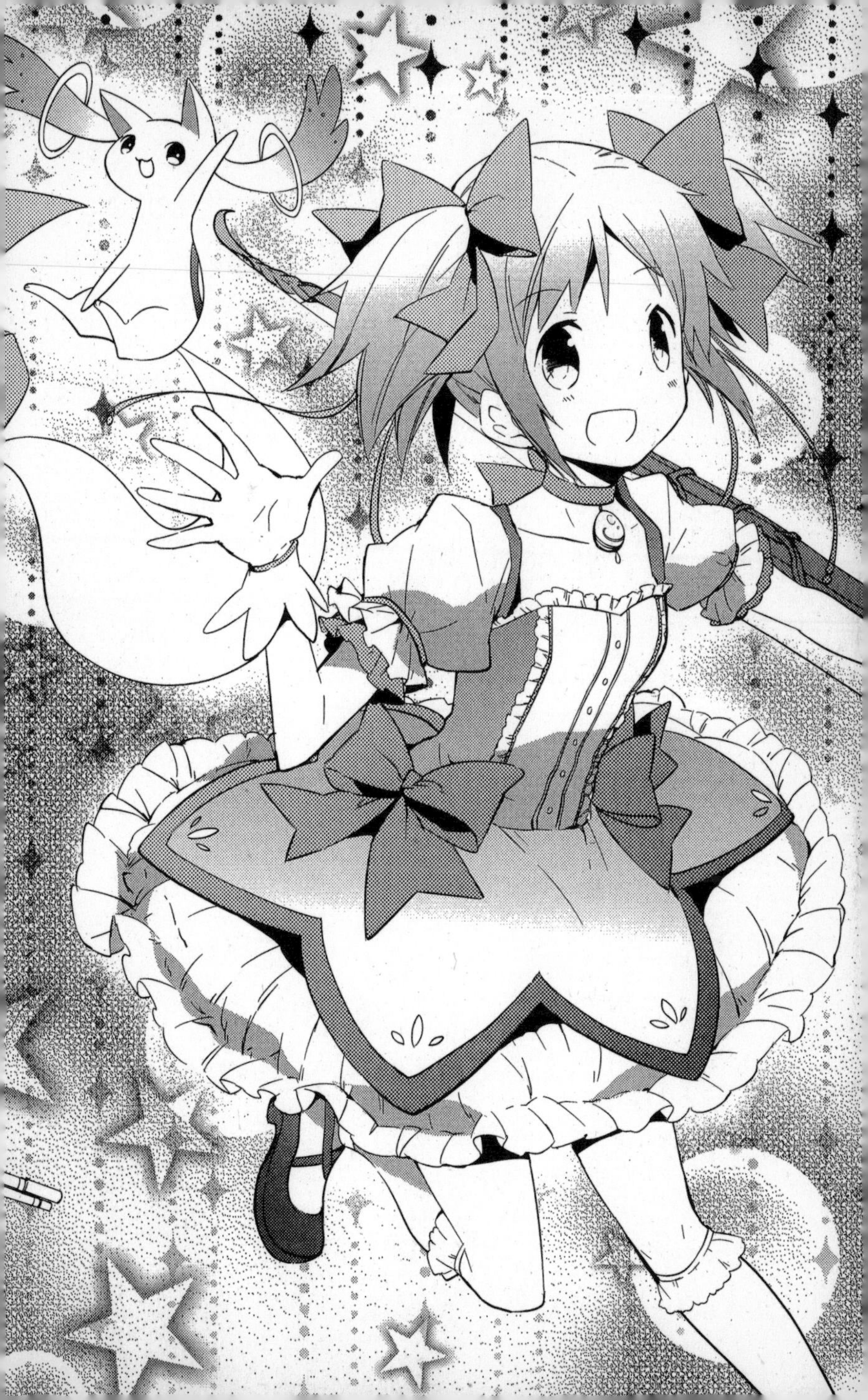

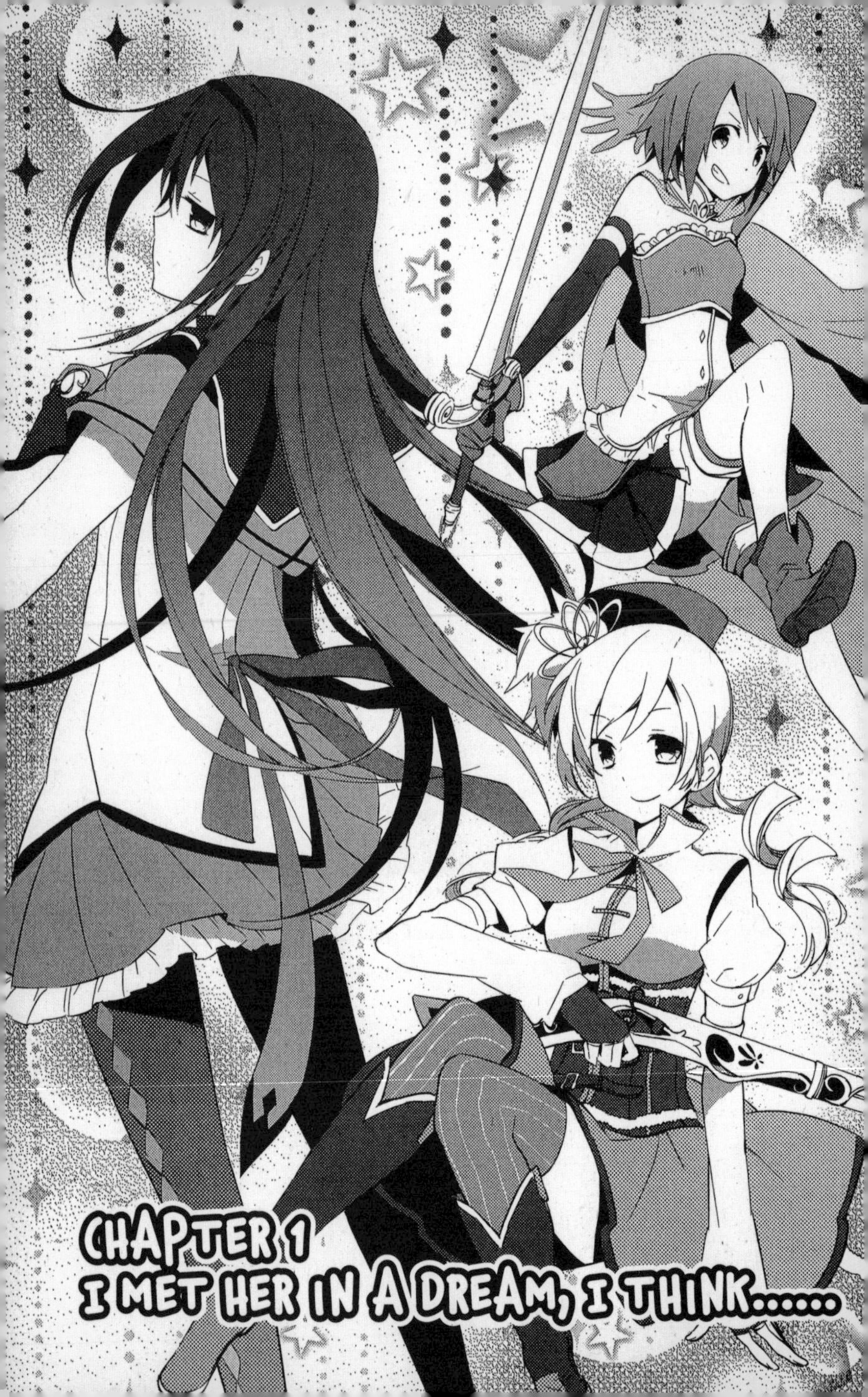
CHAPTER 1
I MET HER IN A DREAM, I THINK......

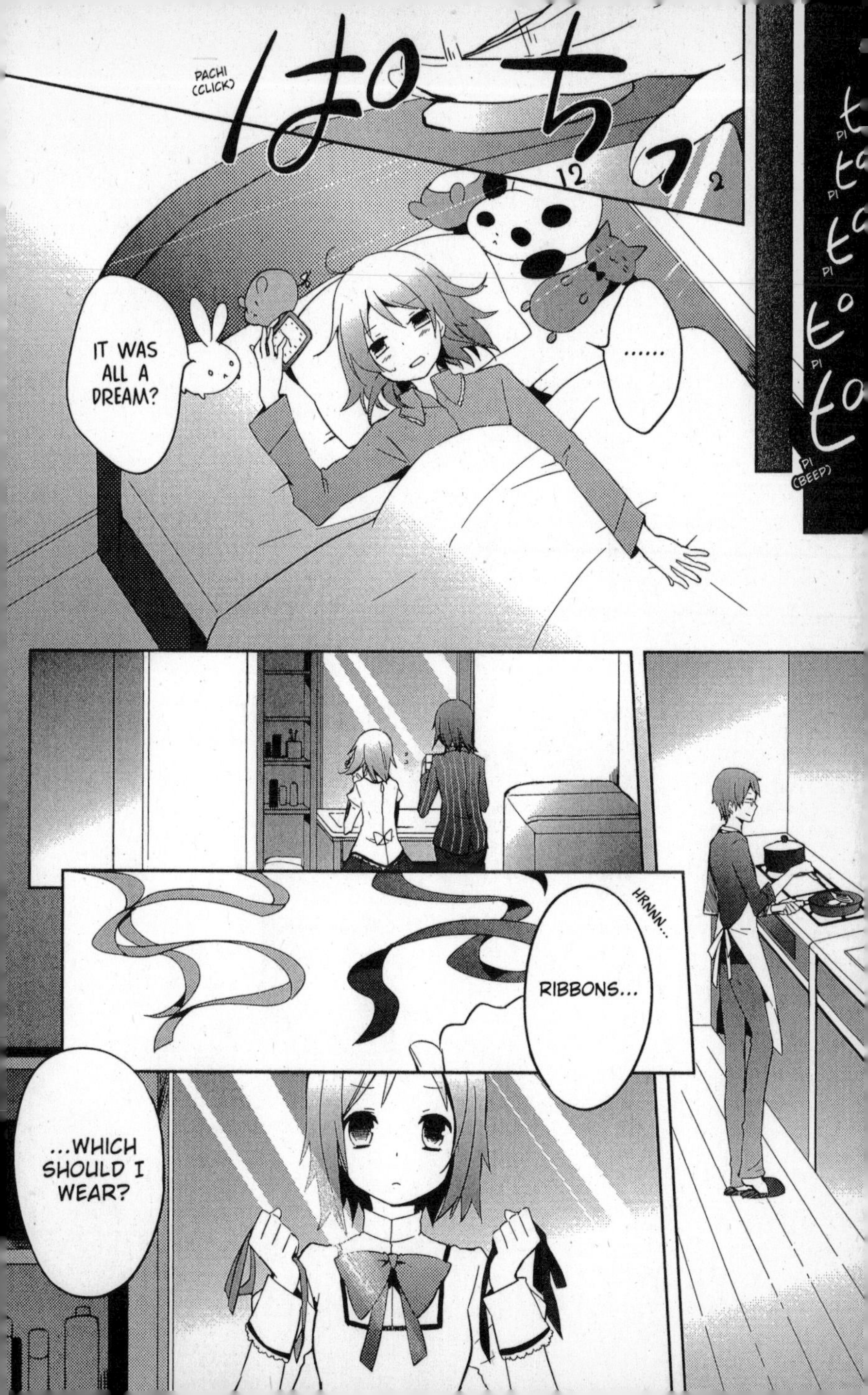
PI PI PI PI PI (BEEP)
PACHI (CLICK)
......
IT WAS ALL A DREAM?
HRNNN...
RIBBONS...
...WHICH SHOULD I WEAR?

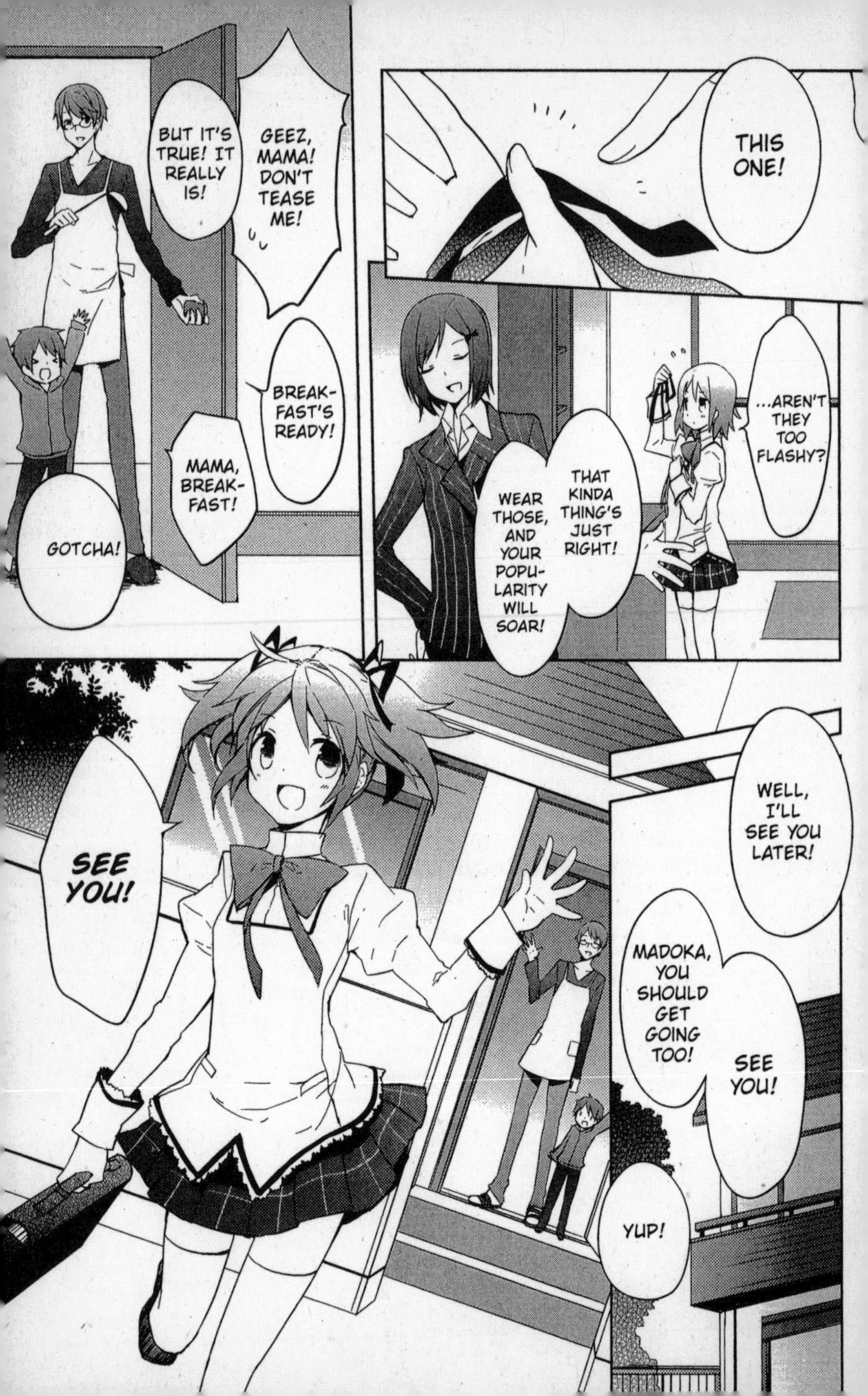
THIS ONE!
...AREN'T THEY TOO FLASHY?
THAT KINDA THING'S JUST RIGHT!
WEAR THOSE, AND YOUR POPULARITY WILL SOAR!
GEEZ, MAMA! DON'T TEASE ME!
BUT IT'S TRUE! IT REALLY IS!
BREAKFAST'S READY!
MAMA, BREAKFAST!
GOTCHA!
WELL, I'LL SEE YOU LATER!
MADOKA, YOU SHOULD GET GOING TOO!
SEE YOU!
YUP!
SEE YOU!

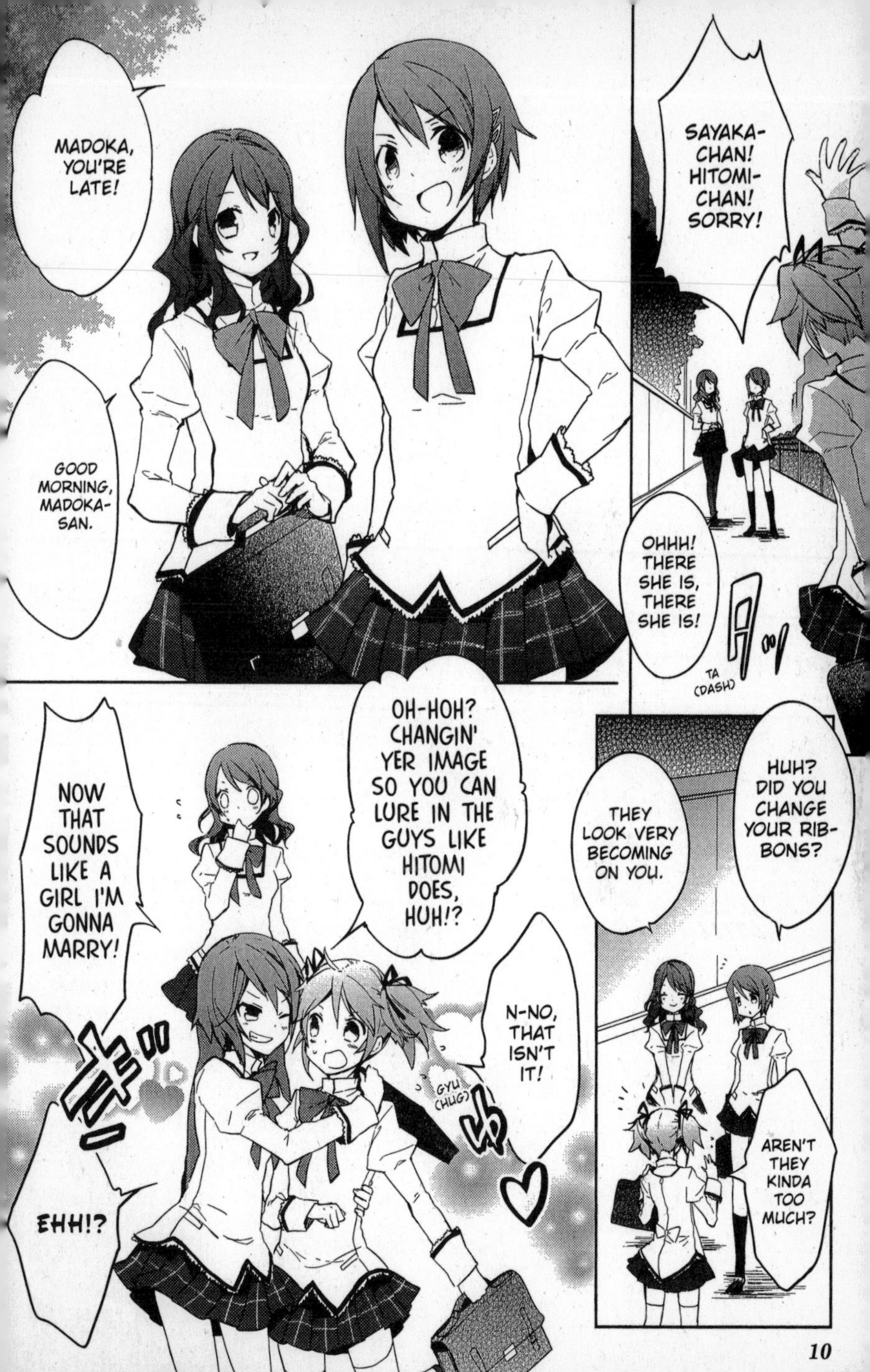

SAYAKA-CHAN! HITOMI-CHAN! SORRY!
OHHH! THERE SHE IS, THERE SHE IS!
TA (DASH)
MADOKA, YOU'RE LATE!
GOOD MORNING, MADOKA-SAN.
HUH? DID YOU CHANGE YOUR RIB-BONS?
THEY LOOK VERY BECOMING ON YOU.
AREN'T THEY KINDA TOO MUCH?
OH-HOH? CHANGIN' YER IMAGE SO YOU CAN LURE IN THE GUYS LIKE HITOMI DOES, HUH!?
NOW THAT SOUNDS LIKE A GIRL I'M GONNA MARRY!
N-NO, THAT ISN'T IT!
GYU (HUG)
EHH!?

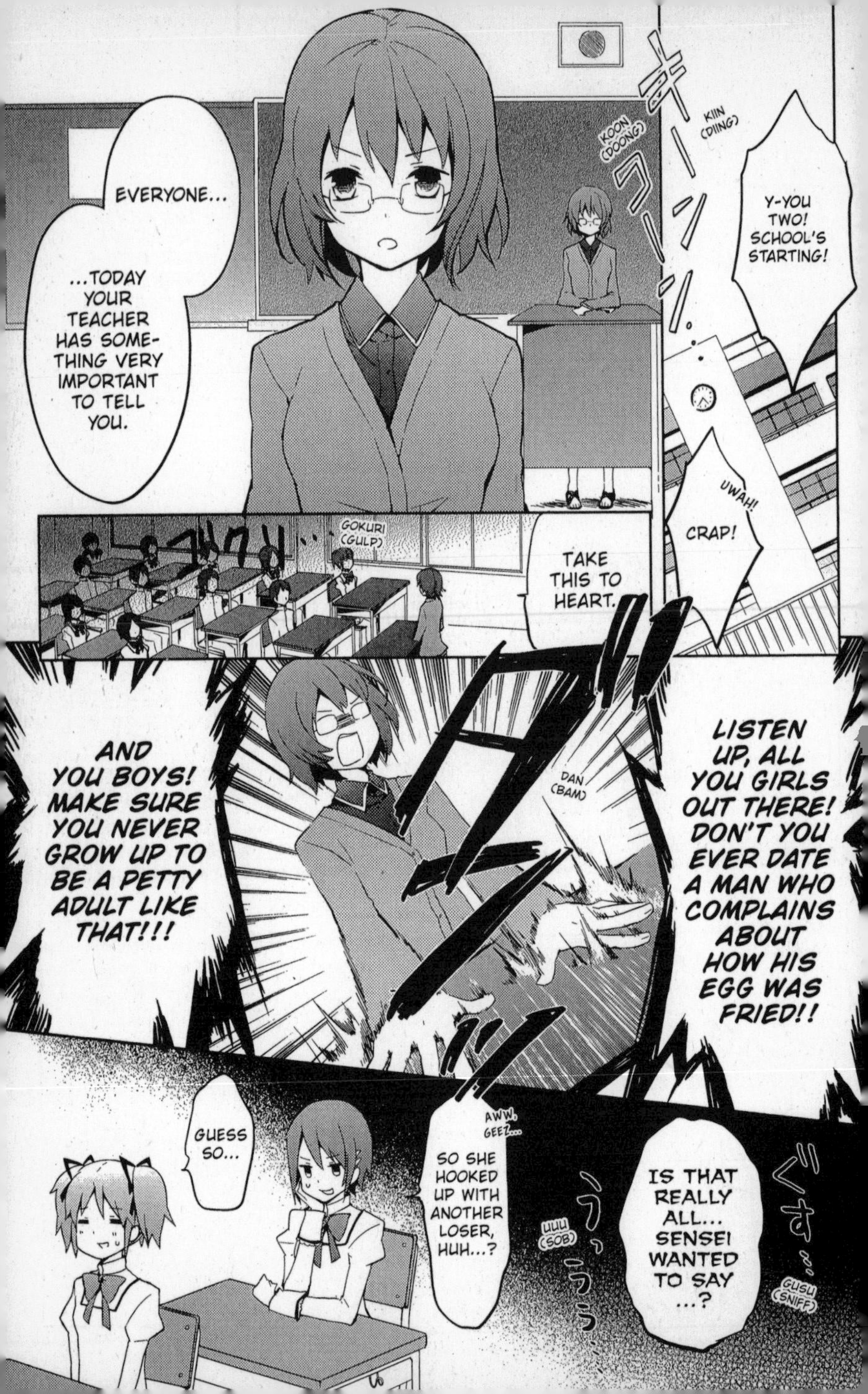
KIIN (DIING)
KOON (DOONG)
Y-YOU TWO! SCHOOL'S STARTING!
UWAH!
CRAP!
EVERYONE...
...TODAY YOUR TEACHER HAS SOME-THING VERY IMPORTANT TO TELL YOU.
TAKE THIS TO HEART.
GOKURI (GULP)
LISTEN UP, ALL YOU GIRLS OUT THERE! DON'T YOU EVER DATE A MAN WHO COMPLAINS ABOUT HOW HIS EGG WAS FRIED!!
DAN (BAM)
AND YOU BOYS! MAKE SURE YOU NEVER GROW UP TO BE A PETTY ADULT LIKE THAT!!!
GUSU (SNIFF)
IS THAT REALLY ALL... SENSEI WANTED TO SAY ...?
UUU (SOB)
AWW, GEEZ...
SO SHE HOOKED UP WITH ANOTHER LOSER, HUH...?
GUESS SO...

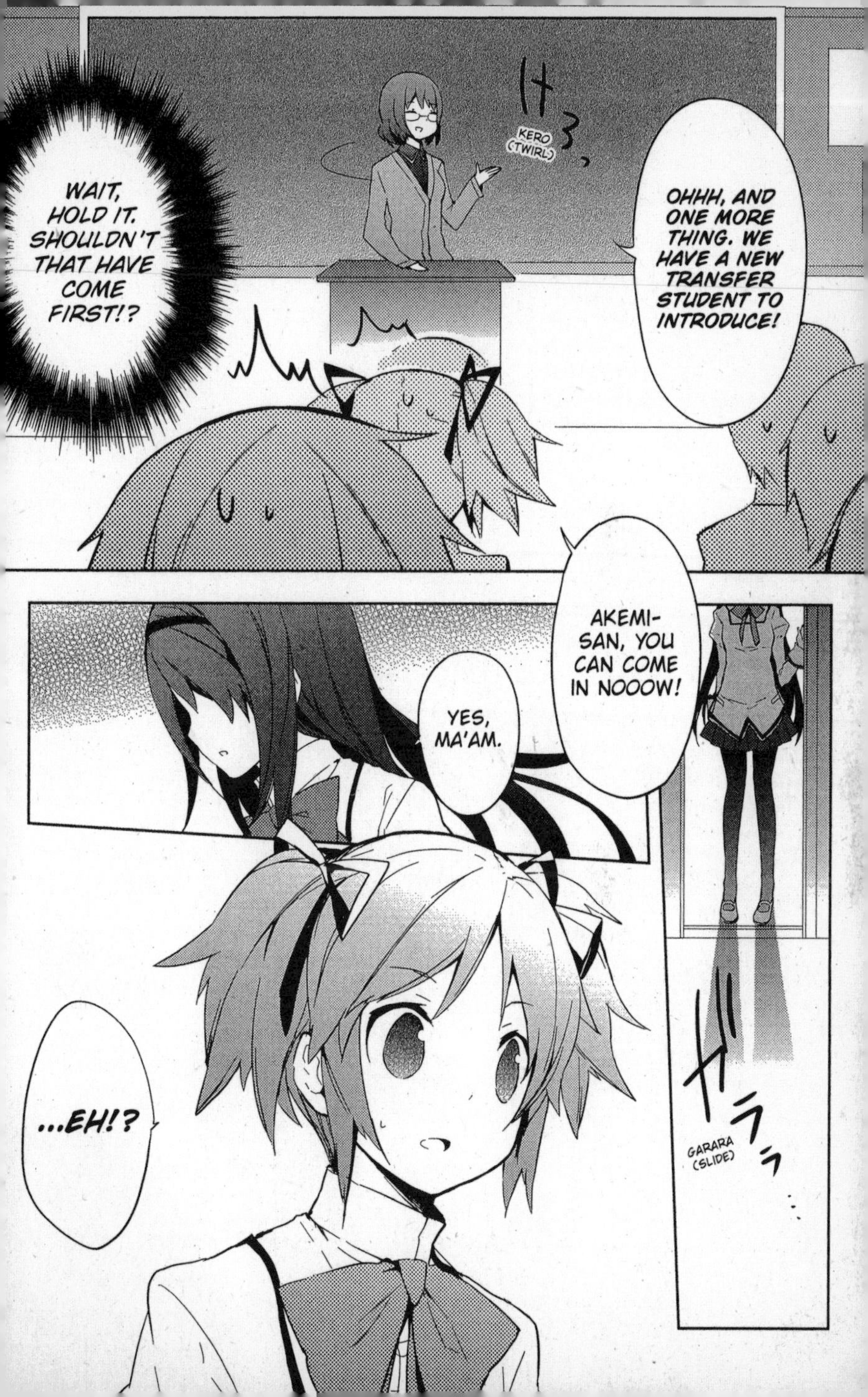
OHHH, AND ONE MORE THING. WE HAVE A NEW TRANSFER STUDENT TO INTRODUCE!
KERO (TWIRL)
WAIT, HOLD IT. SHOULDN'T THAT HAVE COME FIRST!?
AKEMI-SAN, YOU CAN COME IN NOOOW!
YES, MA'AM.
GARARA (SLIDE)
...EH!?

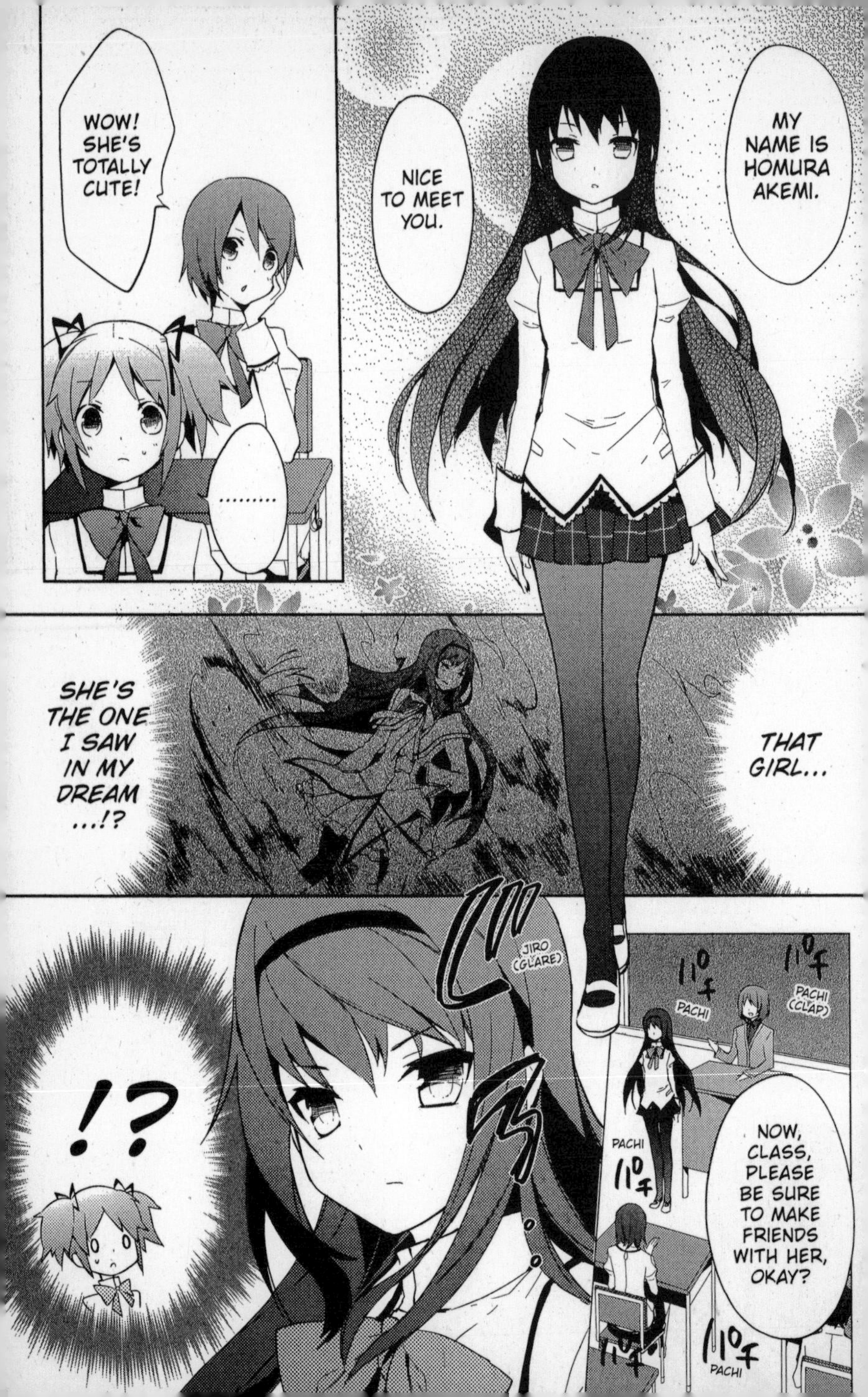
MY NAME IS HOMURA AKEMI.
NICE TO MEET YOU.
WOW! SHE'S TOTALLY CUTE!
....
THAT GIRL...
SHE'S THE ONE I SAW IN MY DREAM ...!?
PACHI (CLAP)
PACHI
PACHI
NOW, CLASS, PLEASE BE SURE TO MAKE FRIENDS WITH HER, OKAY?
PACHI
JIRO (GLARE)
!?

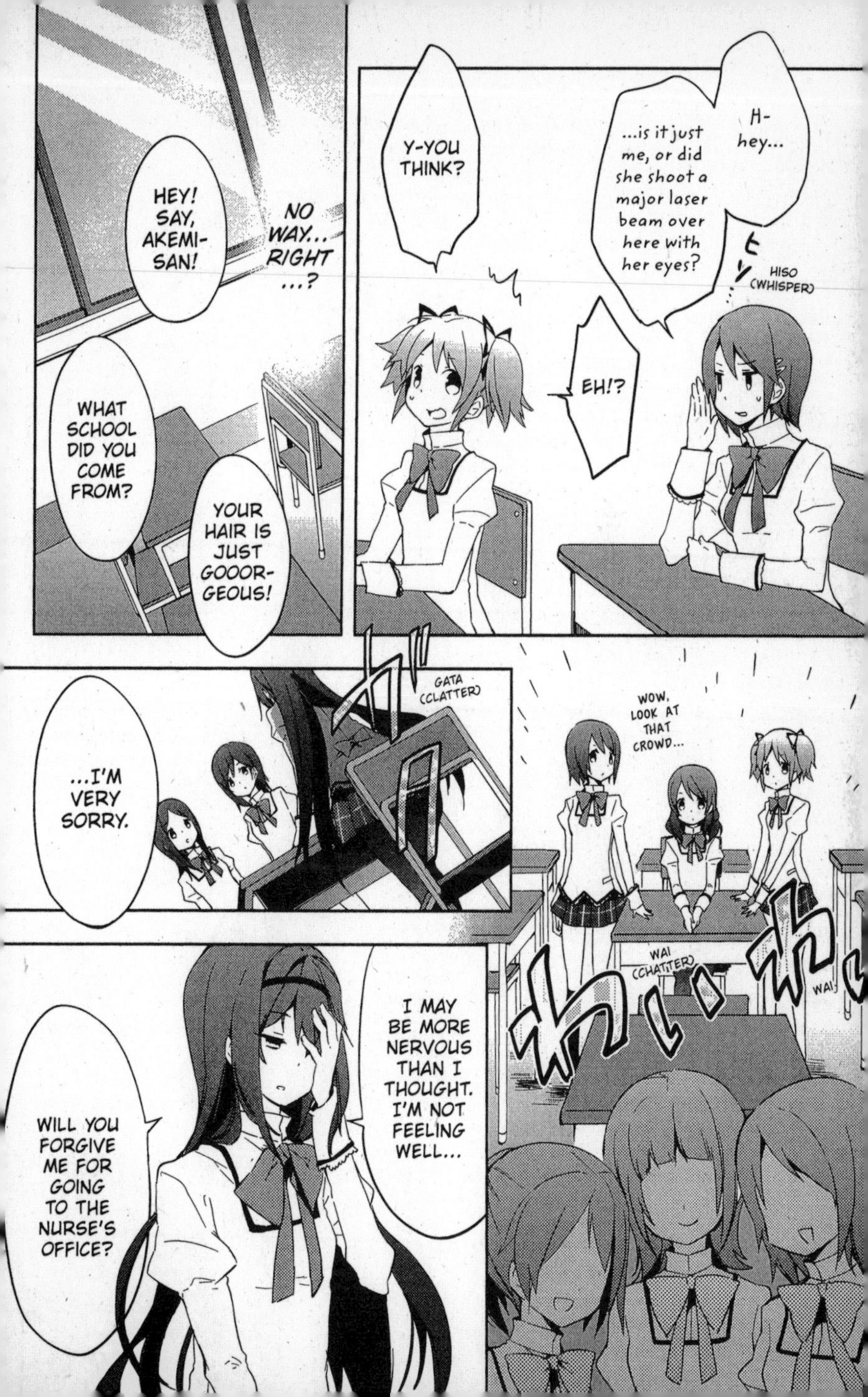
H- hey...
...is it just me, or did she shoot a major laser beam over here with her eyes?
HISO (WHISPER)
EH!?
Y-YOU THINK?
NO WAY... RIGHT...?
HEY! SAY, AKEMI-SAN!
WHAT SCHOOL DID YOU COME FROM?
YOUR HAIR IS JUST GOOOR-GEOUS!
WOW, LOOK AT THAT CROWD...
GATA (CLATTER)
...I'M VERY SORRY.
WAI (CHATTER)
WAI
I MAY BE MORE NERVOUS THAN I THOUGHT. I'M NOT FEELING WELL...
WILL YOU FORGIVE ME FOR GOING TO THE NURSE'S OFFICE?

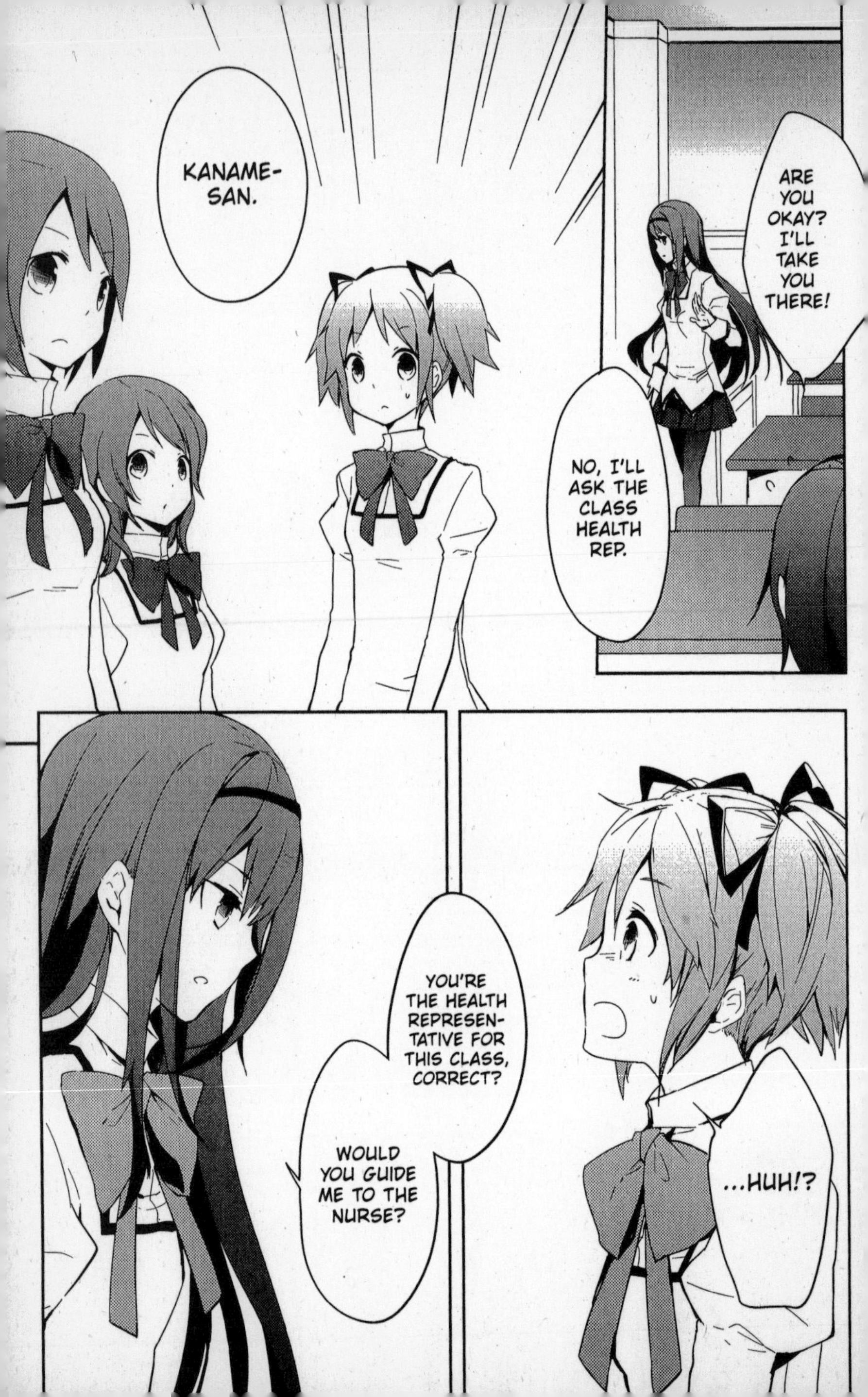
ARE YOU OKAY? I'LL TAKE YOU THERE!
NO, I'LL ASK THE CLASS HEALTH REP.
KANAME-SAN.
YOU'RE THE HEALTH REPRESENTATIVE FOR THIS CLASS, CORRECT?
WOULD YOU GUIDE ME TO THE NURSE?
...HUH!?

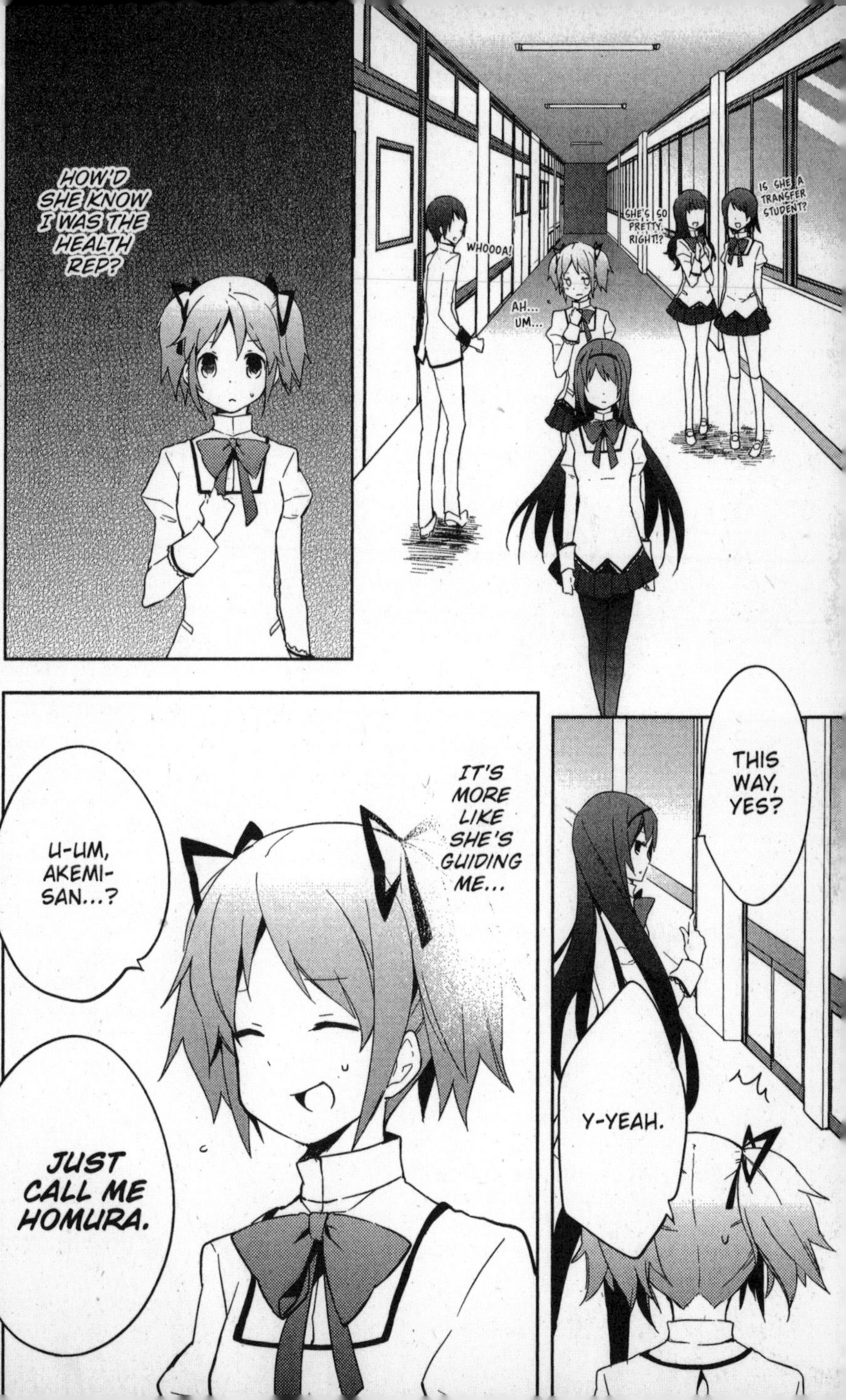
IS SHE A TRANSFER STUDENT?
SHE'S SO PRETTY, RIGHT!?
WHOOOA!
AH... UM...
HOW'D SHE KNOW I WAS THE HEALTH REP?
THIS WAY, YES?
Y-YEAH.
IT'S MORE LIKE SHE'S GUIDING ME...
U-UM, AKEMI-SAN...?
JUST CALL ME HOMURA.

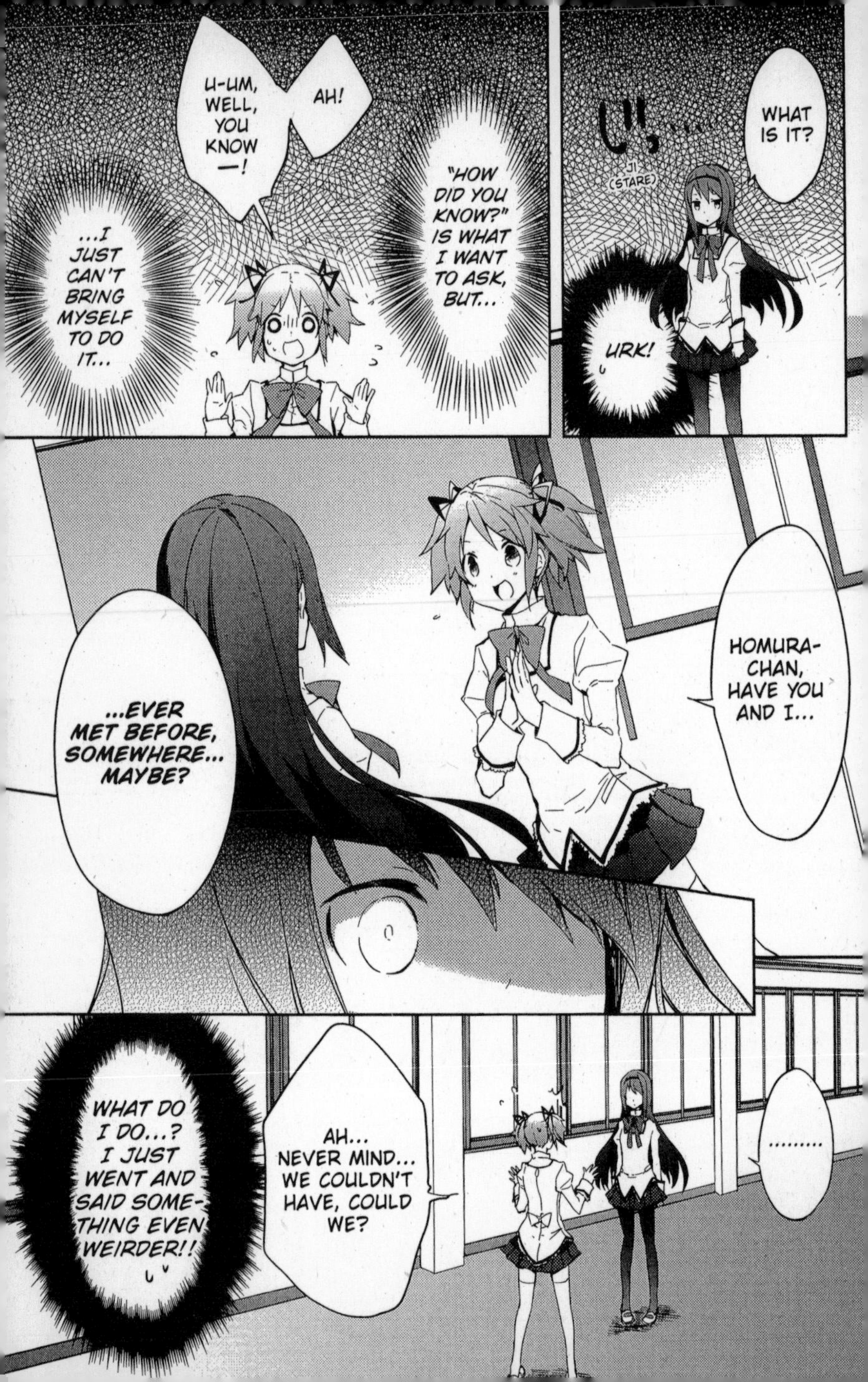
WHAT IS IT?
JI (STARE)
URK!
AH!
U-UM, WELL, YOU KNOW—!
"HOW DID YOU KNOW?" IS WHAT I WANT TO ASK, BUT...
...I JUST CAN'T BRING MYSELF TO DO IT...
HOMURA-CHAN, HAVE YOU AND I...
...EVER MET BEFORE, SOMEWHERE... MAYBE?
....
AH... NEVER MIND... WE COULDN'T HAVE, COULD WE?
WHAT DO I DO...? I JUST WENT AND SAID SOME-THING EVEN WEIRDER!!

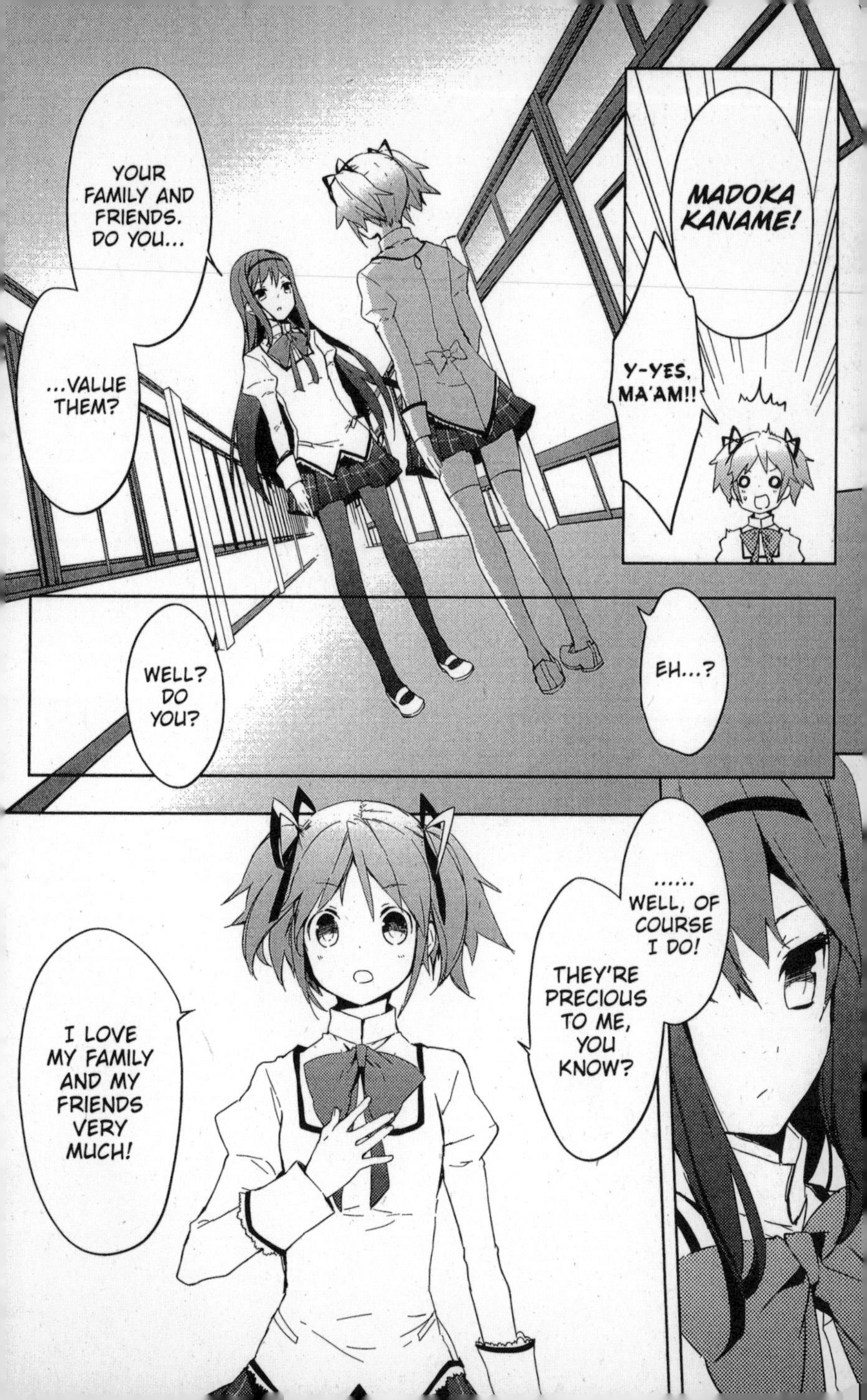
MADOKA KANAME!
Y-YES, MA'AM!!
YOUR FAMILY AND FRIENDS. DO YOU...
...VALUE THEM?
EH...?
WELL? DO YOU?
......
WELL, OF COURSE I DO!
THEY'RE PRECIOUS TO ME, YOU KNOW?
I LOVE MY FAMILY AND MY FRIENDS VERY MUCH!

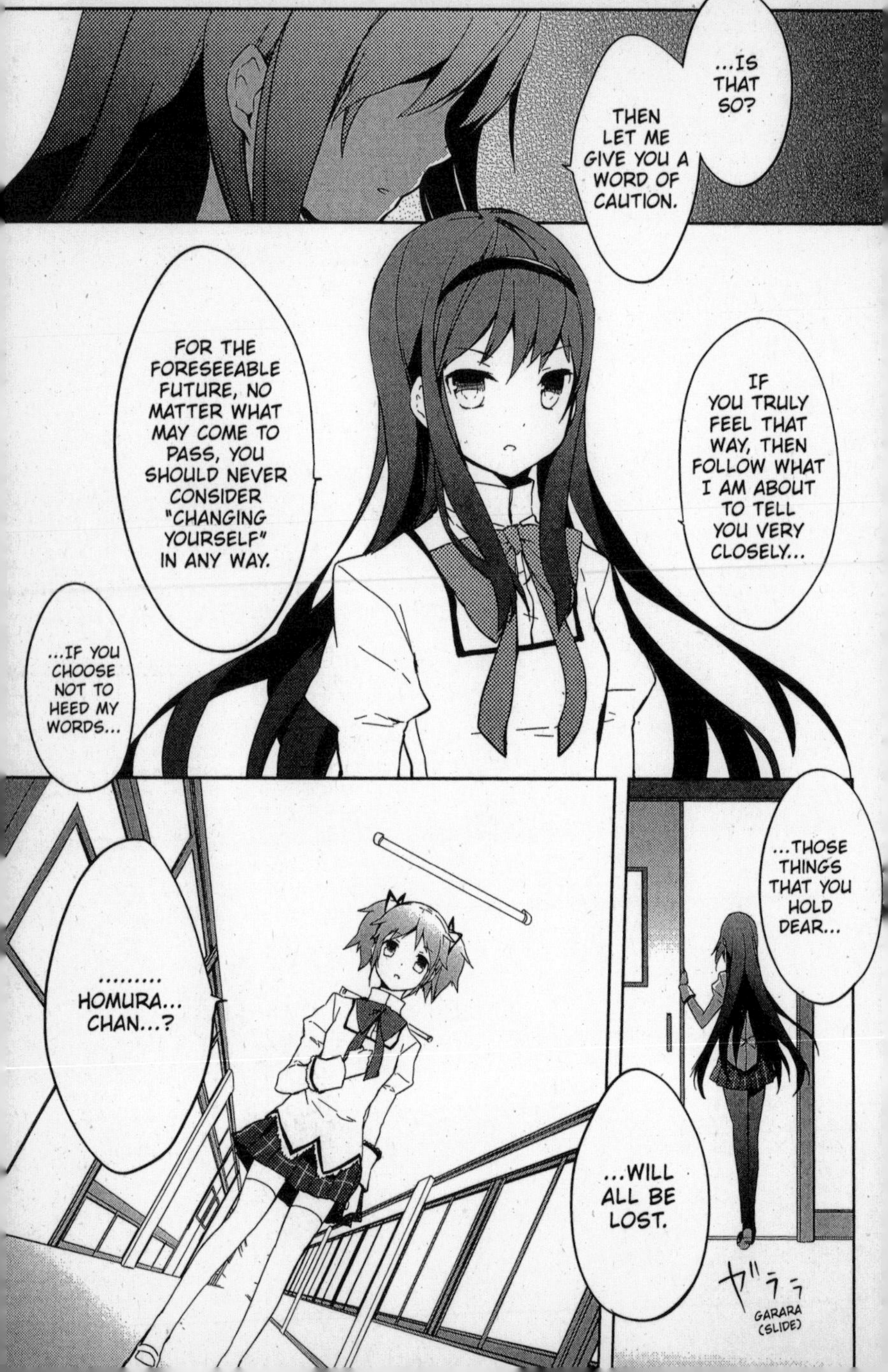
...IS THAT SO?
THEN LET ME GIVE YOU A WORD OF CAUTION.
IF YOU TRULY FEEL THAT WAY, THEN FOLLOW WHAT I AM ABOUT TO TELL YOU VERY CLOSELY...
FOR THE FORESEEABLE FUTURE, NO MATTER WHAT MAY COME TO PASS, YOU SHOULD NEVER CONSIDER "CHANGING YOURSELF" IN ANY WAY.
...IF YOU CHOOSE NOT TO HEED MY WORDS...
...THOSE THINGS THAT YOU HOLD DEAR...
...WILL ALL BE LOST.
ガラララ
GARARA (SLIDE)
.... HOMURA... CHAN...?

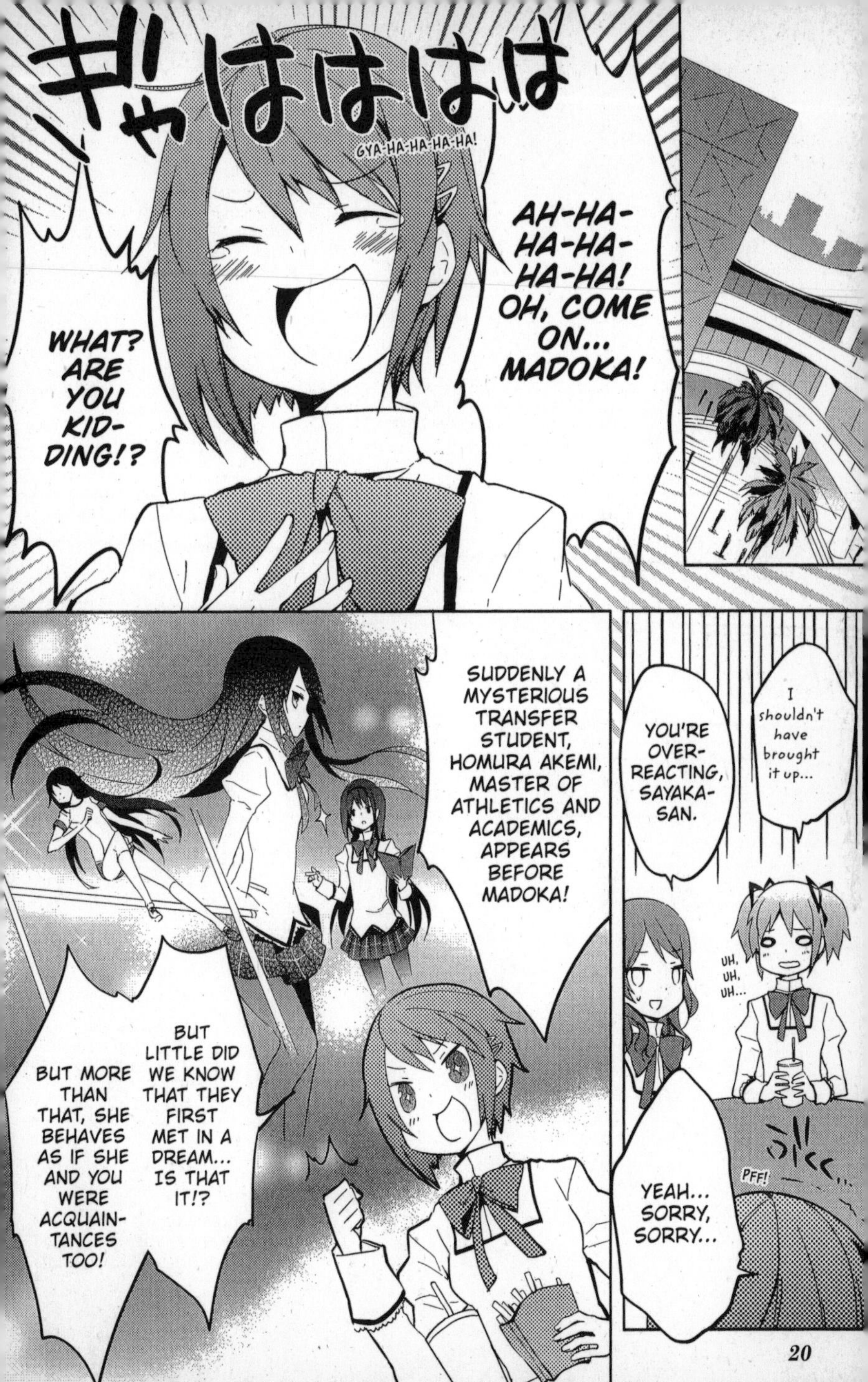
ぎゃはははは
GYA-HA-HA-HA-HA!
AH-HA-HA-HA-HA-HA! OH, COME ON... MADOKA!
WHAT? ARE YOU KID-DING!?
I shouldn't have brought it up...
YOU'RE OVER-REACTING, SAYAKA-SAN.
UH, UH, UH...
ぷくく...
PFF!
YEAH... SORRY, SORRY...
SUDDENLY A MYSTERIOUS TRANSFER STUDENT, HOMURA AKEMI, MASTER OF ATHLETICS AND ACADEMICS, APPEARS BEFORE MADOKA!
BUT LITTLE DID WE KNOW THAT THEY FIRST MET IN A DREAM... IS THAT IT!?
BUT MORE THAN THAT, SHE BEHAVES AS IF SHE AND YOU WERE ACQUAIN-TANCES TOO!

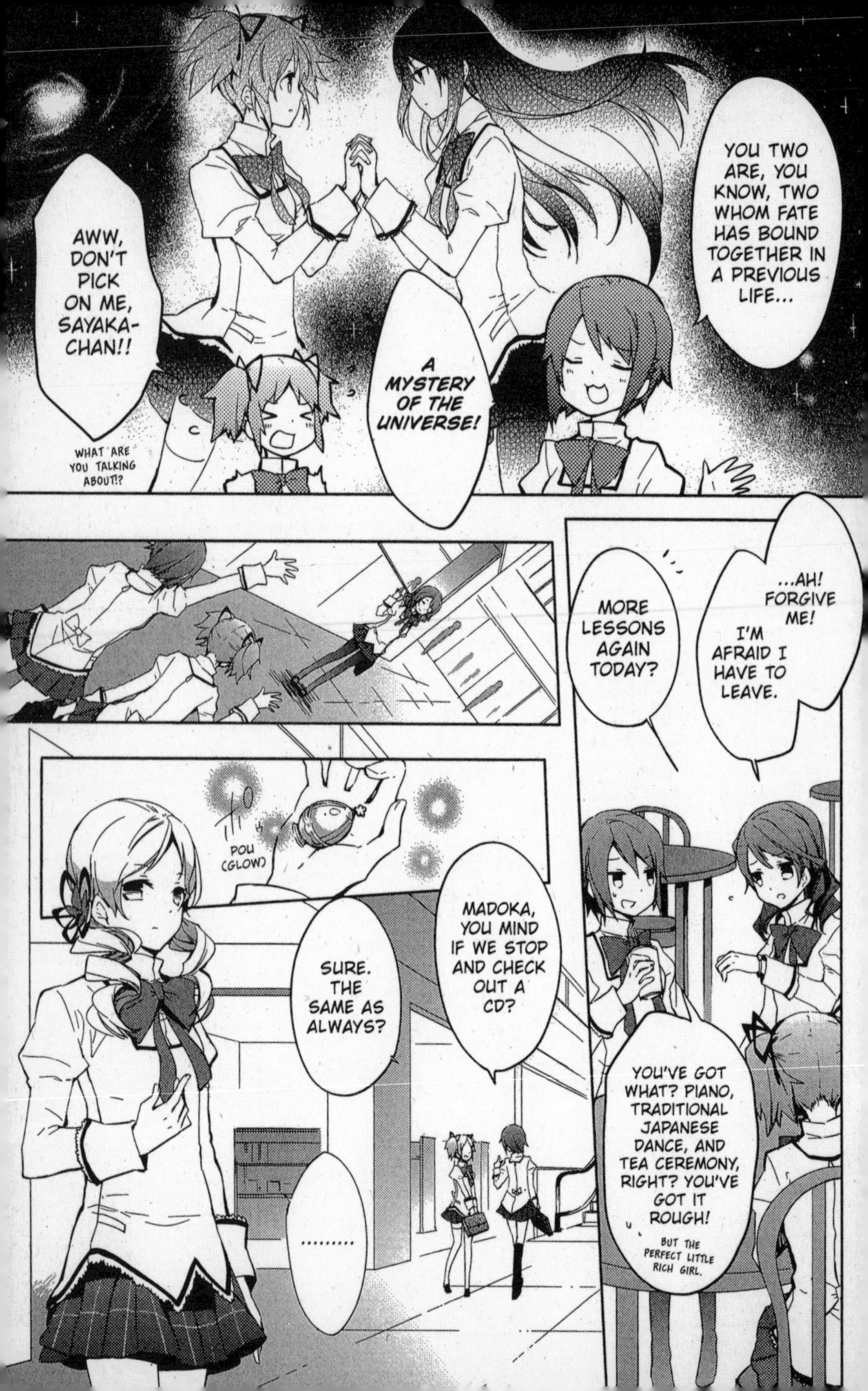
YOU TWO ARE, YOU KNOW, TWO WHOM FATE HAS BOUND TOGETHER IN A PREVIOUS LIFE...
A *MYSTERY OF THE UNIVERSE!*
AWW, DON'T PICK ON ME, SAYAKA-CHAN!!
WHAT ARE YOU TALKING ABOUT!?
...AH! FORGIVE ME!
I'M AFRAID I HAVE TO LEAVE.
MORE LESSONS AGAIN TODAY?
YOU'VE GOT WHAT? PIANO, TRADITIONAL JAPANESE DANCE, AND TEA CEREMONY, RIGHT? YOU'VE GOT IT ROUGH!
BUT THE PERFECT LITTLE RICH GIRL.
POU (GLOW)
MADOKA, YOU MIND IF WE STOP AND CHECK OUT A CD?
SURE. THE SAME AS ALWAYS?
....

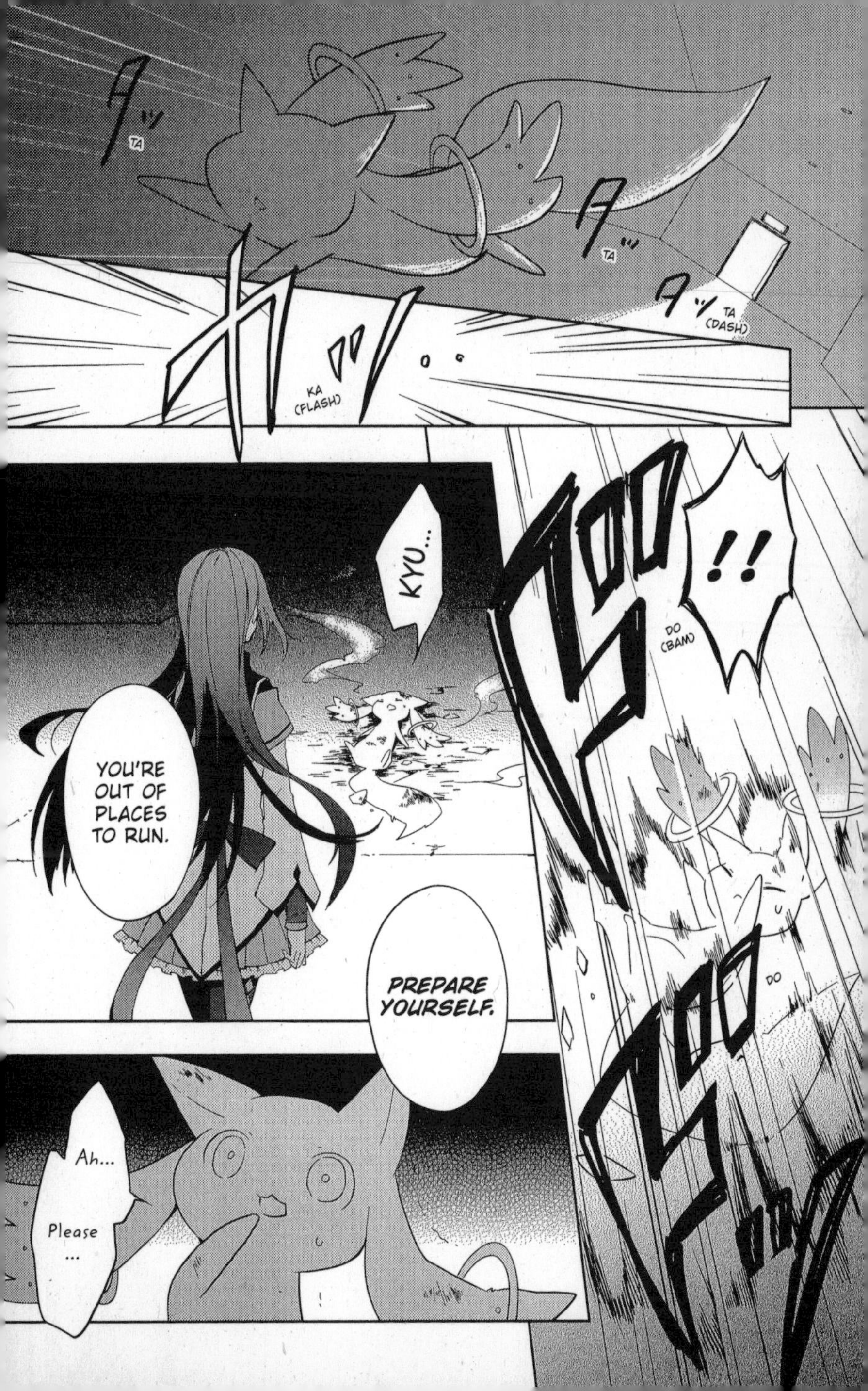
TA
TA
TA (DASH)
KA (FLASH)
!!
DO (BAM)
DO
KYU...
YOU'RE OUT OF PLACES TO RUN.
PREPARE YOURSELF.
Ah...
Please ...

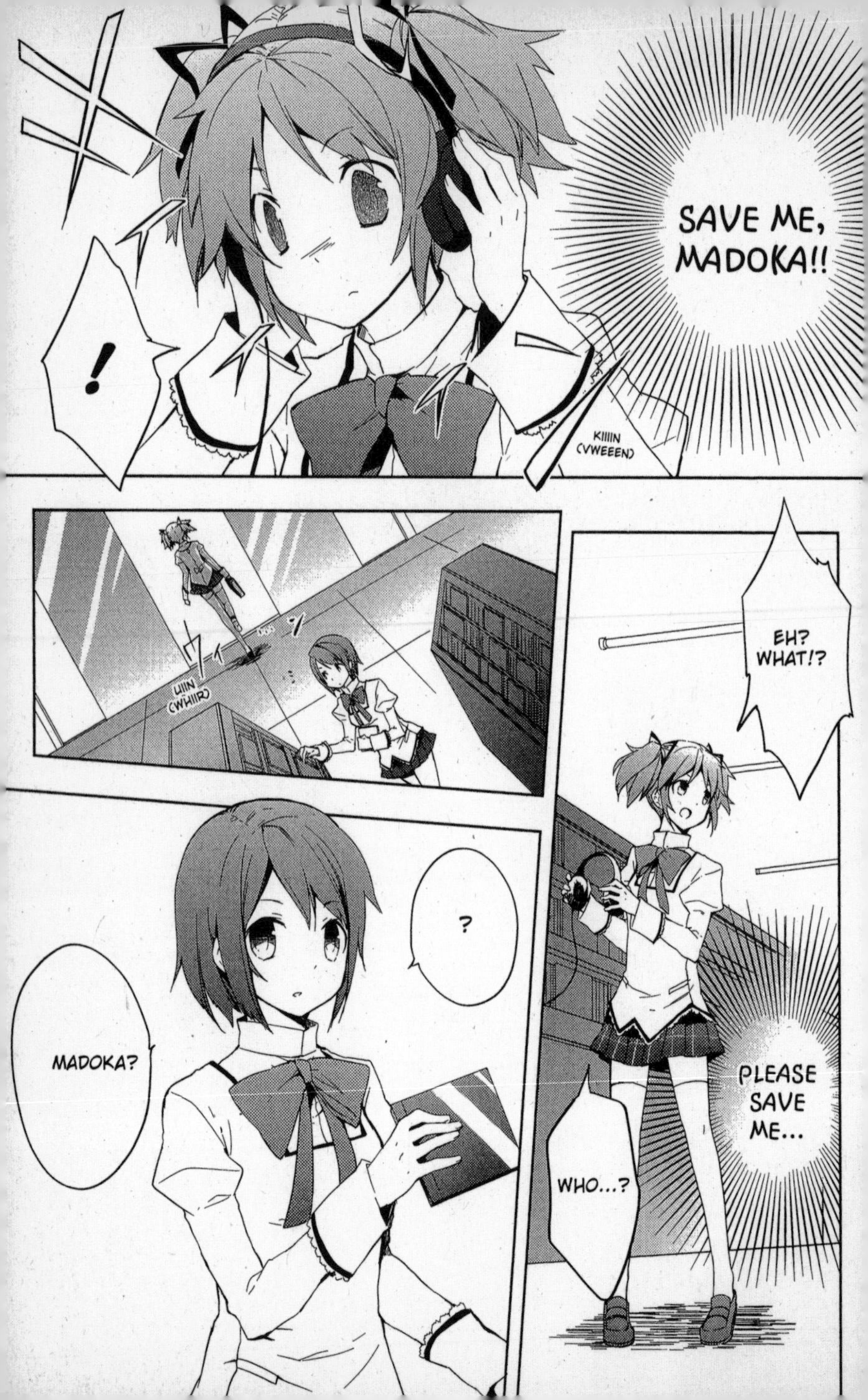
SAVE ME, MADOKA!!
KIIIN (VWEEEN)
!
EH? WHAT!?
PLEASE SAVE ME...
WHO...?
UIIN (WHIIR)
?
MADOKA?

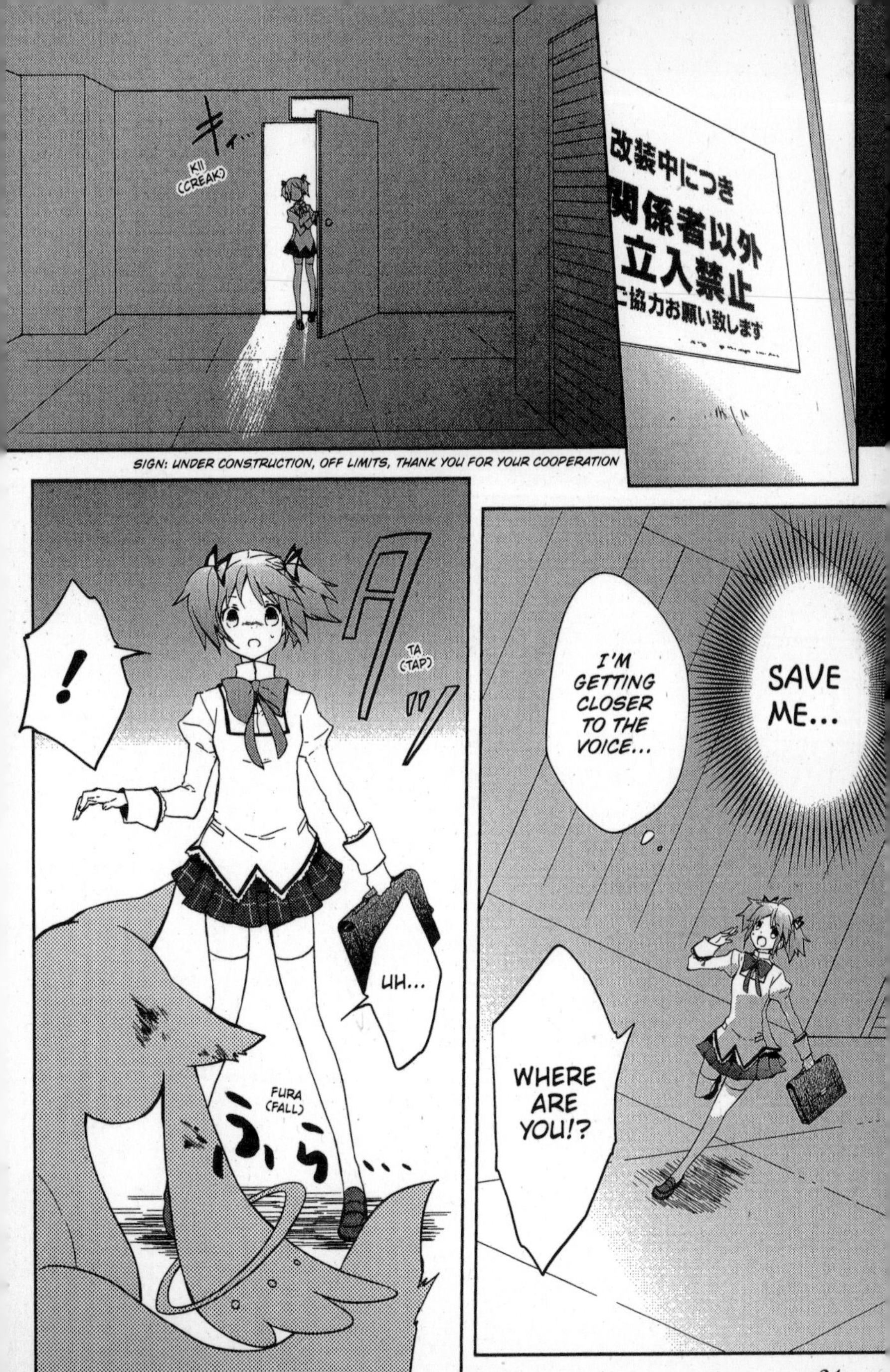
キィ
KII (CREAK)
改装中につき
関係者以外
立入禁止
ご協力お願い致します
SIGN: UNDER CONSTRUCTION, OFF LIMITS, THANK YOU FOR YOUR COOPERATION
SAVE ME...
I'M GETTING CLOSER TO THE VOICE...
WHERE ARE YOU!?
!
TA (TAP)
UH...
FURA (FALL)
ふら...

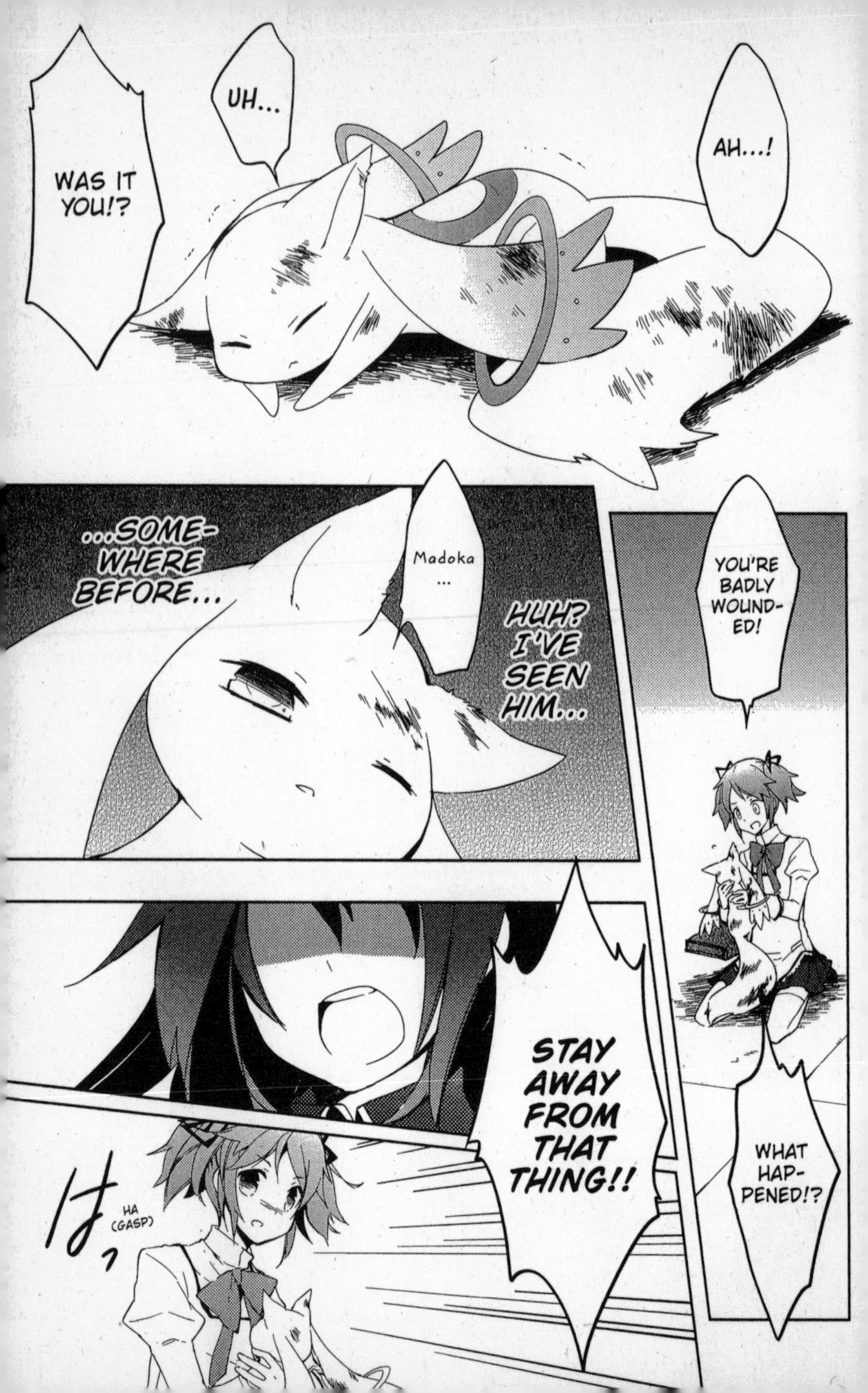
AH...!
UH...
WAS IT YOU!?
YOU'RE BADLY WOUND-ED!
WHAT HAP-PENED!?
Madoka ...
HUH? I'VE SEEN HIM...
...SOME-WHERE BEFORE...
STAY AWAY FROM THAT THING!!
は
HA (GASP)

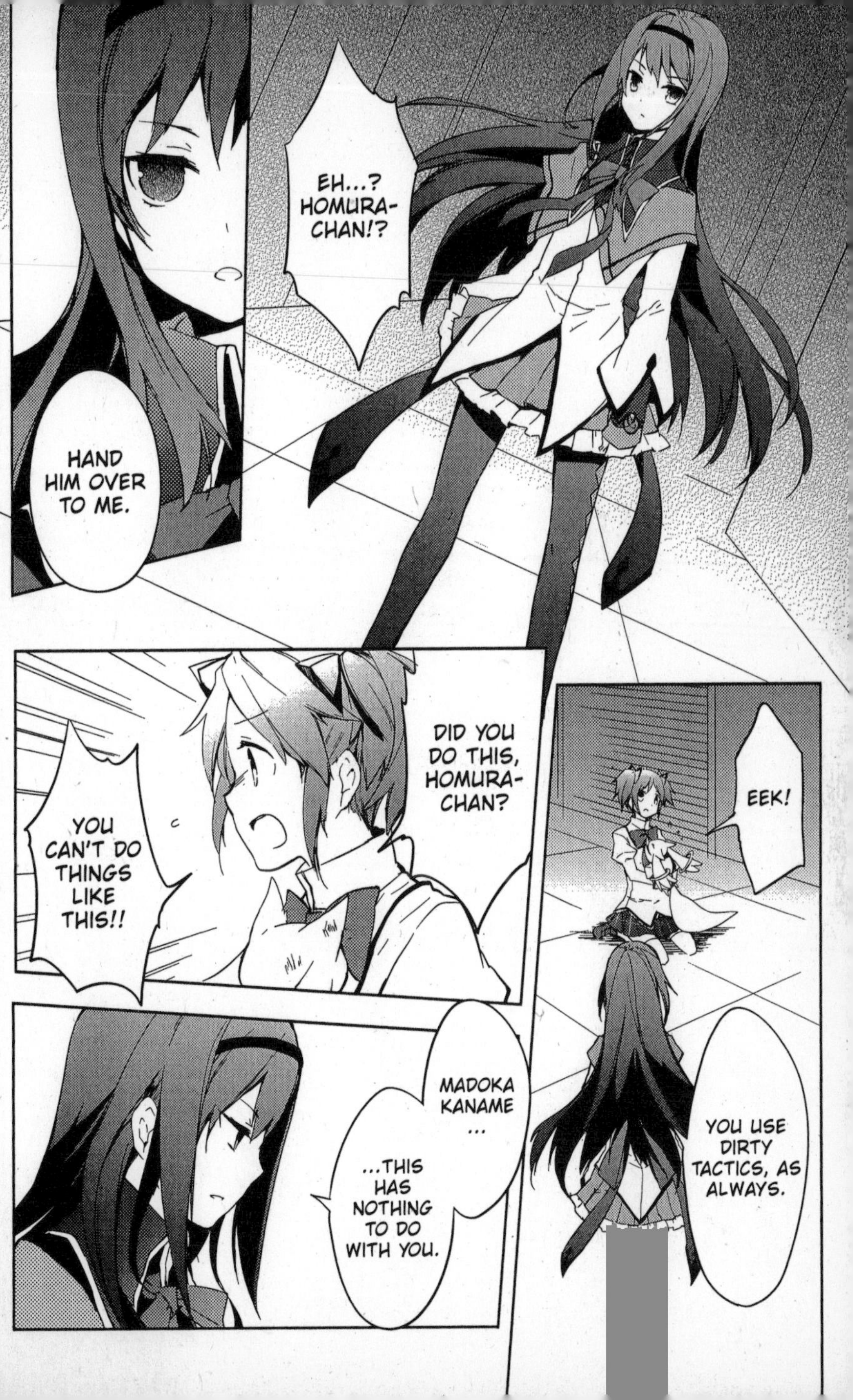
EH...? HOMURA-CHAN!?
HAND HIM OVER TO ME.
EEK!
YOU USE DIRTY TACTICS, AS ALWAYS.
DID YOU DO THIS, HOMURA-CHAN?
YOU CAN'T DO THINGS LIKE THIS!!
MADOKA KANAME ...
...THIS HAS NOTHING TO DO WITH YOU.

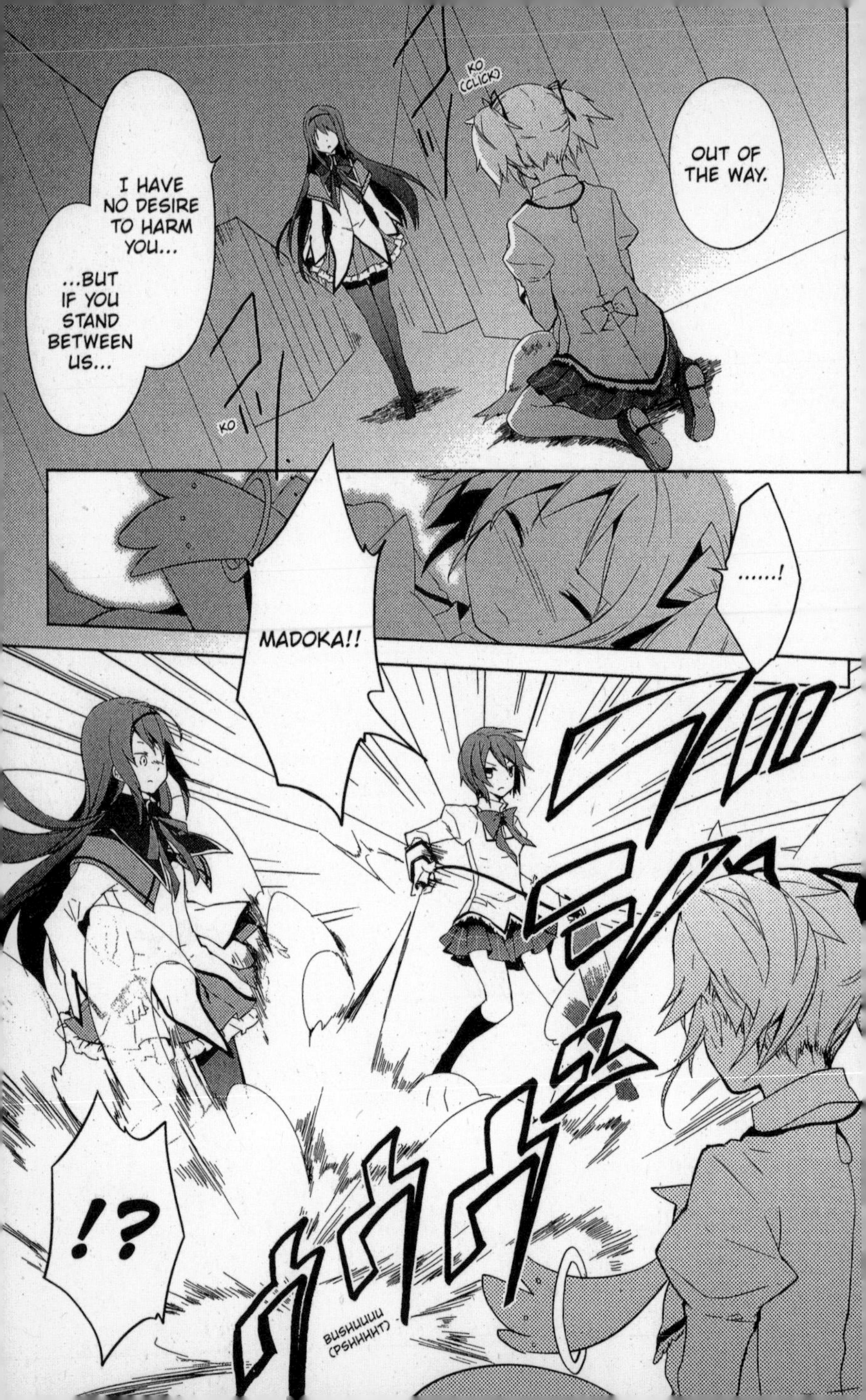
KO (CLICK)
OUT OF THE WAY.
I HAVE NO DESIRE TO HARM YOU...
...BUT IF YOU STAND BETWEEN US...
KO
......!
MADOKA!!
!?
BUSHUUUU (PSHHHHT)

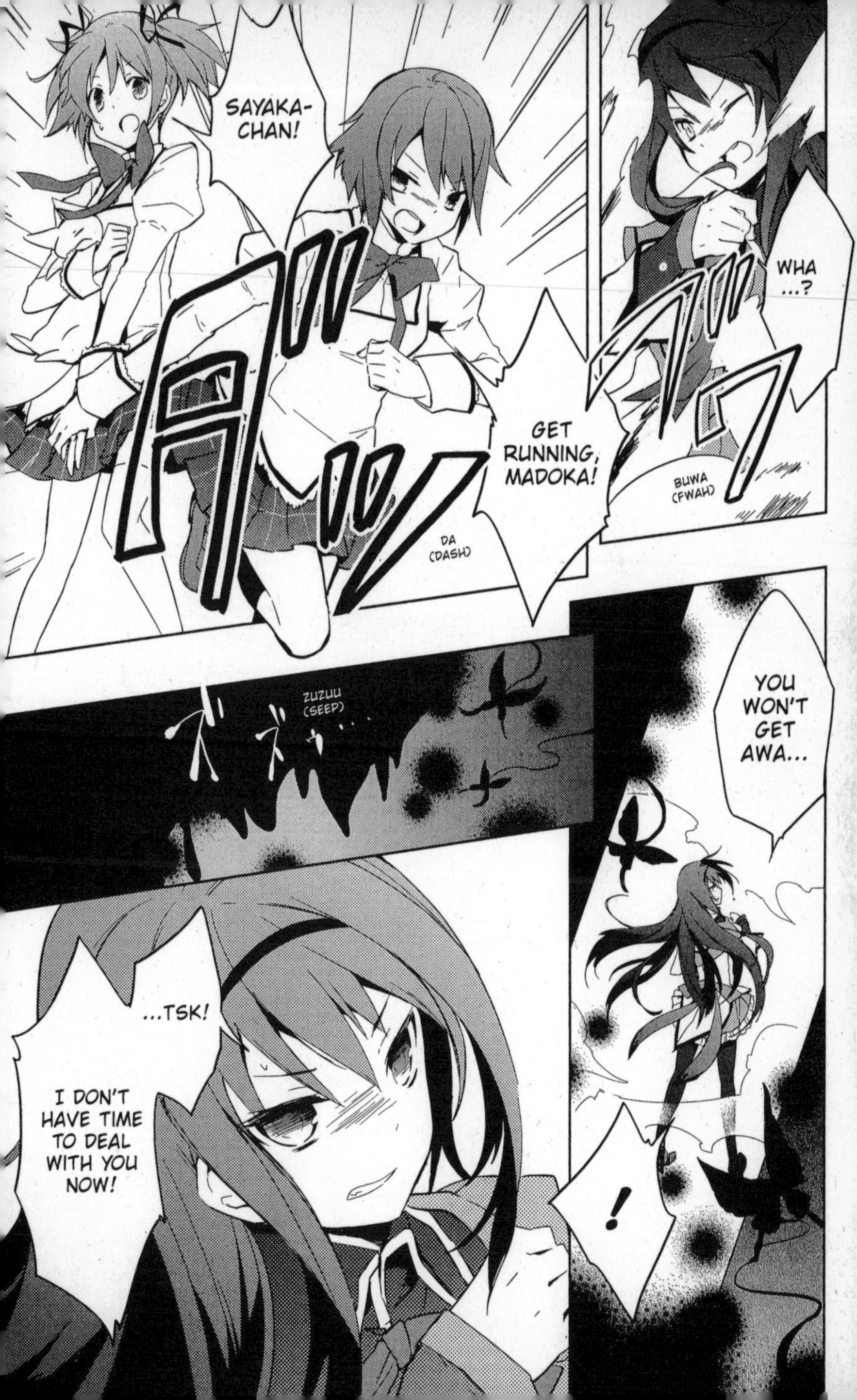
WHA ...?
BUWA (FWAH)
SAYAKA-CHAN!
GET RUNNING, MADOKA!
DA (DASH)
YOU WON'T GET AWA...
!
ZUZUU (SEEP)
...TSK!
I DON'T HAVE TIME TO DEAL WITH YOU NOW!

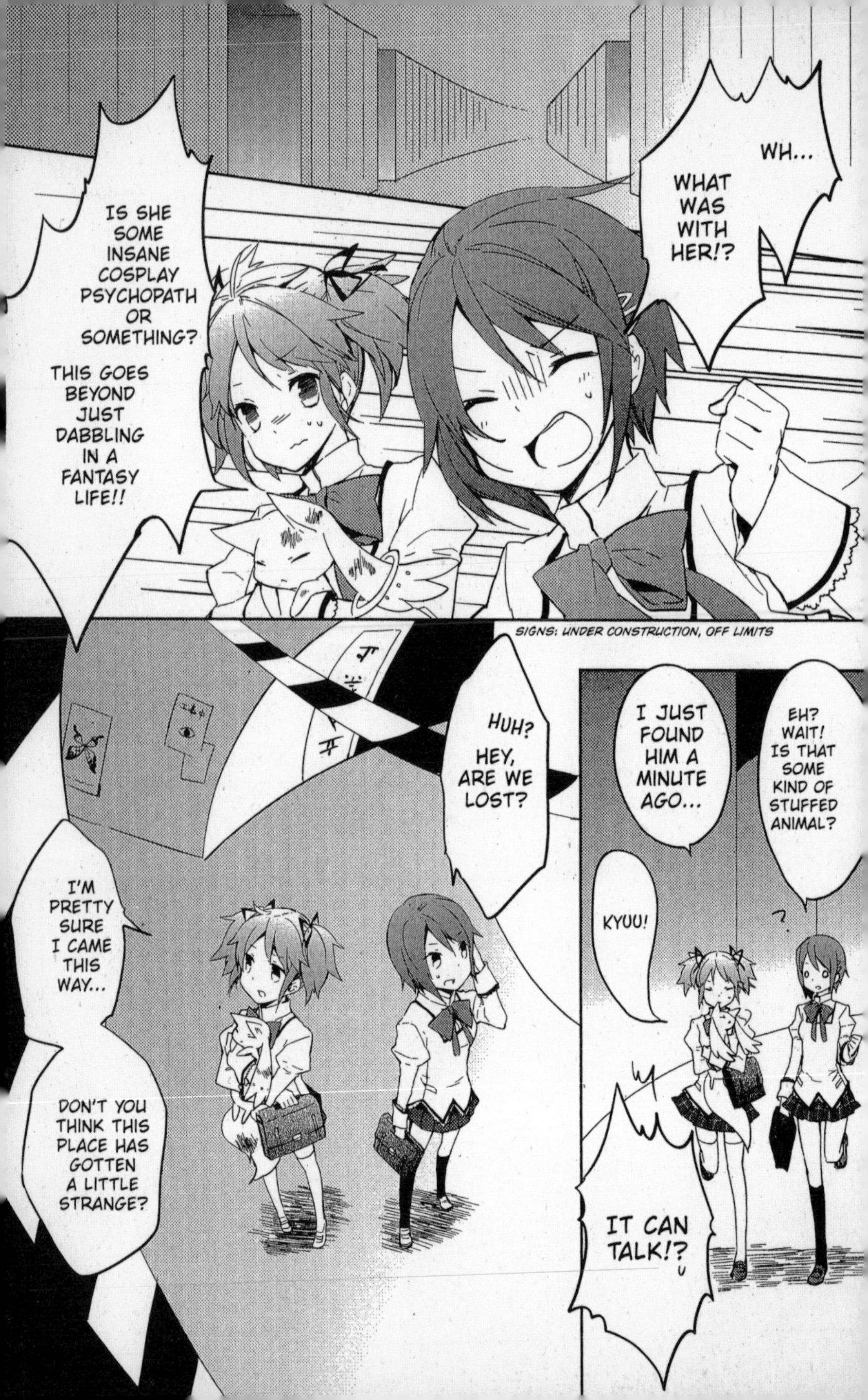
WH... WHAT WAS WITH HER!?
IS SHE SOME INSANE COSPLAY PSYCHOPATH OR SOMETHING?
THIS GOES BEYOND JUST DABBLING IN A FANTASY LIFE!!
EH? WAIT! IS THAT SOME KIND OF STUFFED ANIMAL?
I JUST FOUND HIM A MINUTE AGO...
KYUU!
IT CAN TALK!?
SIGNS: UNDER CONSTRUCTION, OFF LIMITS
HUH? HEY, ARE WE LOST?
I'M PRETTY SURE I CAME THIS WAY...
DON'T YOU THINK THIS PLACE HAS GOTTEN A LITTLE STRANGE?

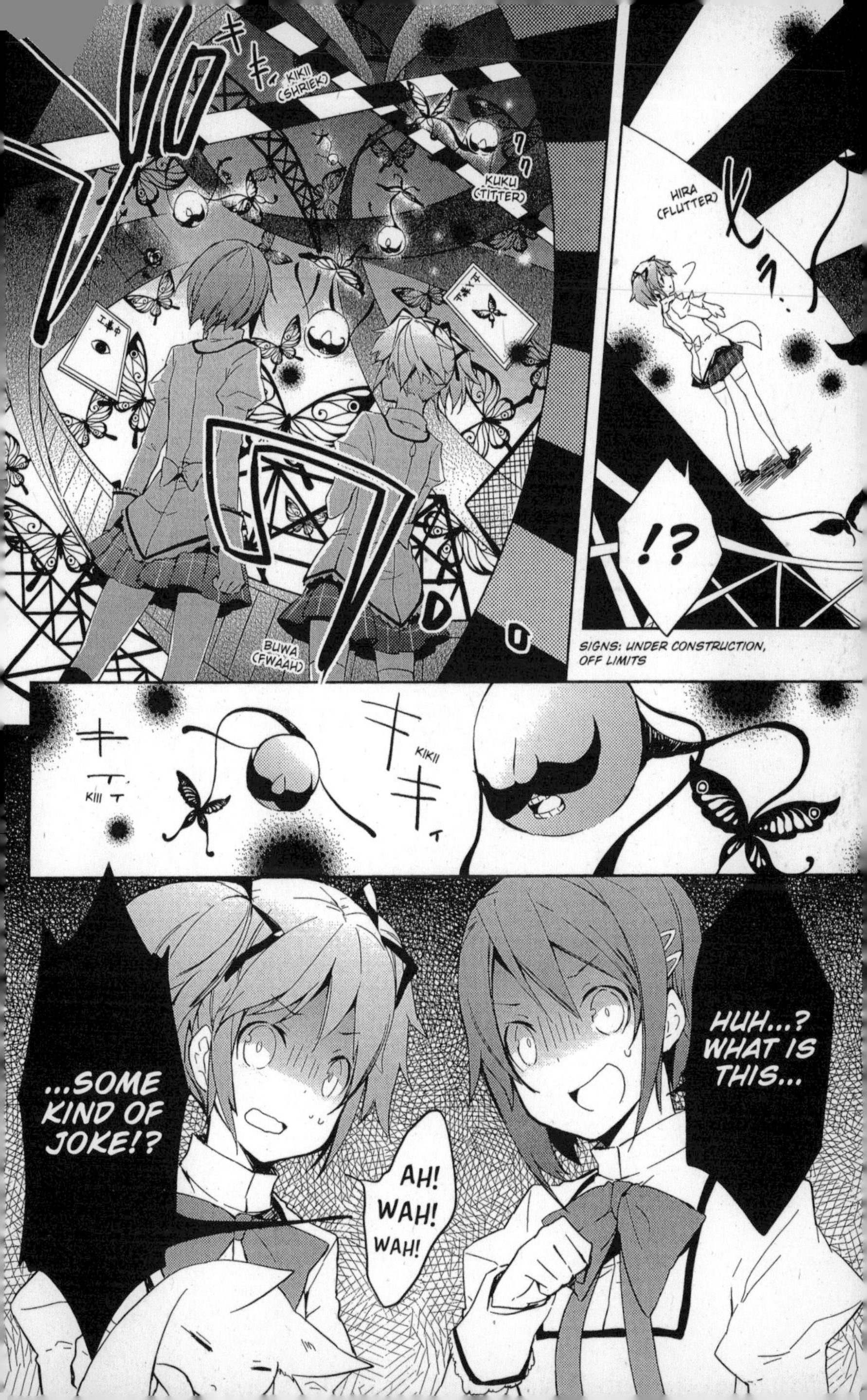
HIRA (FLUTTER)
!?
SIGNS: UNDER CONSTRUCTION, OFF LIMITS
KIKII (SHRIEK)
KUKU (TITTER)
BUWA (FWAAH)
KIKII
KIII
HUH...? WHAT IS THIS...
AH! WAH! WAH!
...SOME KIND OF JOKE!?

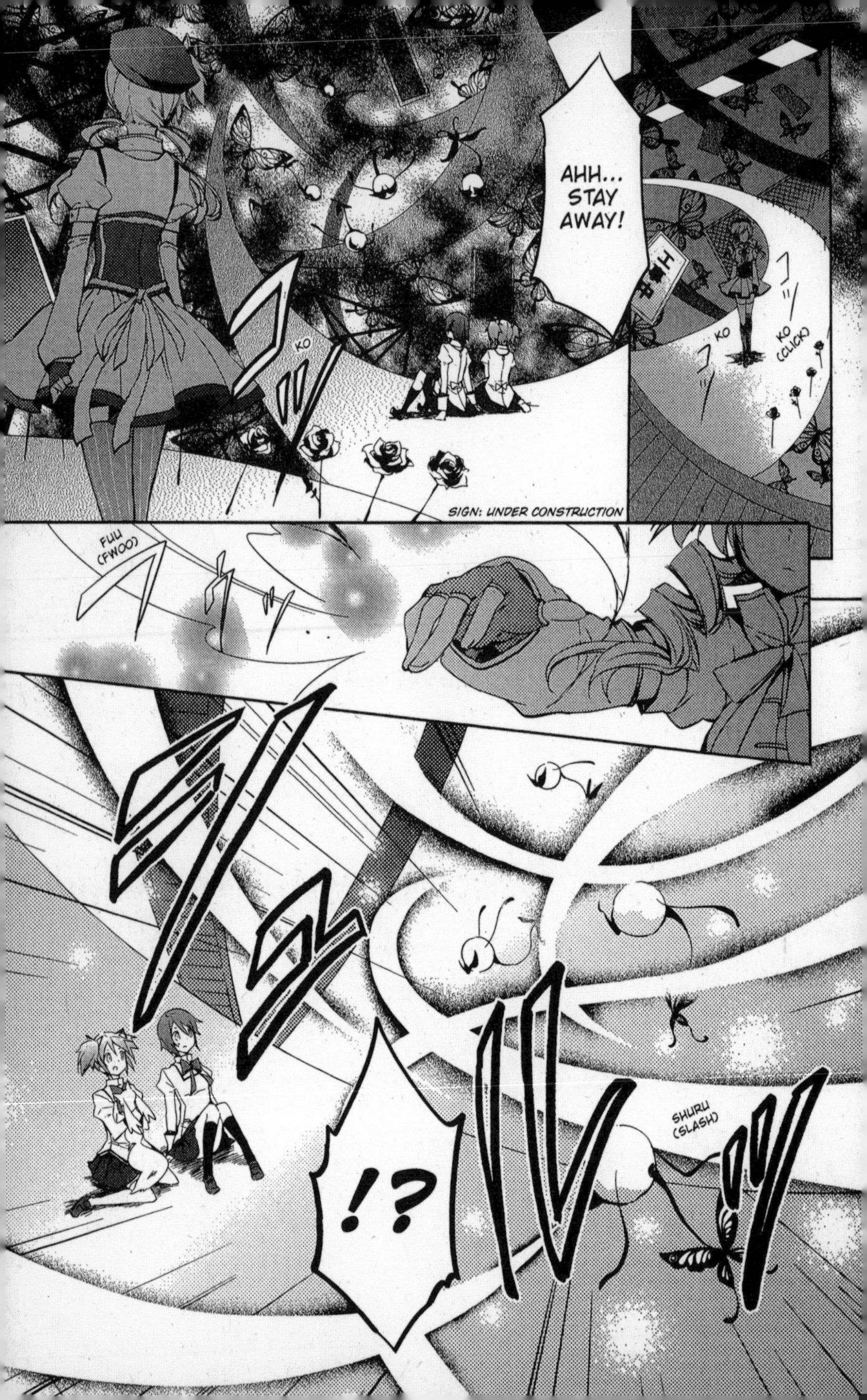
AHH... STAY AWAY!
KO
KO (CLICK)
KO
SIGN: UNDER CONSTRUCTION
FUU (FWOO)
SHURU (SLASH)
!?

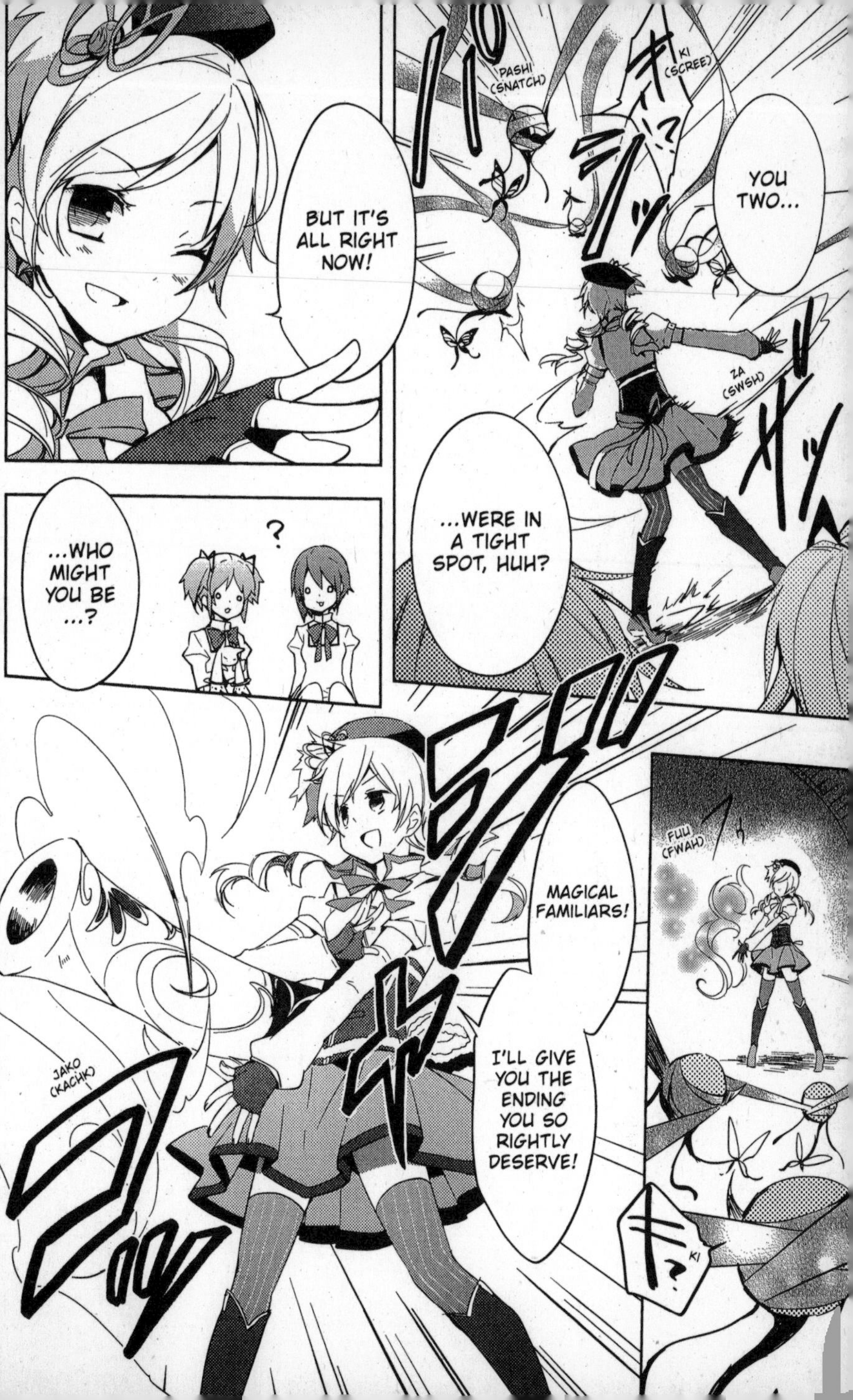
KI (SCREE)
YOU TWO...
PASHI (SNATCH)
ZA (SWSH)
...WERE IN A TIGHT SPOT, HUH?
BUT IT'S ALL RIGHT NOW!
...WHO MIGHT YOU BE ...?
?
FUU (FWAH)
KI
MAGICAL FAMILIARS!
I'LL GIVE YOU THE ENDING YOU SO RIGHTLY DESERVE!
JAKO (KACHK)

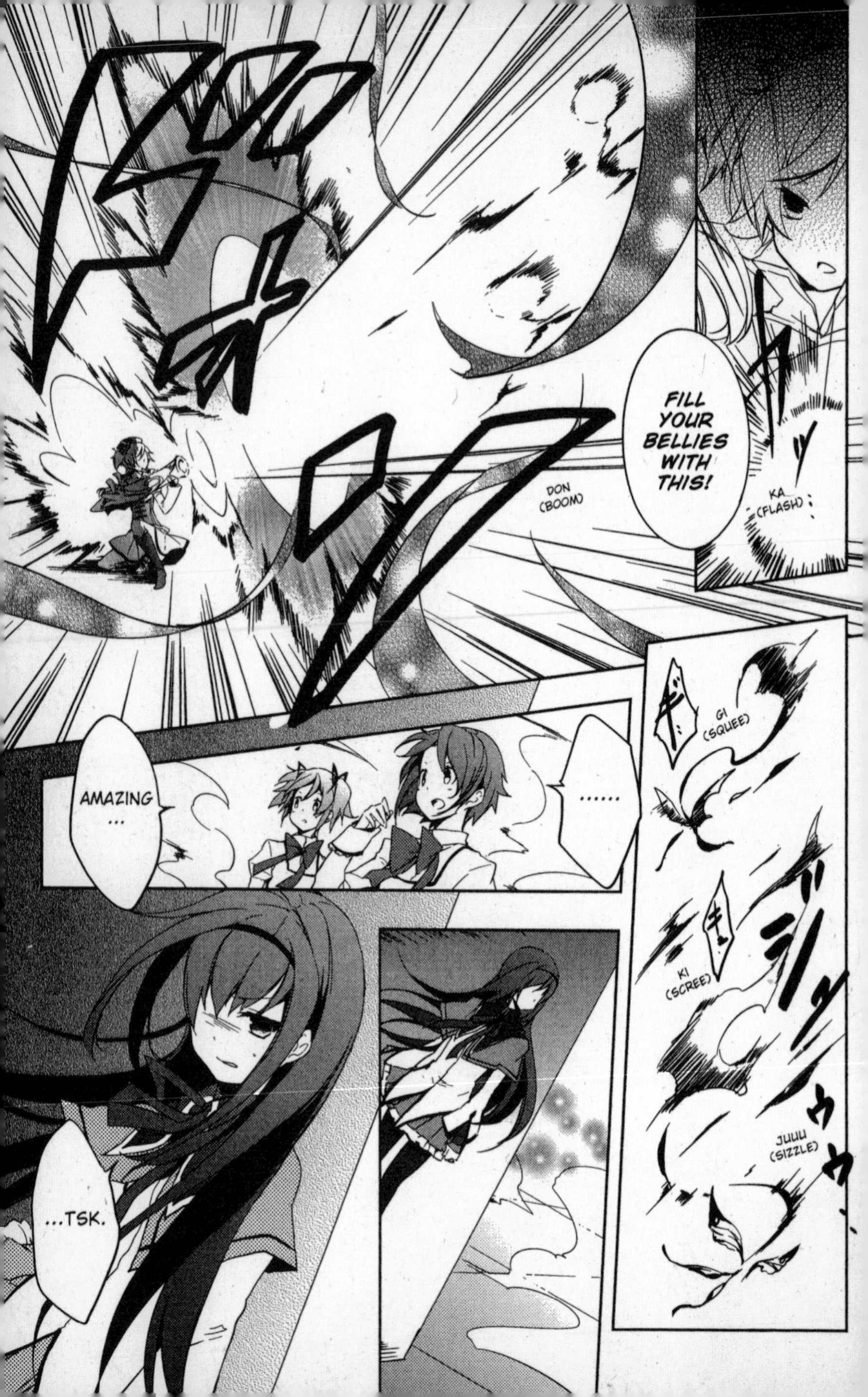
KA (FLASH)
FILL YOUR BELLIES WITH THIS!
DON (BOOM)
GI (SQUEE)
KI (SCREE)
JUUU (SIZZLE)
......
AMAZING ...
...TSK.

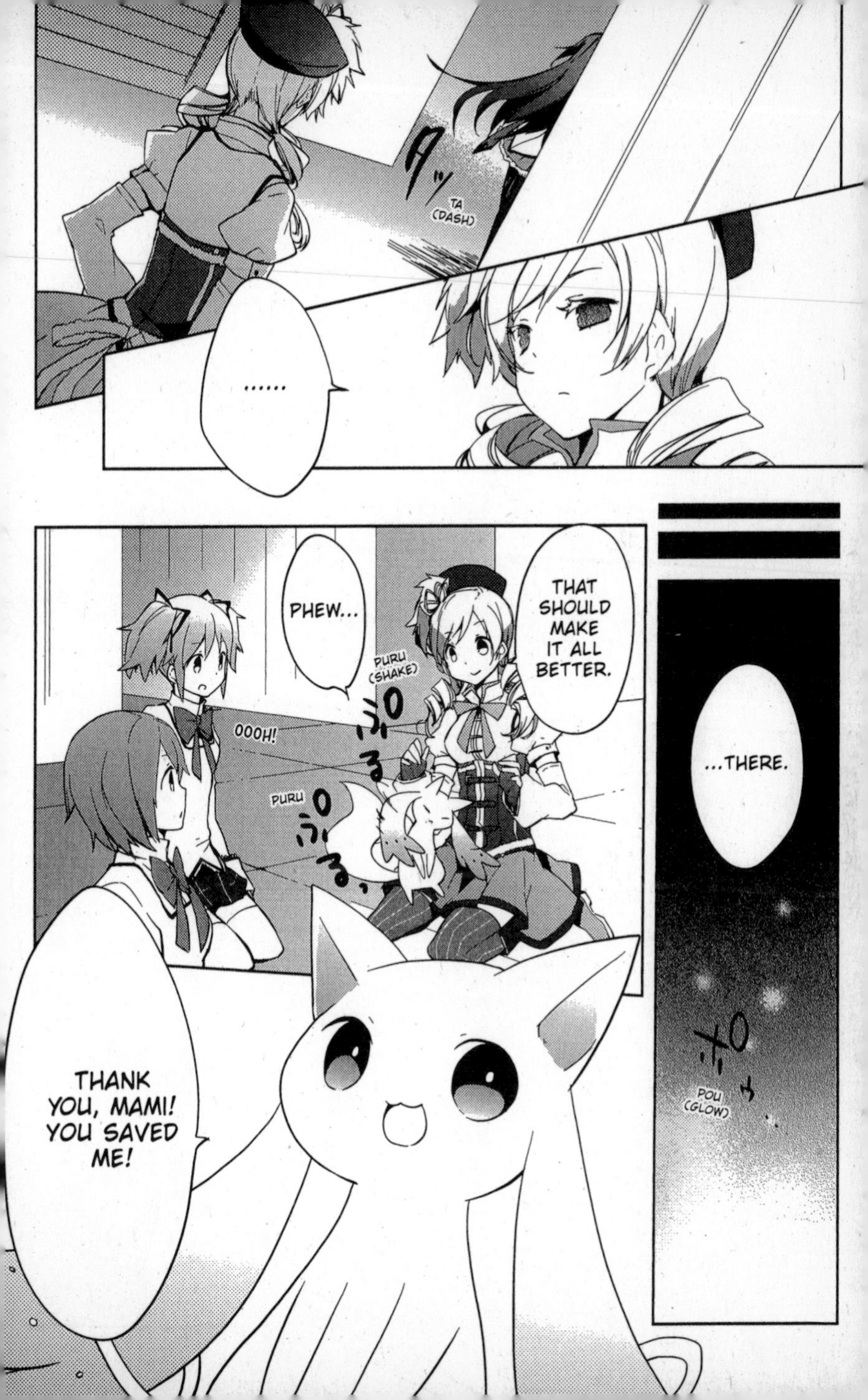
TA (DASH)
......
...THERE.
POU (GLOW)
THAT SHOULD MAKE IT ALL BETTER.
PHEW...
PURU (SHAKE)
OOOH!
PURU
THANK YOU, MAMI! YOU SAVED ME!

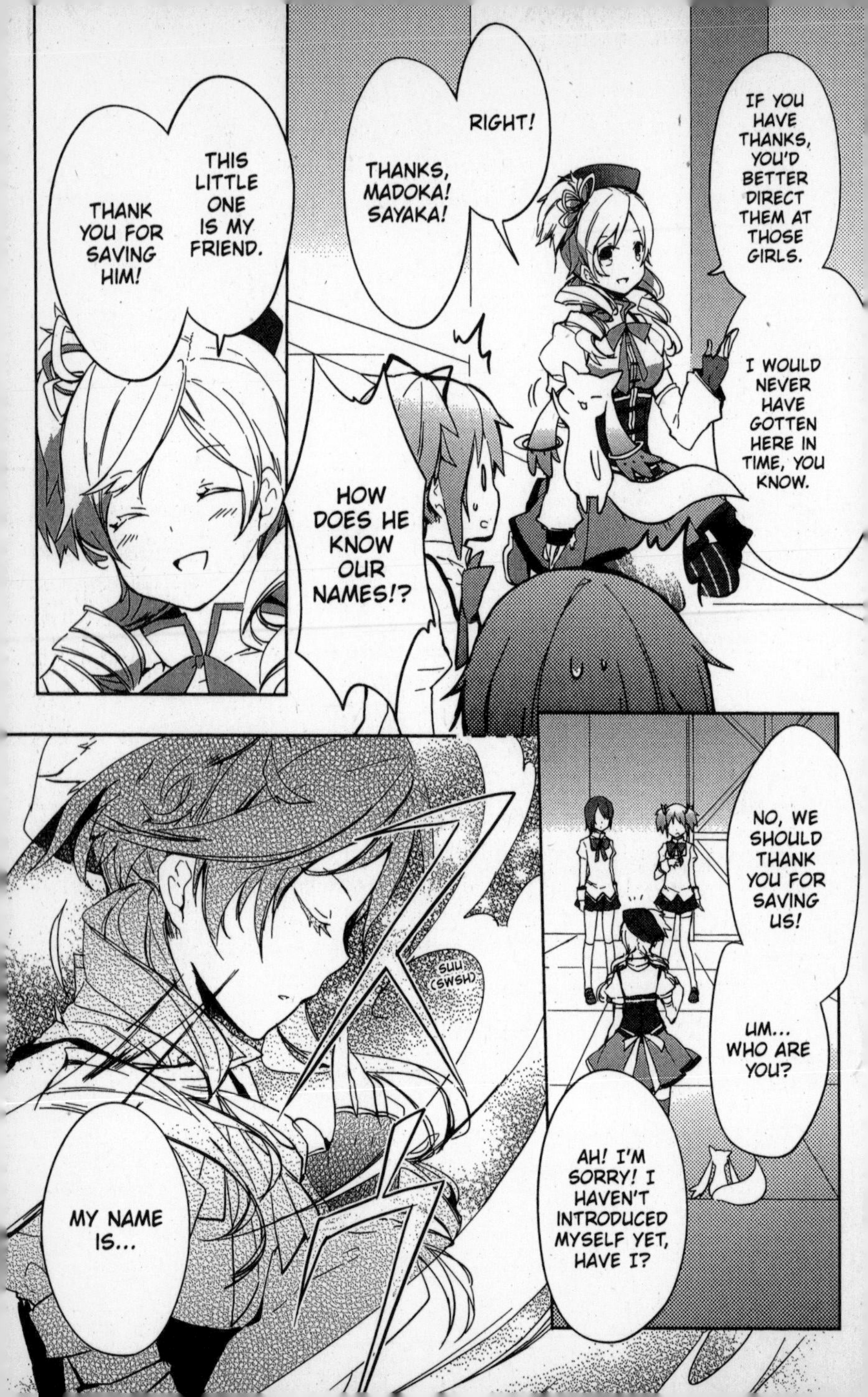

IF YOU HAVE THANKS, YOU'D BETTER DIRECT THEM AT THOSE GIRLS.
I WOULD NEVER HAVE GOTTEN HERE IN TIME, YOU KNOW.
RIGHT!
THANKS, MADOKA! SAYAKA!
HOW DOES HE KNOW OUR NAMES!?
THIS LITTLE ONE IS MY FRIEND.
THANK YOU FOR SAVING HIM!
NO, WE SHOULD THANK YOU FOR SAVING US!
UM... WHO ARE YOU?
AH! I'M SORRY! I HAVEN'T INTRODUCED MYSELF YET, HAVE I?
SUU (SWSH)
MY NAME IS...

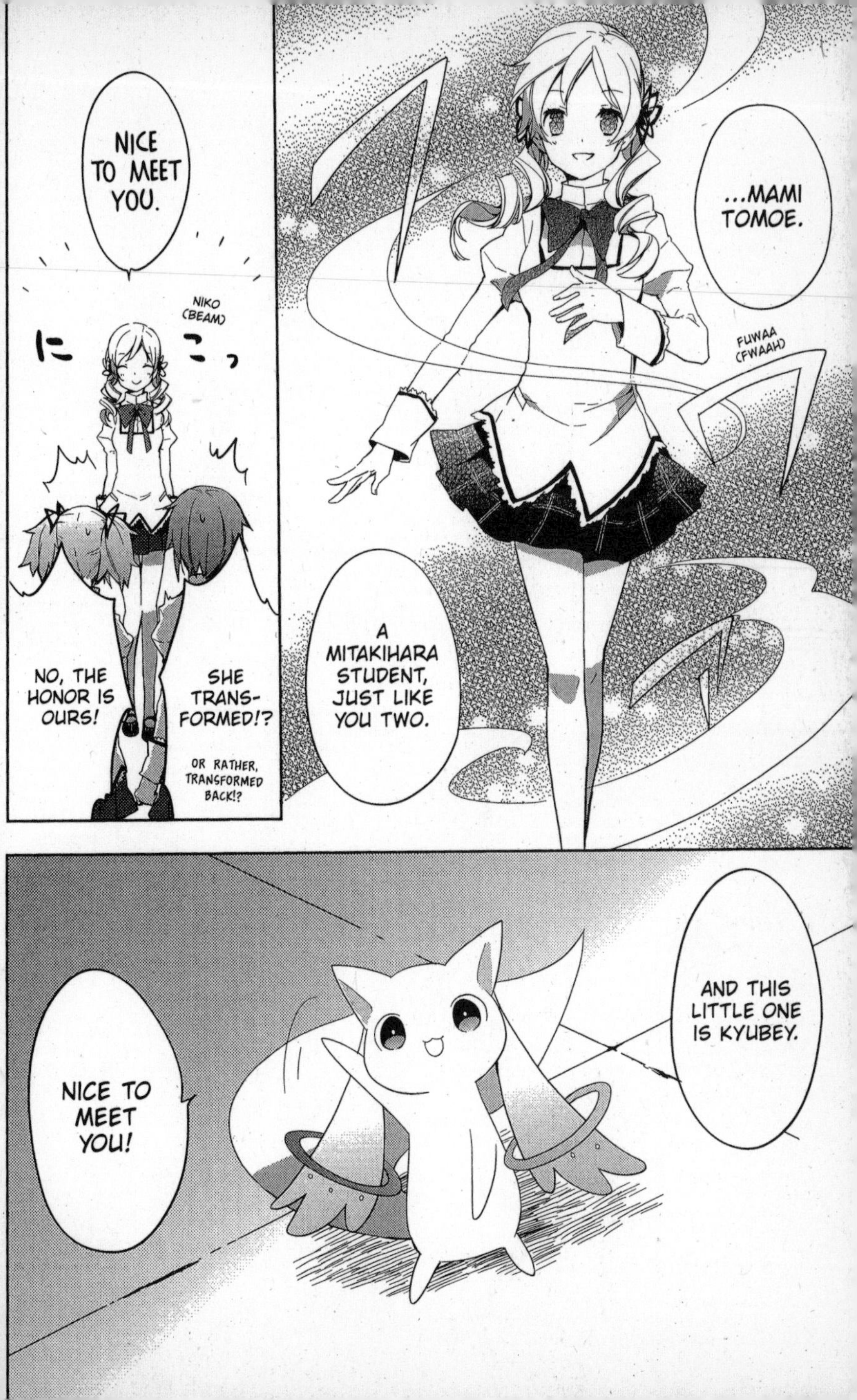
...MAMI TOMOE.
FUWAA (FWAAH)
A MITAKIHARA STUDENT, JUST LIKE YOU TWO.
NICE TO MEET YOU.
にこっ
NIKO (BEAM)
SHE TRANSFORMED!?
OR RATHER, TRANSFORMED BACK!?
NO, THE HONOR IS OURS!
AND THIS LITTLE ONE IS KYUBEY.
NICE TO MEET YOU!

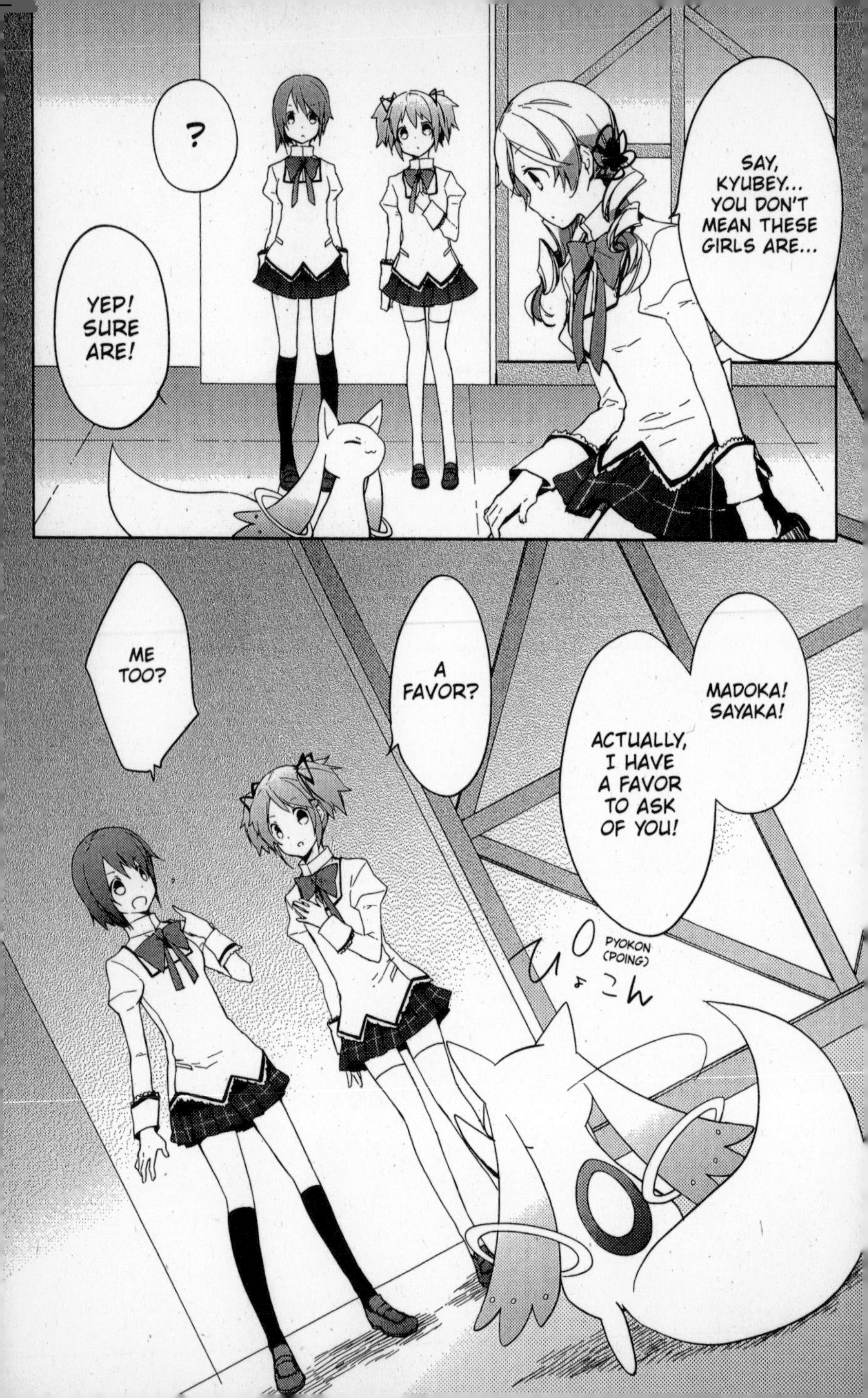

SAY, KYUBEY... YOU DON'T MEAN THESE GIRLS ARE...
?
YEP! SURE ARE!
MADOKA! SAYAKA!
ACTUALLY, I HAVE A FAVOR TO ASK OF YOU!
A FAVOR?
ME TOO?
ぴょこん
PYOKON (POING)

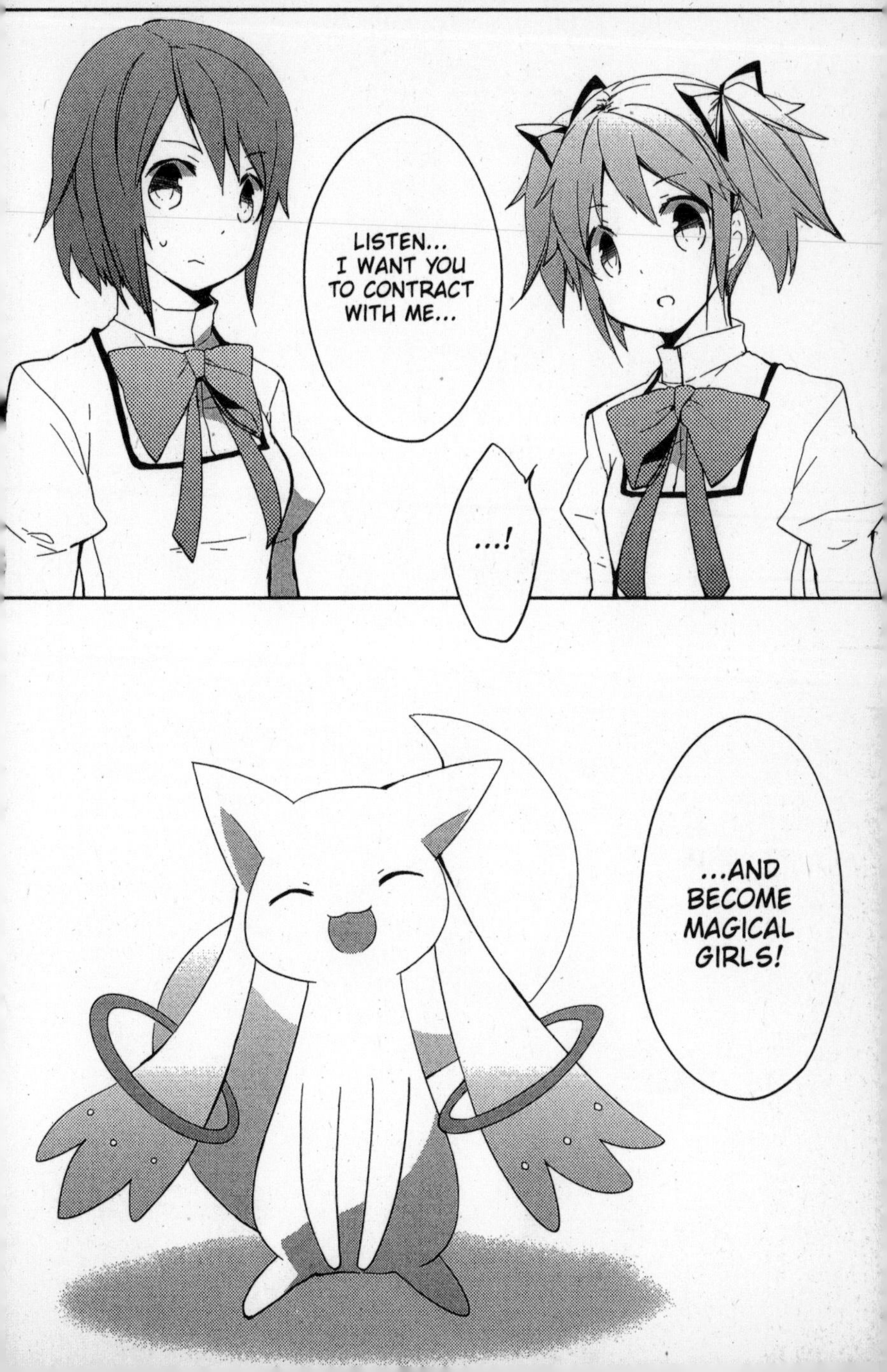
LISTEN... I WANT YOU TO CONTRACT WITH ME...
...!
...AND BECOME MAGICAL GIRLS!

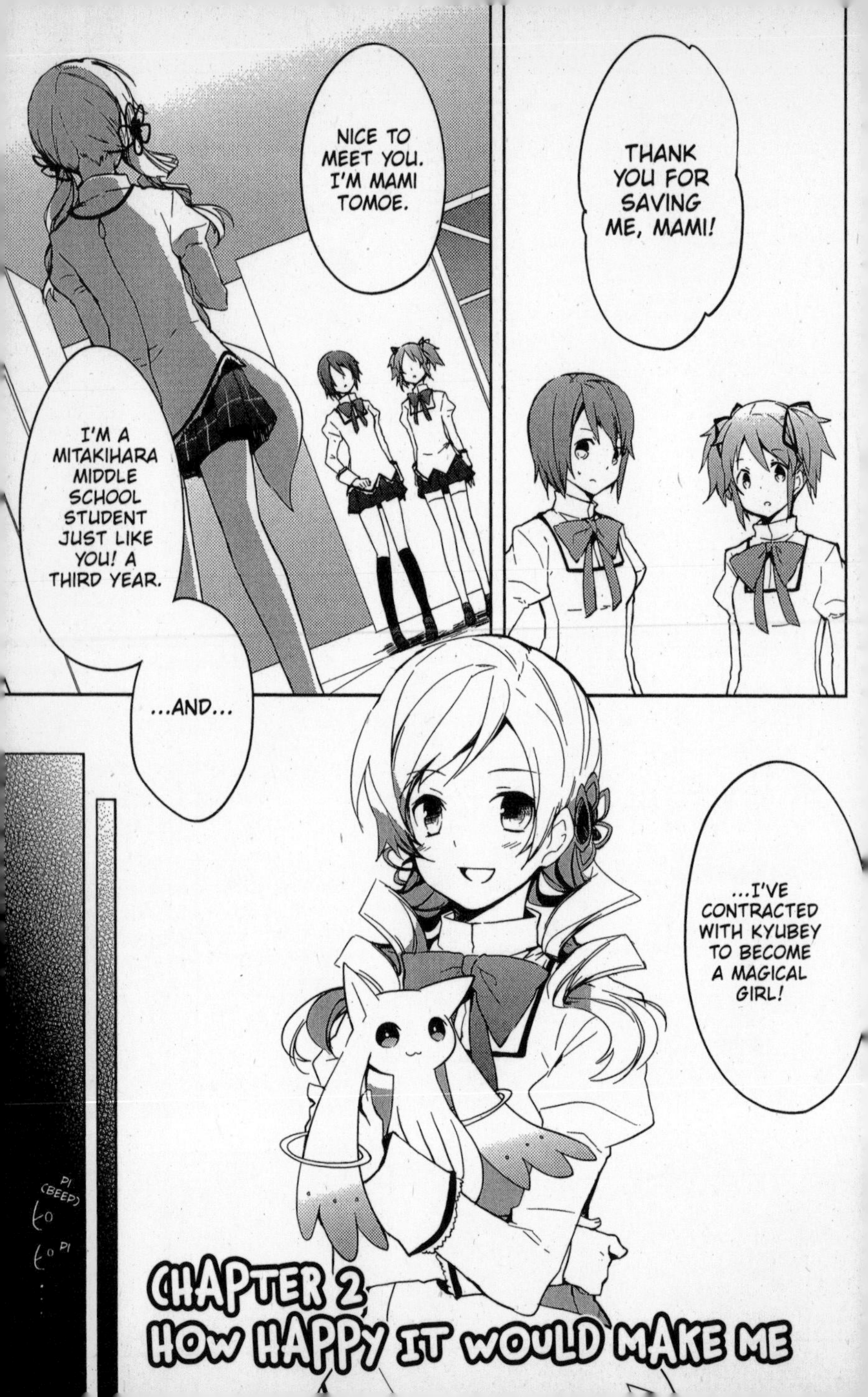
THANK YOU FOR SAVING ME, MAMI!
NICE TO MEET YOU. I'M MAMI TOMOE.
I'M A MITAKIHARA MIDDLE SCHOOL STUDENT JUST LIKE YOU! A THIRD YEAR.
...AND...
...I'VE CONTRACTED WITH KYUBEY TO BECOME A MAGICAL GIRL!
PI (BEEP)
PI
CHAPTER 2
HOW HAPPY IT WOULD MAKE ME

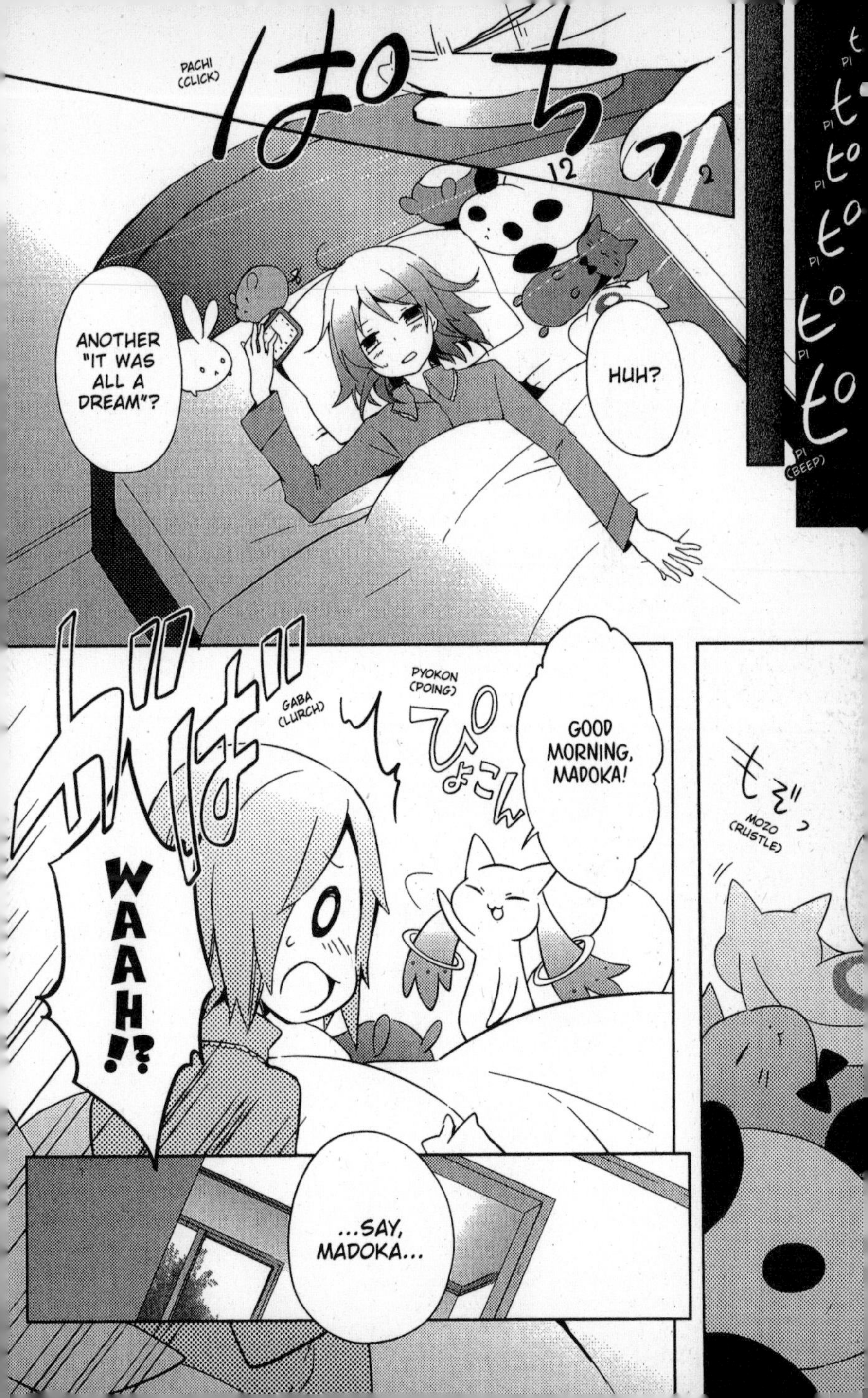

PI PI PI PI PI PI (BEEP)
PACHI (CLICK)
HUH?
ANOTHER "IT WAS ALL A DREAM"?
MOZO (RUSTLE)
GOOD MORNING, MADOKA!
PYOKON (POING)
GABA (LURCH)
WAAAH!?
...SAY, MADOKA...

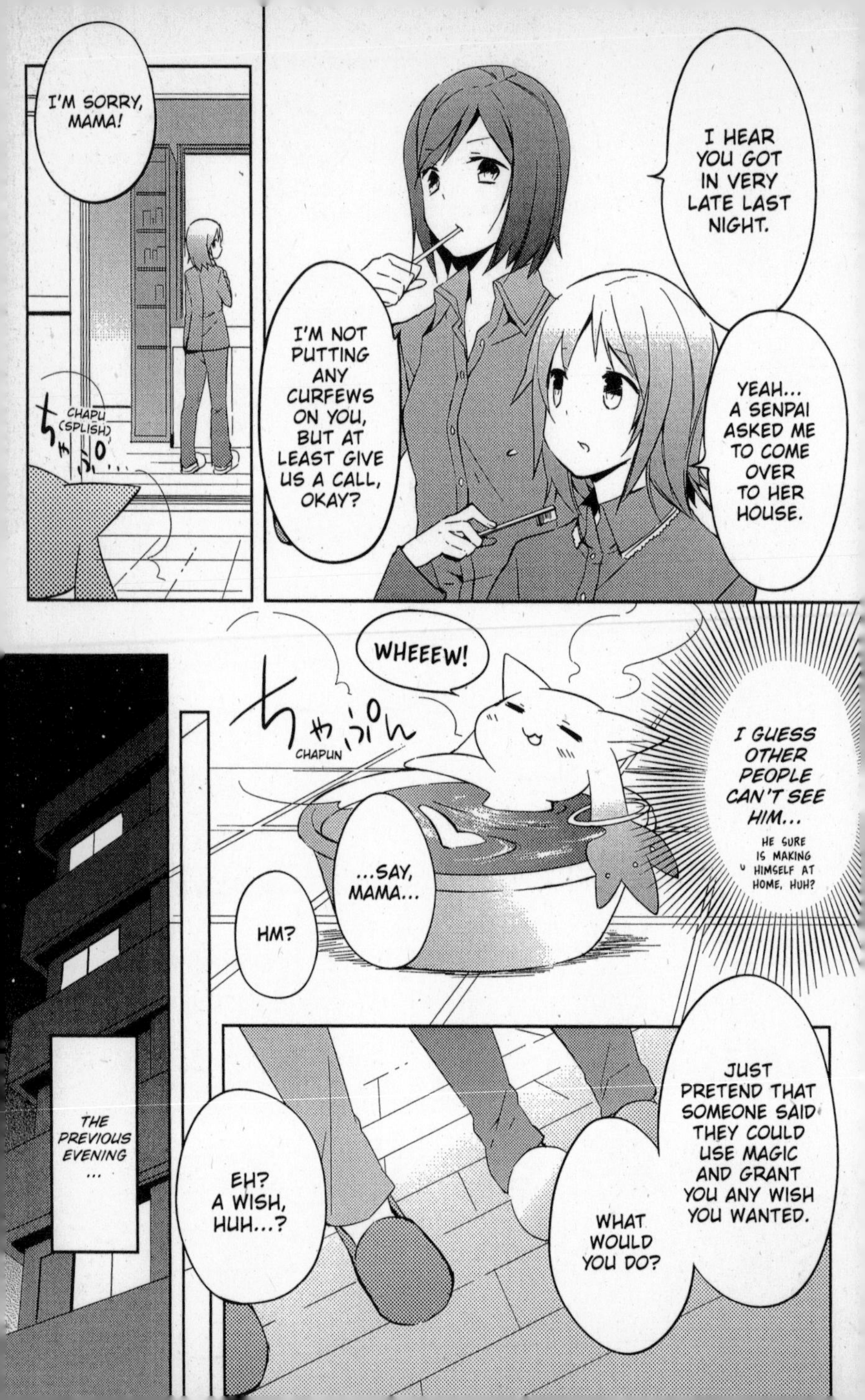
I HEAR YOU GOT IN VERY LATE LAST NIGHT.
YEAH... A SENPAI ASKED ME TO COME OVER TO HER HOUSE.
I'M NOT PUTTING ANY CURFEWS ON YOU, BUT AT LEAST GIVE US A CALL, OKAY?
I'M SORRY, MAMA!
CHAPU (SPLISH)
ちゃぷん
CHAPUN
WHEEEW!
I GUESS OTHER PEOPLE CAN'T SEE HIM...
HE SURE IS MAKING HIMSELF AT HOME, HUH?
...SAY, MAMA...
HM?
JUST PRETEND THAT SOMEONE SAID THEY COULD USE MAGIC AND GRANT YOU ANY WISH YOU WANTED.
WHAT WOULD YOU DO?
EH? A WISH, HUH...?
THE PREVIOUS EVENING...

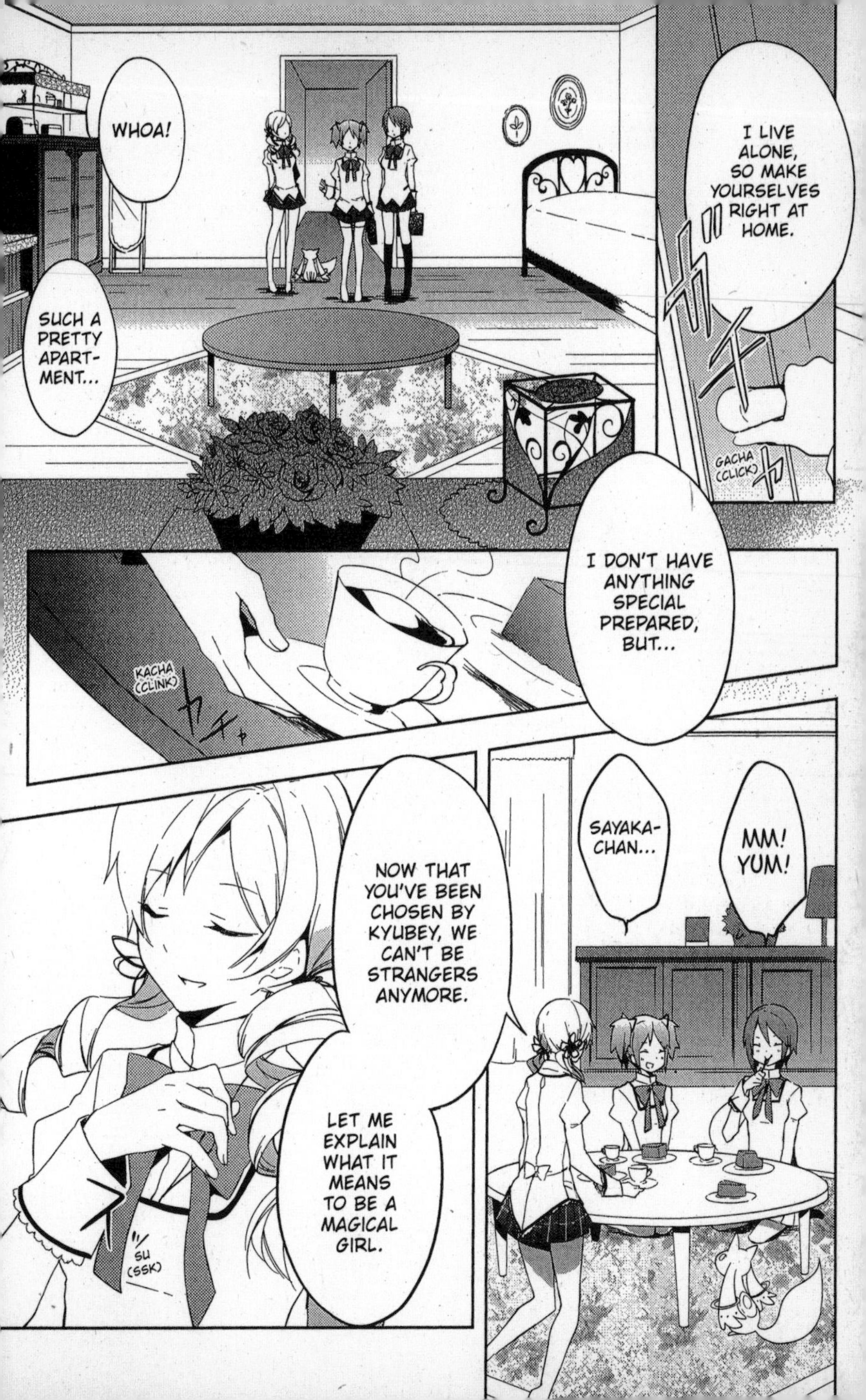
I LIVE ALONE, SO MAKE YOURSELVES RIGHT AT HOME.
GACHA (CLICK)
WHOA!
SUCH A PRETTY APART-MENT...
I DON'T HAVE ANYTHING SPECIAL PREPARED, BUT...
KACHA (CLINK)
MM! YUM!
SAYAKA-CHAN...
NOW THAT YOU'VE BEEN CHOSEN BY KYUBEY, WE CAN'T BE STRANGERS ANYMORE.
LET ME EXPLAIN WHAT IT MEANS TO BE A MAGICAL GIRL.
SU (SSK)

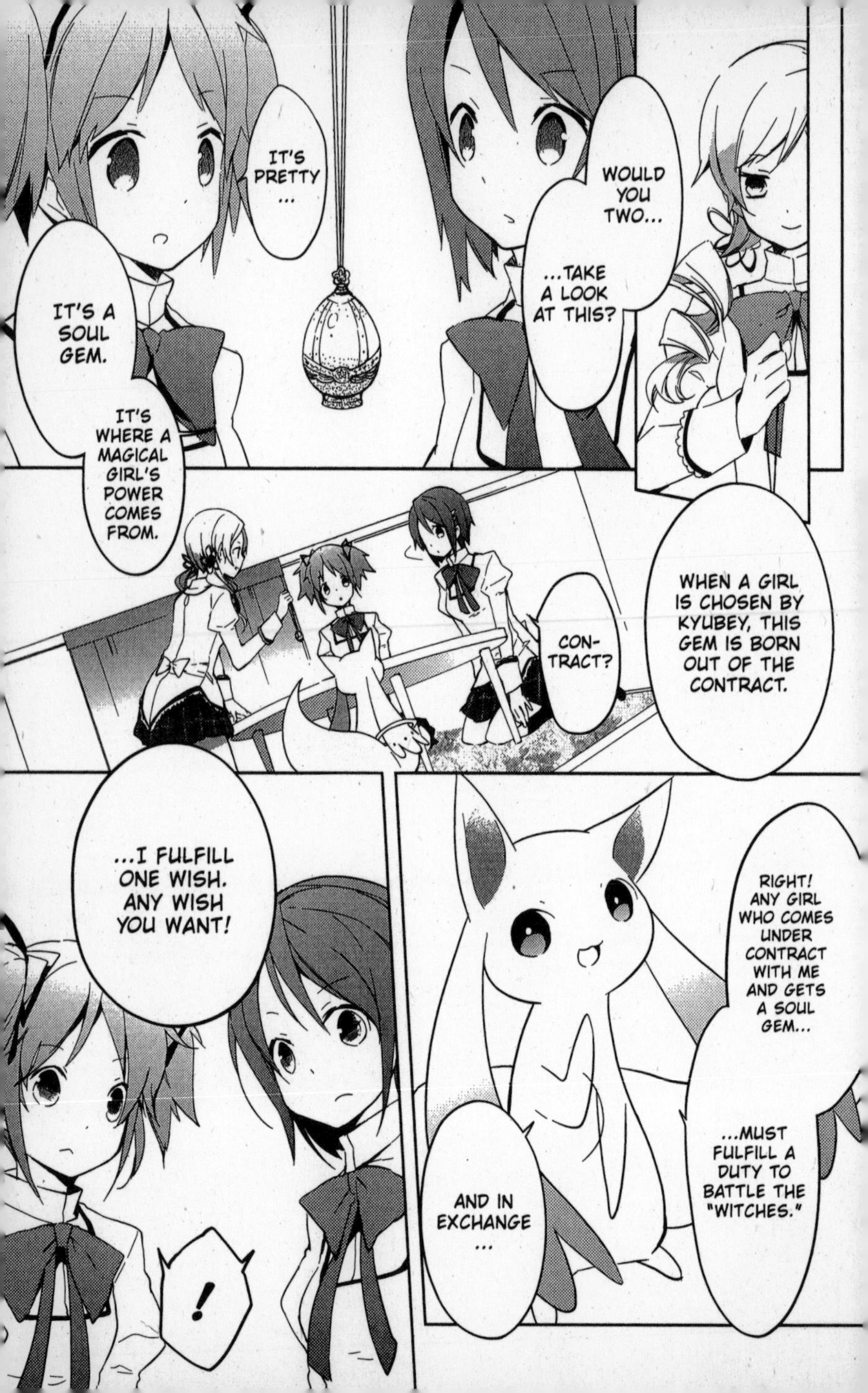
WOULD YOU TWO...
...TAKE A LOOK AT THIS?
IT'S PRETTY...
IT'S A SOUL GEM.
IT'S WHERE A MAGICAL GIRL'S POWER COMES FROM.
WHEN A GIRL IS CHOSEN BY KYUBEY, THIS GEM IS BORN OUT OF THE CONTRACT.
CON-TRACT?
RIGHT! ANY GIRL WHO COMES UNDER CONTRACT WITH ME AND GETS A SOUL GEM...
...MUST FULFILL A DUTY TO BATTLE THE "WITCHES."
AND IN EXCHANGE...
...I FULFILL ONE WISH. ANY WISH YOU WANT!
!

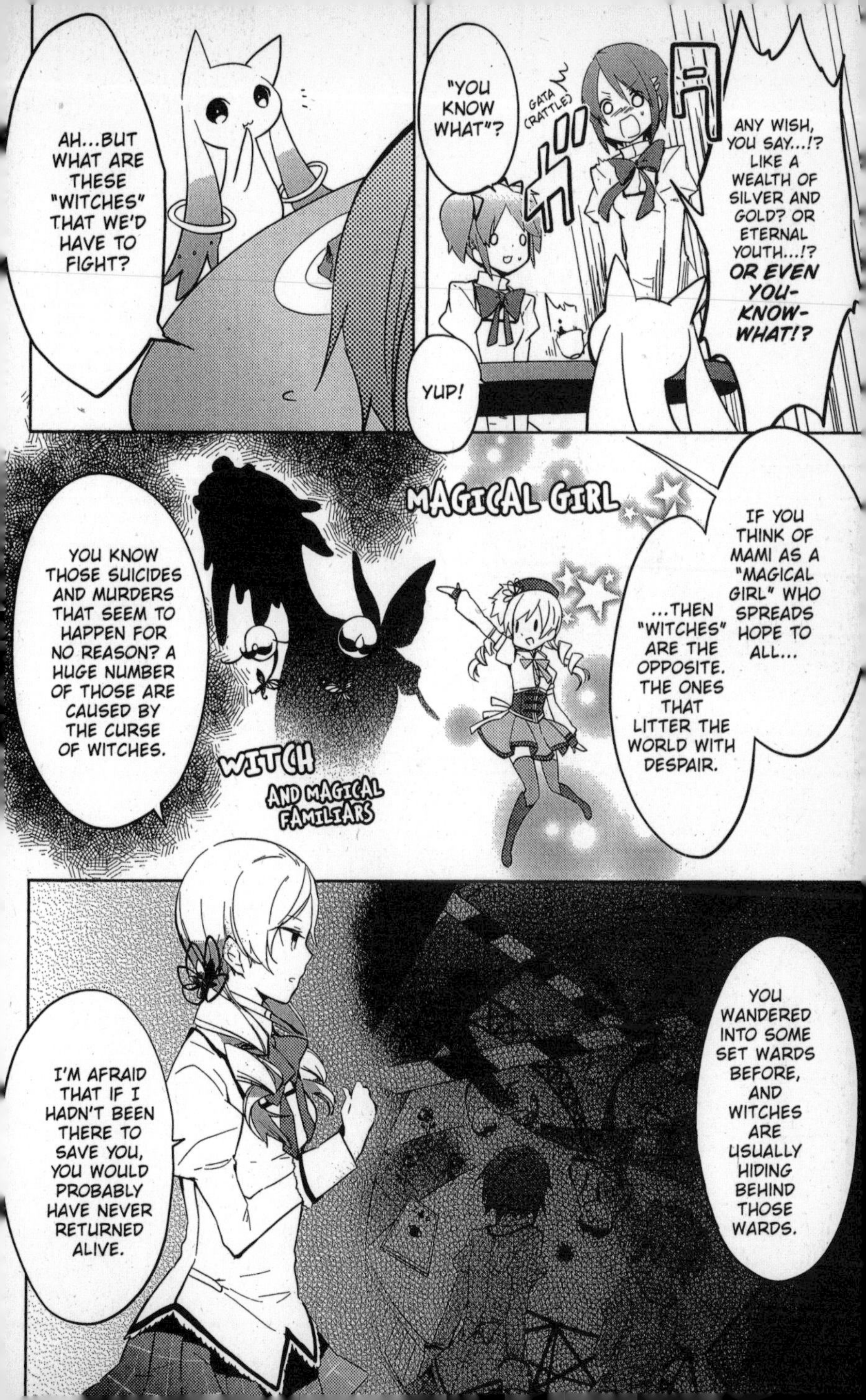
ANY WISH, YOU SAY...!? LIKE A WEALTH OF SILVER AND GOLD? OR ETERNAL YOUTH...!? OR EVEN YOU-KNOW-WHAT!?
GATA (RATTLE)
"YOU KNOW WHAT"?
YUP!
AH...BUT WHAT ARE THESE "WITCHES" THAT WE'D HAVE TO FIGHT?
IF YOU THINK OF MAMI AS A "MAGICAL GIRL" WHO SPREADS HOPE TO ALL...
...THEN "WITCHES" ARE THE OPPOSITE. THE ONES THAT LITTER THE WORLD WITH DESPAIR.
MAGICAL GIRL
YOU KNOW THOSE SUICIDES AND MURDERS THAT SEEM TO HAPPEN FOR NO REASON? A HUGE NUMBER OF THOSE ARE CAUSED BY THE CURSE OF WITCHES.
WITCH
AND MAGICAL FAMILIARS
YOU WANDERED INTO SOME SET WARDS BEFORE, AND WITCHES ARE USUALLY HIDING BEHIND THOSE WARDS.
I'M AFRAID THAT IF I HADN'T BEEN THERE TO SAVE YOU, YOU WOULD PROBABLY HAVE NEVER RETURNED ALIVE.

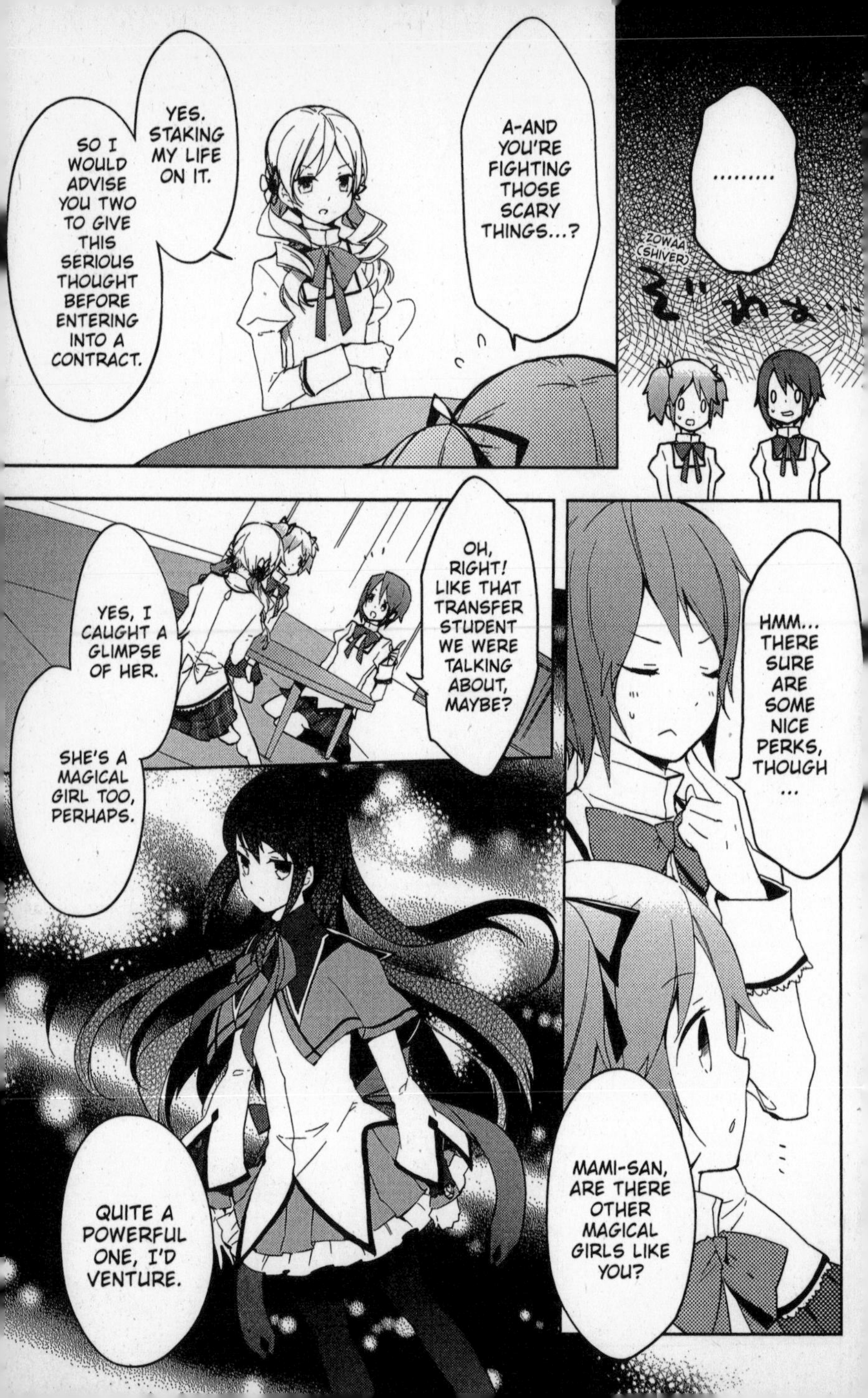
....
ZOWAA (SHIVER)
A-AND YOU'RE FIGHTING THOSE SCARY THINGS...?
YES. STAKING MY LIFE ON IT.
SO I WOULD ADVISE YOU TWO TO GIVE THIS SERIOUS THOUGHT BEFORE ENTERING INTO A CONTRACT.
HMM... THERE SURE ARE SOME NICE PERKS, THOUGH...
MAMI-SAN, ARE THERE OTHER MAGICAL GIRLS LIKE YOU?
OH, RIGHT! LIKE THAT TRANSFER STUDENT WE WERE TALKING ABOUT, MAYBE?
YES, I CAUGHT A GLIMPSE OF HER.
SHE'S A MAGICAL GIRL TOO, PERHAPS.
QUITE A POWERFUL ONE, I'D VENTURE.

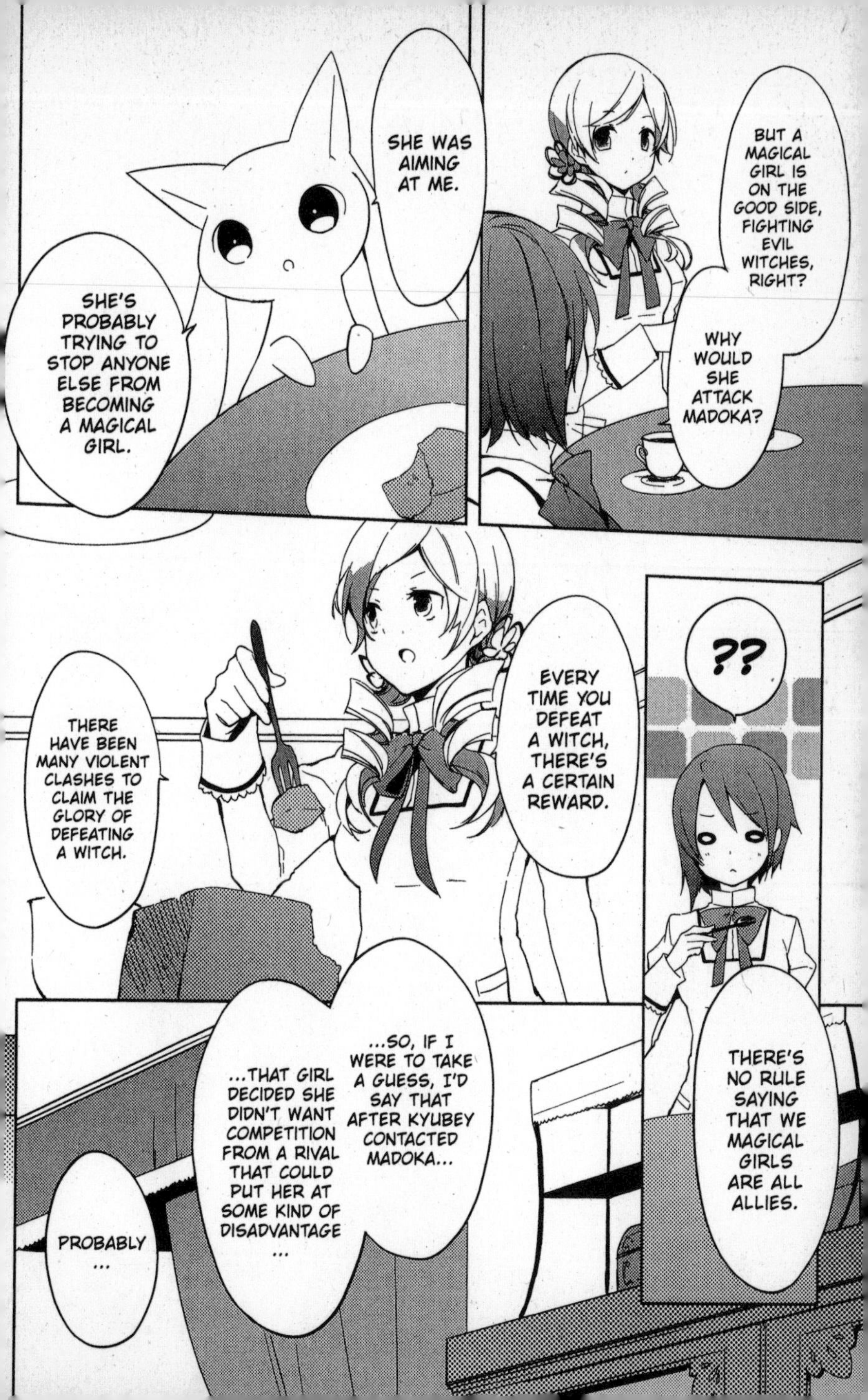
BUT A MAGICAL GIRL IS ON THE GOOD SIDE, FIGHTING EVIL WITCHES, RIGHT?
WHY WOULD SHE ATTACK MADOKA?
SHE WAS AIMING AT ME.
SHE'S PROBABLY TRYING TO STOP ANYONE ELSE FROM BECOMING A MAGICAL GIRL.
??
EVERY TIME YOU DEFEAT A WITCH, THERE'S A CERTAIN REWARD.
THERE HAVE BEEN MANY VIOLENT CLASHES TO CLAIM THE GLORY OF DEFEATING A WITCH.
THERE'S NO RULE SAYING THAT WE MAGICAL GIRLS ARE ALL ALLIES.
...SO, IF I WERE TO TAKE A GUESS, I'D SAY THAT AFTER KYUBEY CONTACTED MADOKA...
...THAT GIRL DECIDED SHE DIDN'T WANT COMPETITION FROM A RIVAL THAT COULD PUT HER AT SOME KIND OF DISADVANTAGE...
PROBABLY...

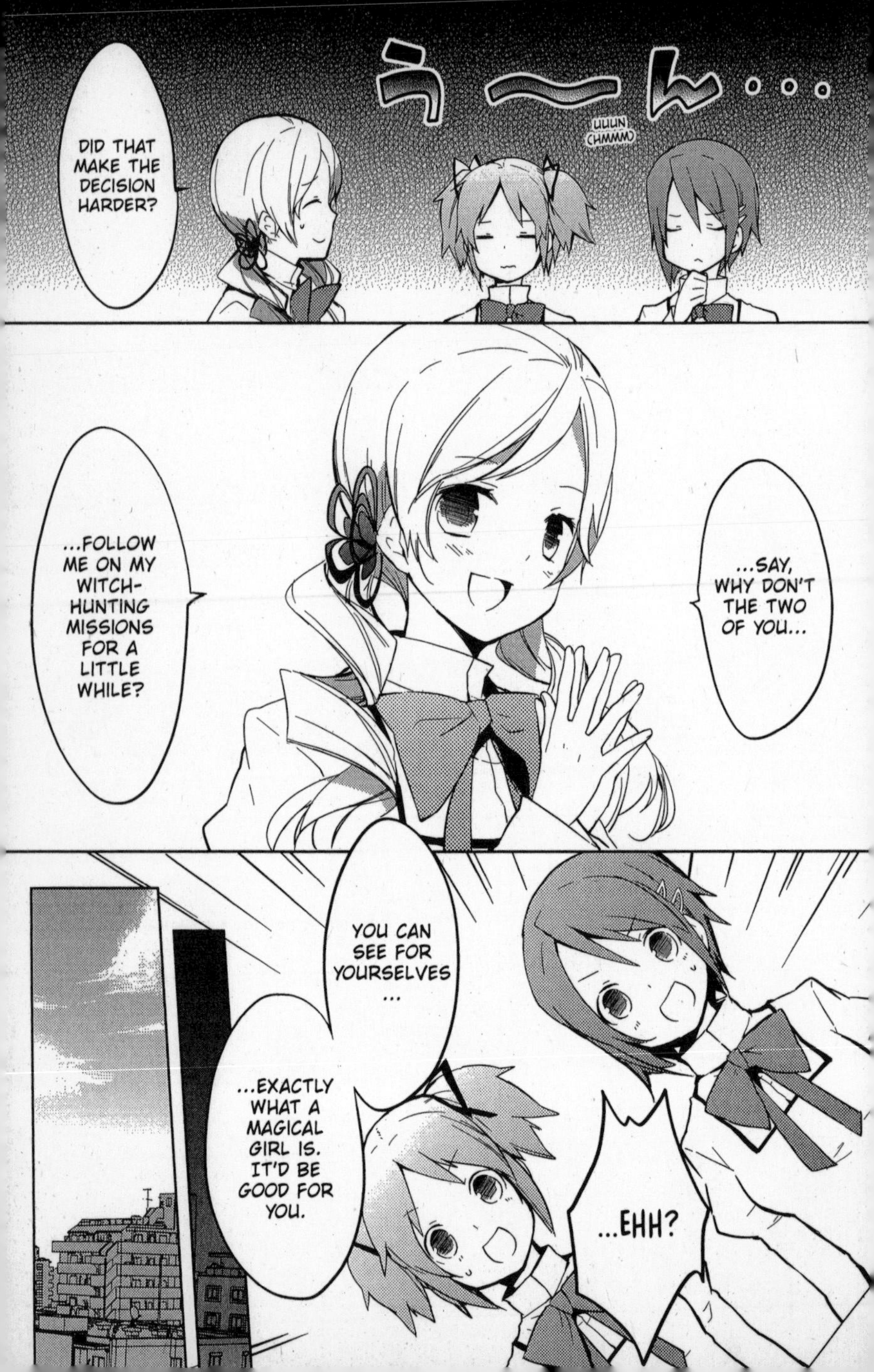
うーん…
UUUN (HMMM)
DID THAT MAKE THE DECISION HARDER?
...SAY, WHY DON'T THE TWO OF YOU...
...FOLLOW ME ON MY WITCH-HUNTING MISSIONS FOR A LITTLE WHILE?
YOU CAN SEE FOR YOURSELVES...
...EXACTLY WHAT A MAGICAL GIRL IS. IT'D BE GOOD FOR YOU.
...EHH?

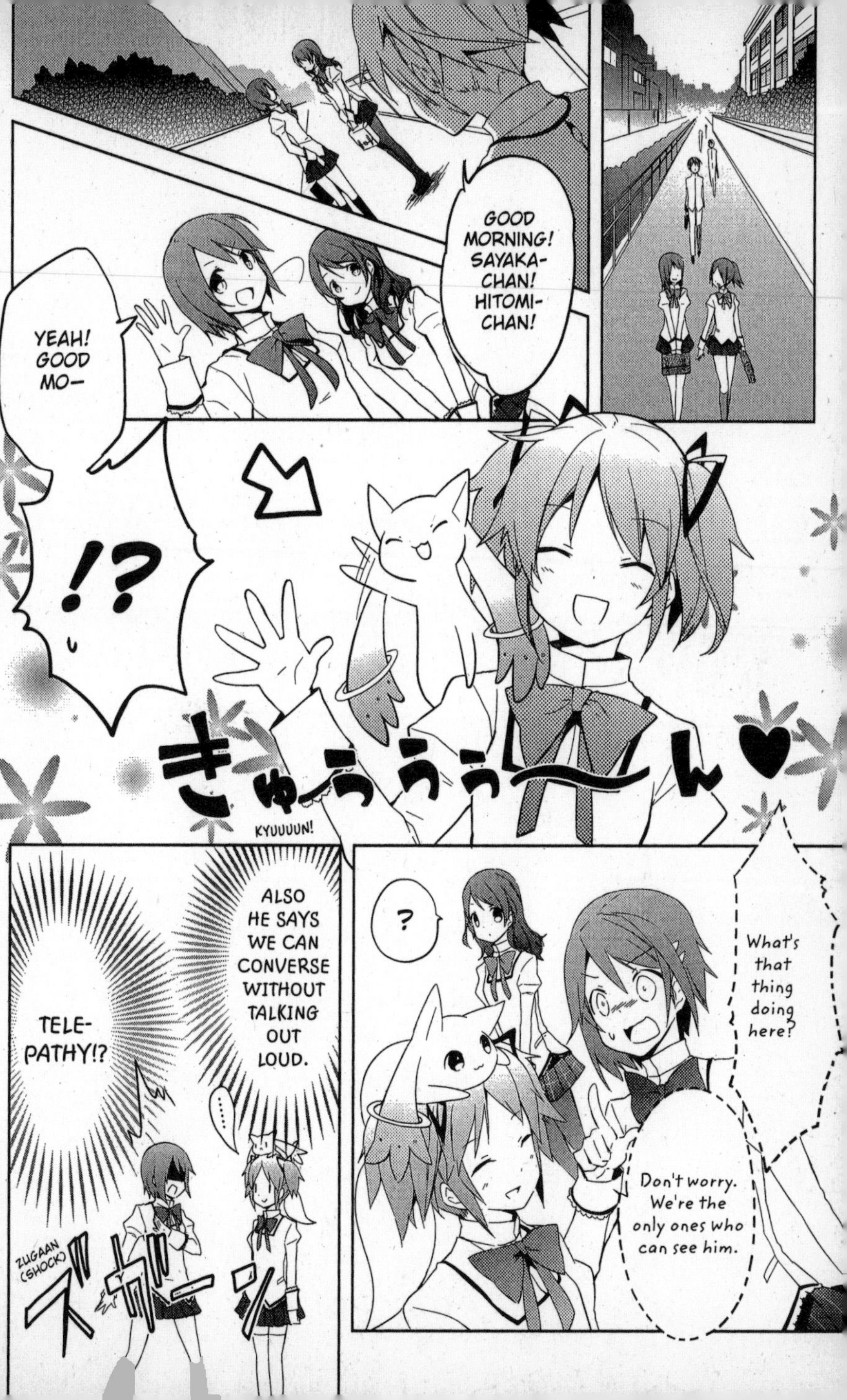
GOOD MORNING! SAYAKA-CHAN! HITOMI-CHAN!
YEAH! GOOD MO—
!?
きゅうううーん♥
KYUUUUN!
What's that thing doing here?
?
Don't worry. We're the only ones who can see him.
ALSO HE SAYS WE CAN CONVERSE WITHOUT TALKING OUT LOUD.
TELE-PATHY!?
......
ZUGAAN (SHOCK)

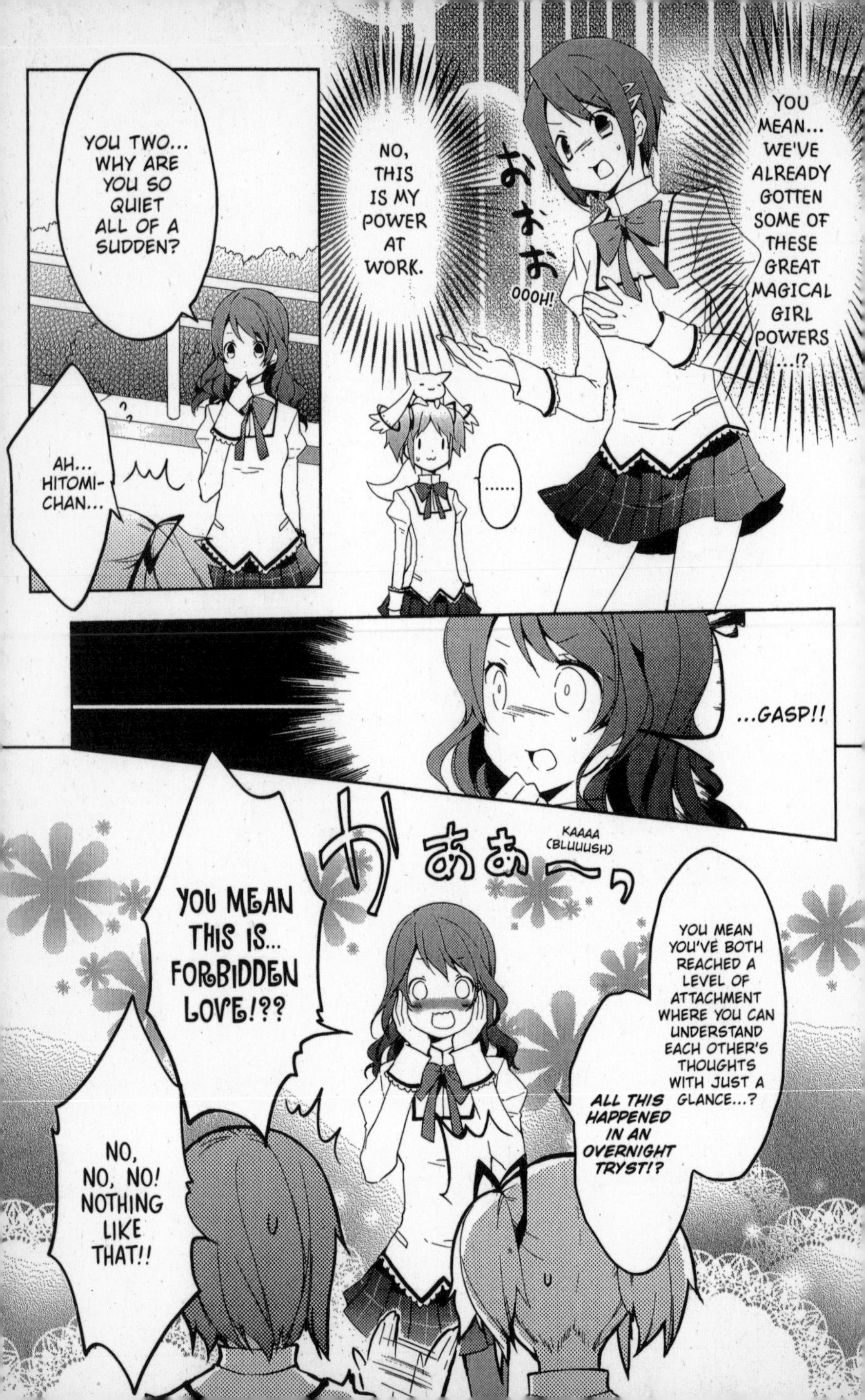

YOU MEAN... WE'VE ALREADY GOTTEN SOME OF THESE GREAT MAGICAL GIRL POWERS...!?
おおお
OOOH!
NO, THIS IS MY POWER AT WORK.
......
YOU TWO... WHY ARE YOU SO QUIET ALL OF A SUDDEN?
AH... HITOMI-CHAN...
...GASP!!
かぁぁ〜
KAAAA (BLUUUSH)
YOU MEAN YOU'VE BOTH REACHED A LEVEL OF ATTACHMENT WHERE YOU CAN UNDERSTAND EACH OTHER'S THOUGHTS WITH JUST A GLANCE...?
ALL THIS HAPPENED IN AN OVERNIGHT TRYST!?
YOU MEAN THIS IS... FORBIDDEN LOVE!??
NO, NO, NO! NOTHING LIKE THAT!!

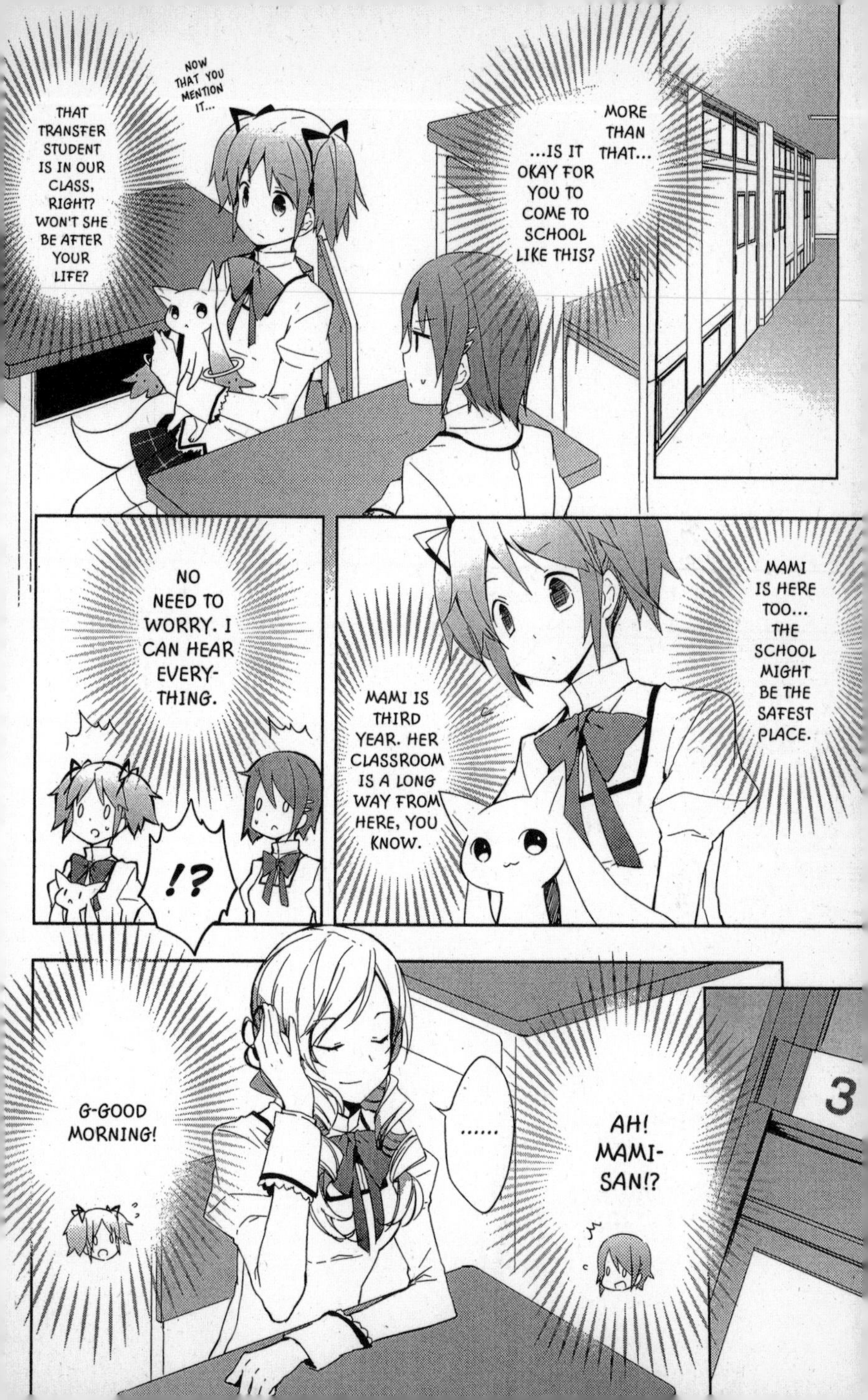
MORE THAN THAT...
...IS IT OKAY FOR YOU TO COME TO SCHOOL LIKE THIS?
NOW THAT YOU MENTION IT...
THAT TRANSFER STUDENT IS IN OUR CLASS, RIGHT? WON'T SHE BE AFTER YOUR LIFE?
MAMI IS HERE TOO... THE SCHOOL MIGHT BE THE SAFEST PLACE.
MAMI IS THIRD YEAR. HER CLASSROOM IS A LONG WAY FROM HERE, YOU KNOW.
NO NEED TO WORRY. I CAN HEAR EVERY-THING.
!?
3
AH! MAMI-SAN!?
......
G-GOOD MORNING!

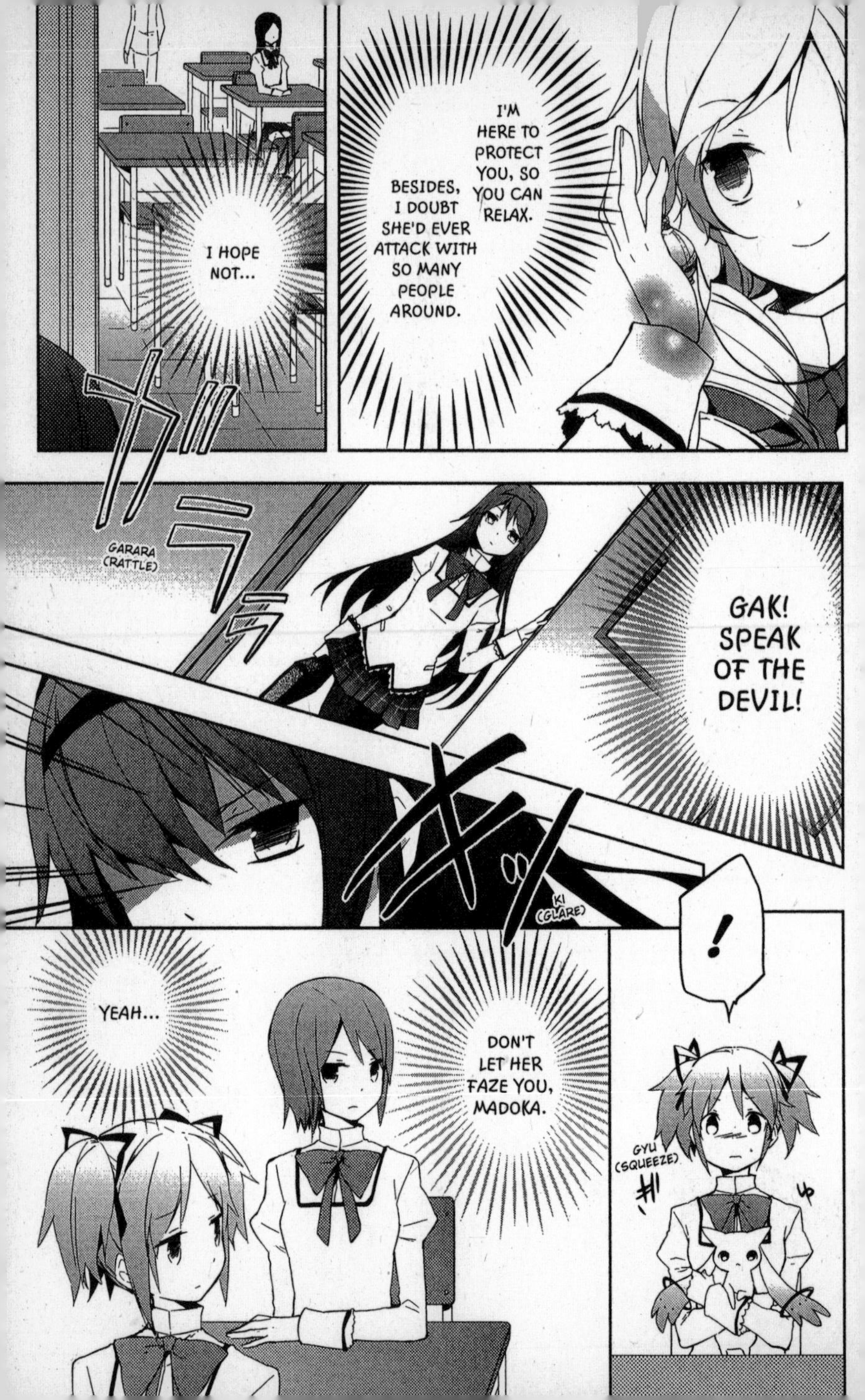
I'M HERE TO PROTECT YOU, SO YOU CAN RELAX.
BESIDES, I DOUBT SHE'D EVER ATTACK WITH SO MANY PEOPLE AROUND.
I HOPE NOT...
GAK! SPEAK OF THE DEVIL!
GARARA (RATTLE)
KI (GLARE)
!
GYU (SQUEEZE)
DON'T LET HER FAZE YOU, MADOKA.
YEAH...

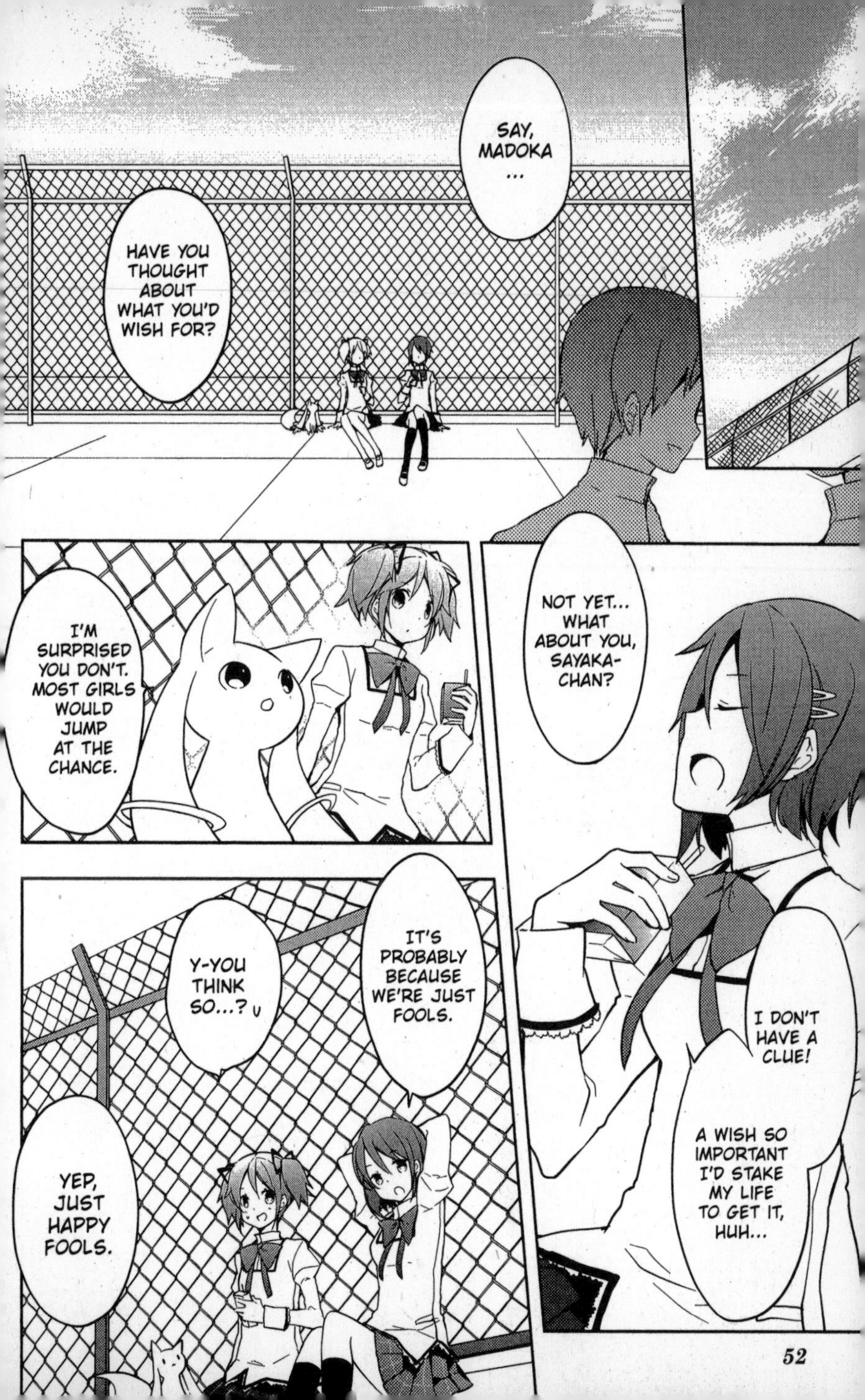
SAY, MADOKA ...
HAVE YOU THOUGHT ABOUT WHAT YOU'D WISH FOR?
NOT YET... WHAT ABOUT YOU, SAYAKA-CHAN?
I DON'T HAVE A CLUE!
A WISH SO IMPORTANT I'D STAKE MY LIFE TO GET IT, HUH...
I'M SURPRISED YOU DON'T. MOST GIRLS WOULD JUMP AT THE CHANCE.
IT'S PROBABLY BECAUSE WE'RE JUST FOOLS.
Y-YOU THINK SO...?
YEP, JUST HAPPY FOOLS.

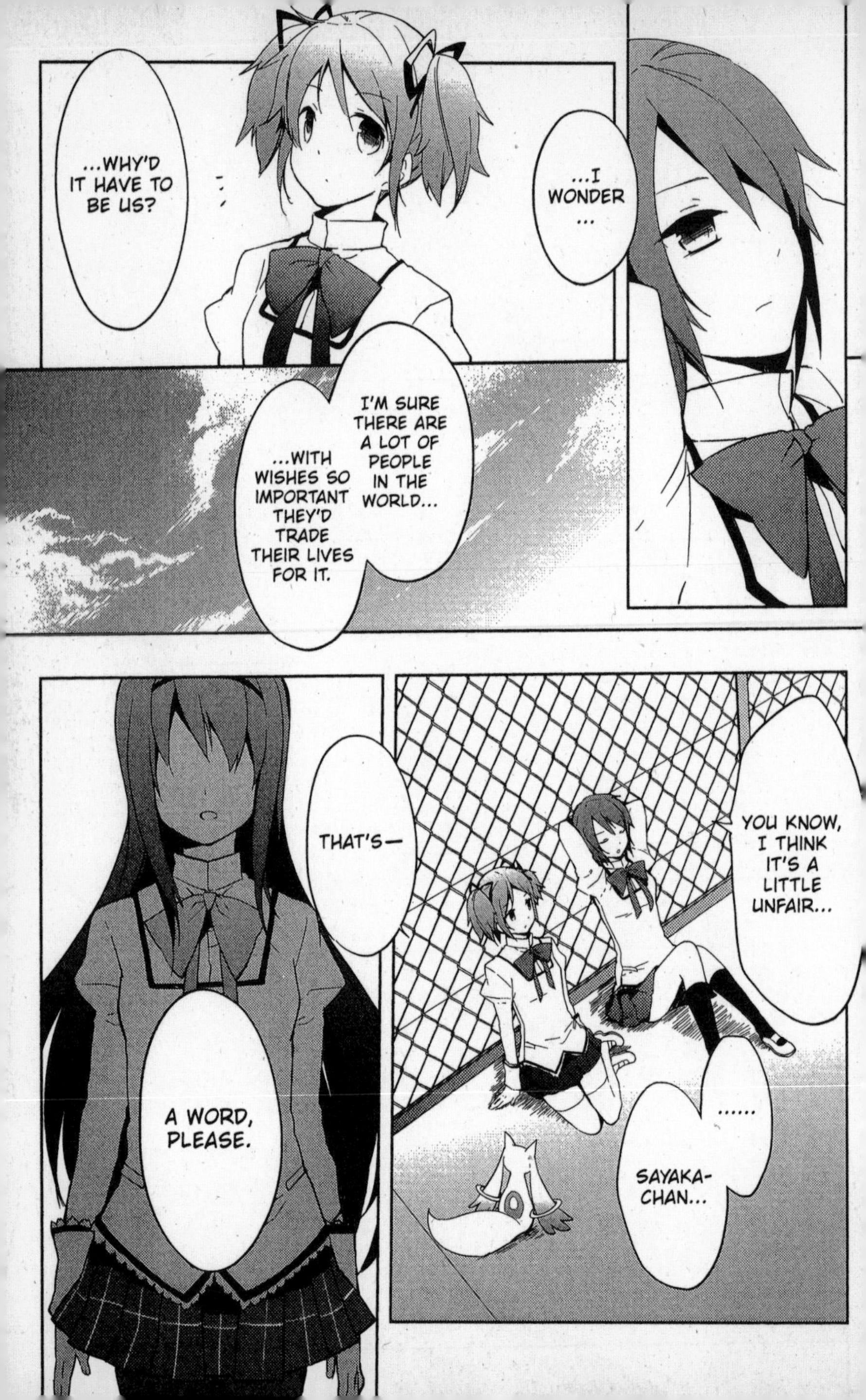
...I WONDER ...
...WHY'D IT HAVE TO BE US?
I'M SURE THERE ARE A LOT OF PEOPLE IN THE WORLD...
...WITH WISHES SO IMPORTANT THEY'D TRADE THEIR LIVES FOR IT.
YOU KNOW, I THINK IT'S A LITTLE UNFAIR...
THAT'S—
......
SAYAKA-CHAN...
A WORD, PLEASE.

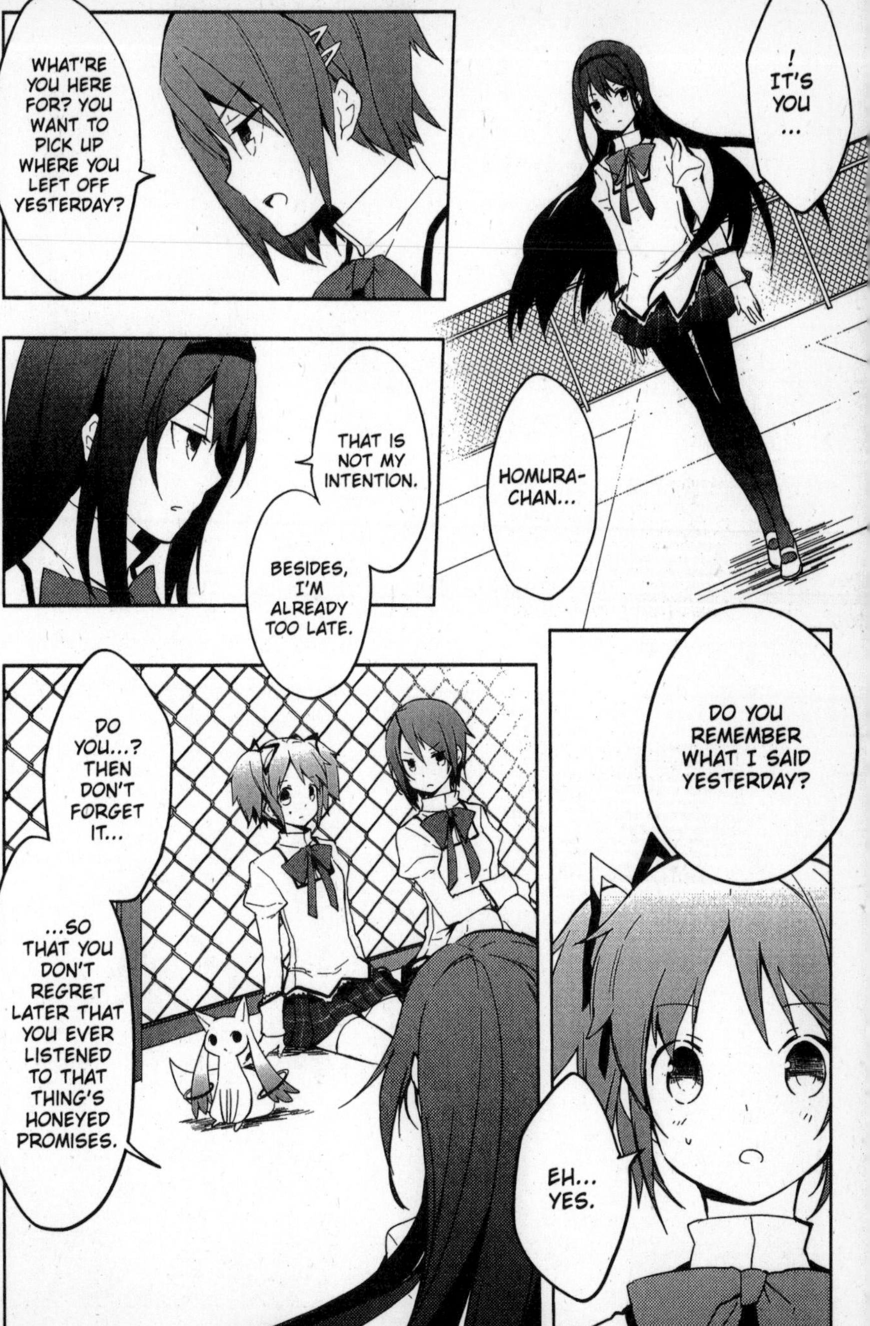
! IT'S YOU ...
HOMURA-CHAN...
WHAT'RE YOU HERE FOR? YOU WANT TO PICK UP WHERE YOU LEFT OFF YESTERDAY?
THAT IS NOT MY INTENTION.
BESIDES, I'M ALREADY TOO LATE.
DO YOU REMEMBER WHAT I SAID YESTERDAY?
EH... YES.
DO YOU...? THEN DON'T FORGET IT...
...SO THAT YOU DON'T REGRET LATER THAT YOU EVER LISTENED TO THAT THING'S HONEYED PROMISES.

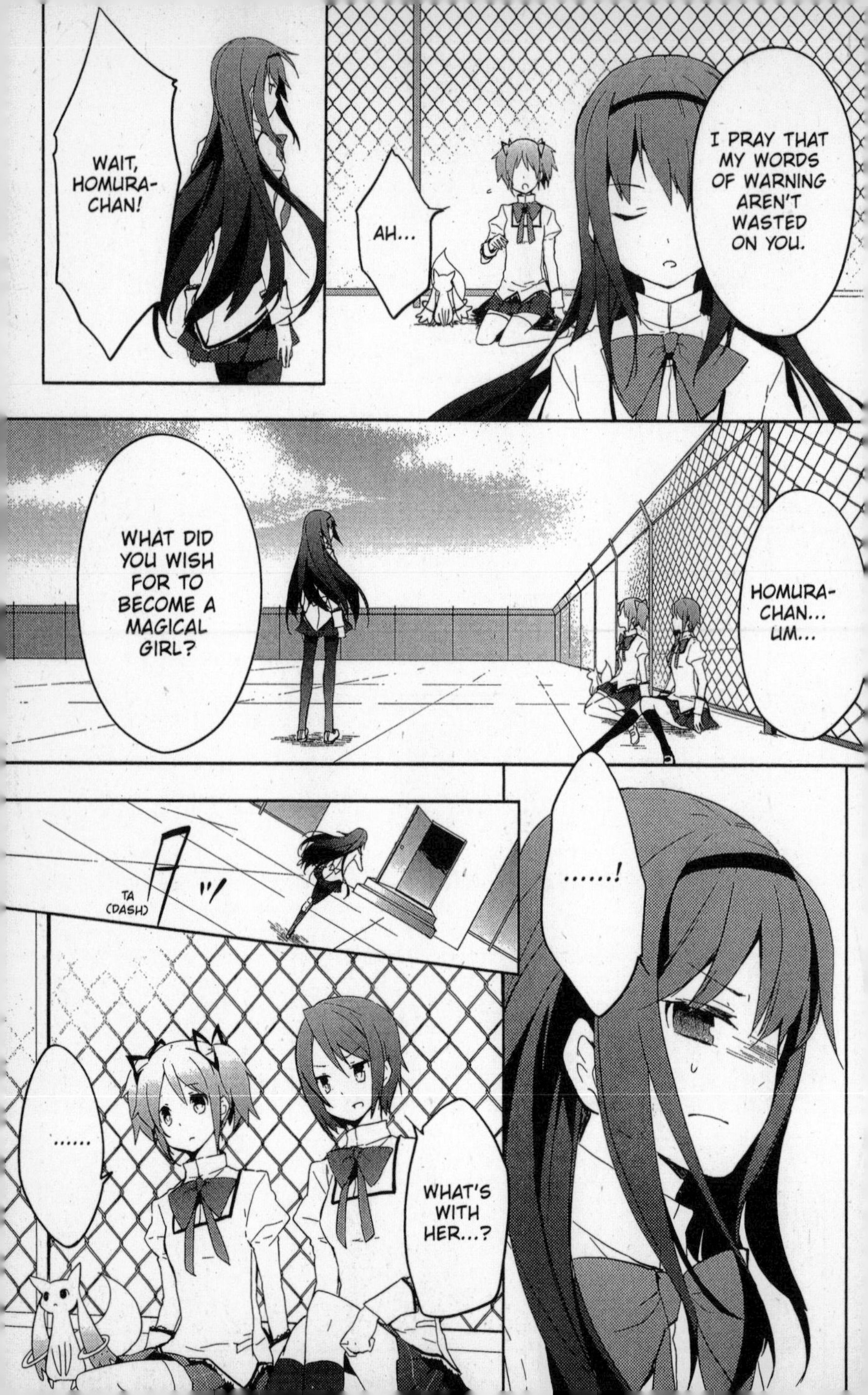
I PRAY THAT MY WORDS OF WARNING AREN'T WASTED ON YOU.
AH...
WAIT, HOMURA-CHAN!
HOMURA-CHAN... UM...
WHAT DID YOU WISH FOR TO BECOME A MAGICAL GIRL?
......!
TA (DASH)
WHAT'S WITH HER...?
......

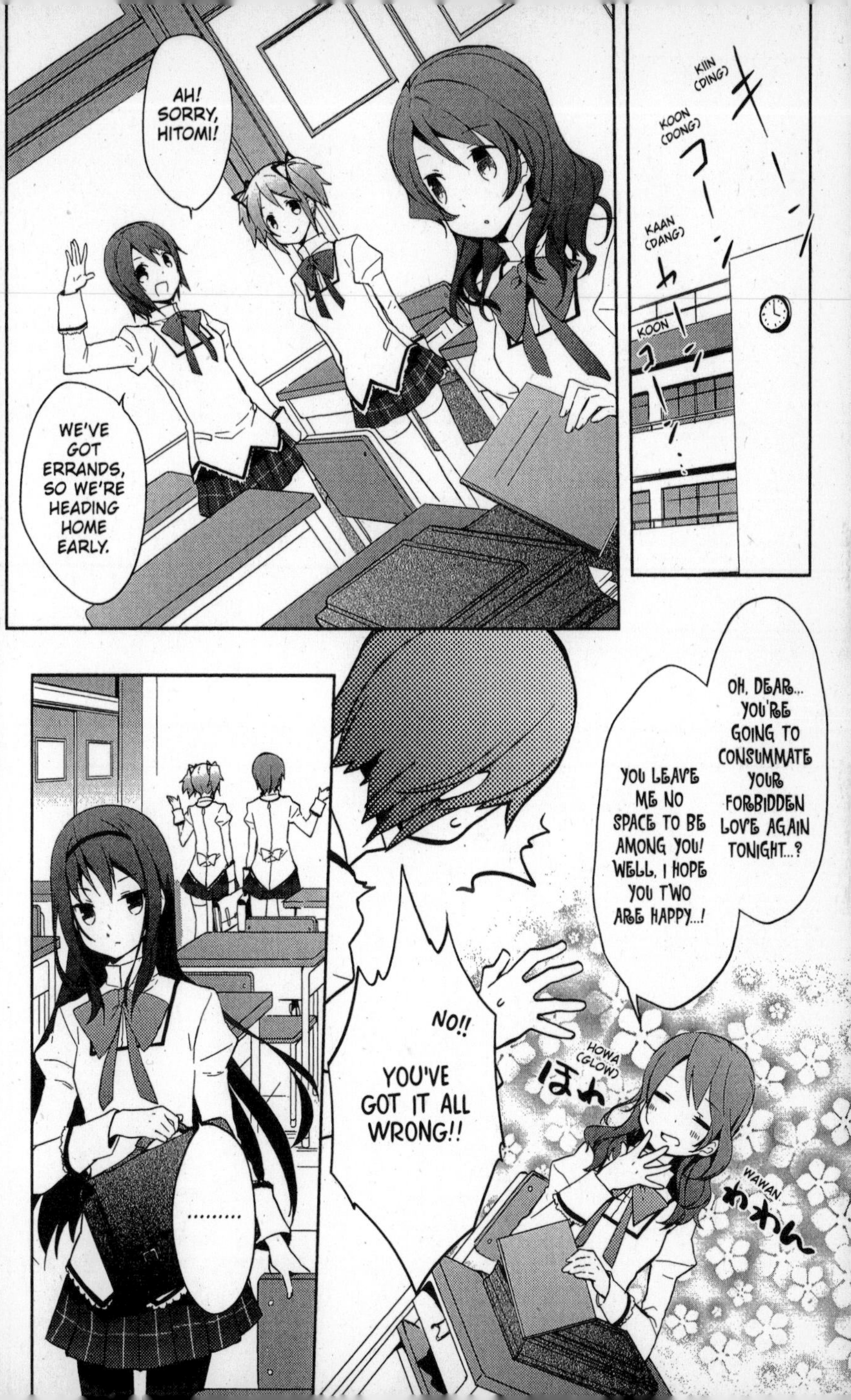
KIIN (DING)
KOON (DONG)
KAAN (DANG)
KOON
AH! SORRY, HITOMI!
WE'VE GOT ERRANDS, SO WE'RE HEADING HOME EARLY.
OH, DEAR... YOU'RE GOING TO CONSUMMATE YOUR FORBIDDEN LOVE AGAIN TONIGHT...?
YOU LEAVE ME NO SPACE TO BE AMONG YOU! WELL, I HOPE YOU TWO ARE HAPPY...!
NO!!
HOWA (GLOW)
YOU'VE GOT IT ALL WRONG!!
WAWAN
....

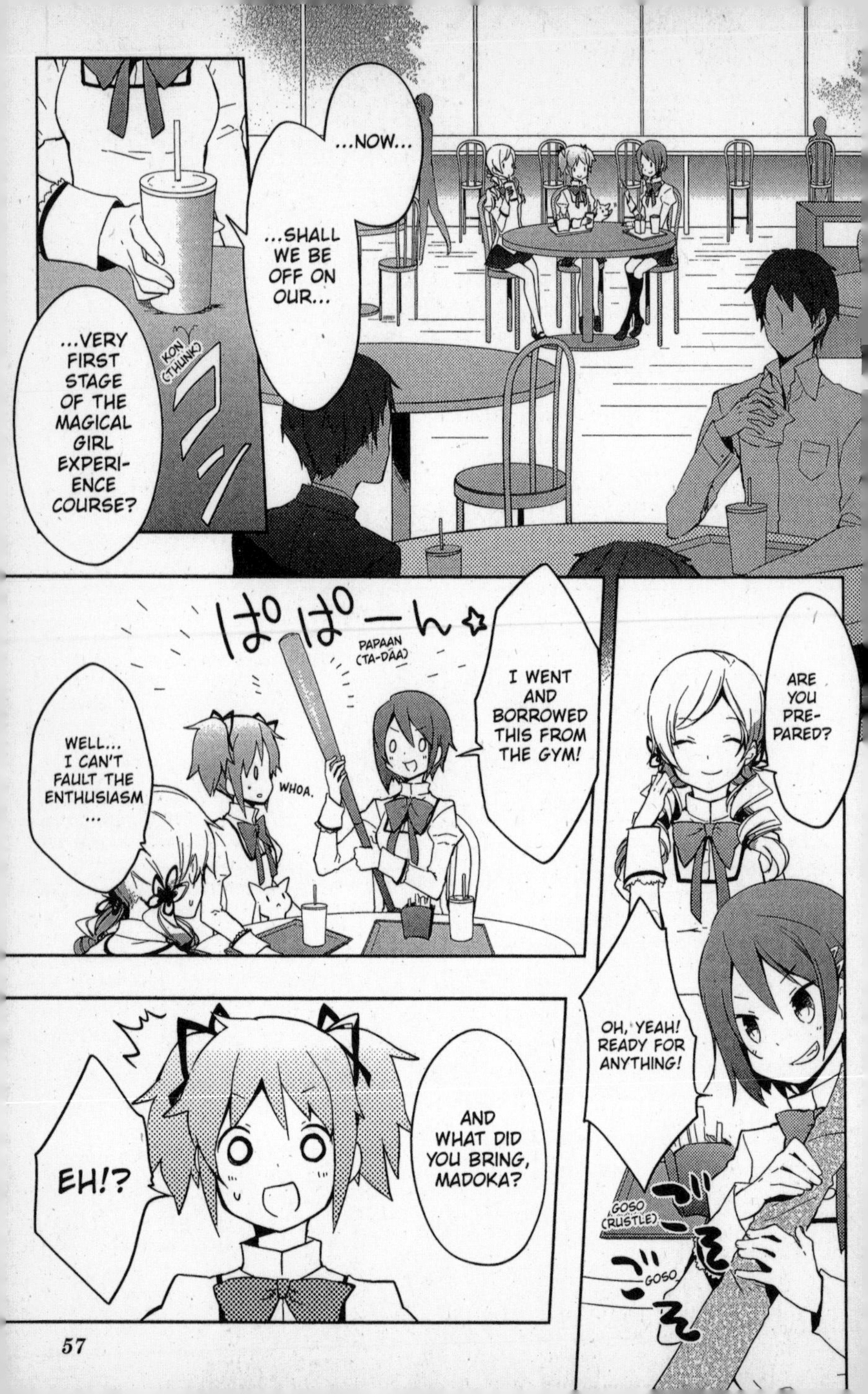
...NOW...
...SHALL WE BE OFF ON OUR...
...VERY FIRST STAGE OF THE MAGICAL GIRL EXPERIENCE COURSE?
KON (THUNK)
ARE YOU PREPARED?
OH, YEAH! READY FOR ANYTHING!
GOSO (RUSTLE)
GOSO
ぱぱーん☆
PAPAAN (TA-DAA)
I WENT AND BORROWED THIS FROM THE GYM!
WHOA.
WELL... I CAN'T FAULT THE ENTHUSIASM ...
AND WHAT DID YOU BRING, MADOKA?
EH!?

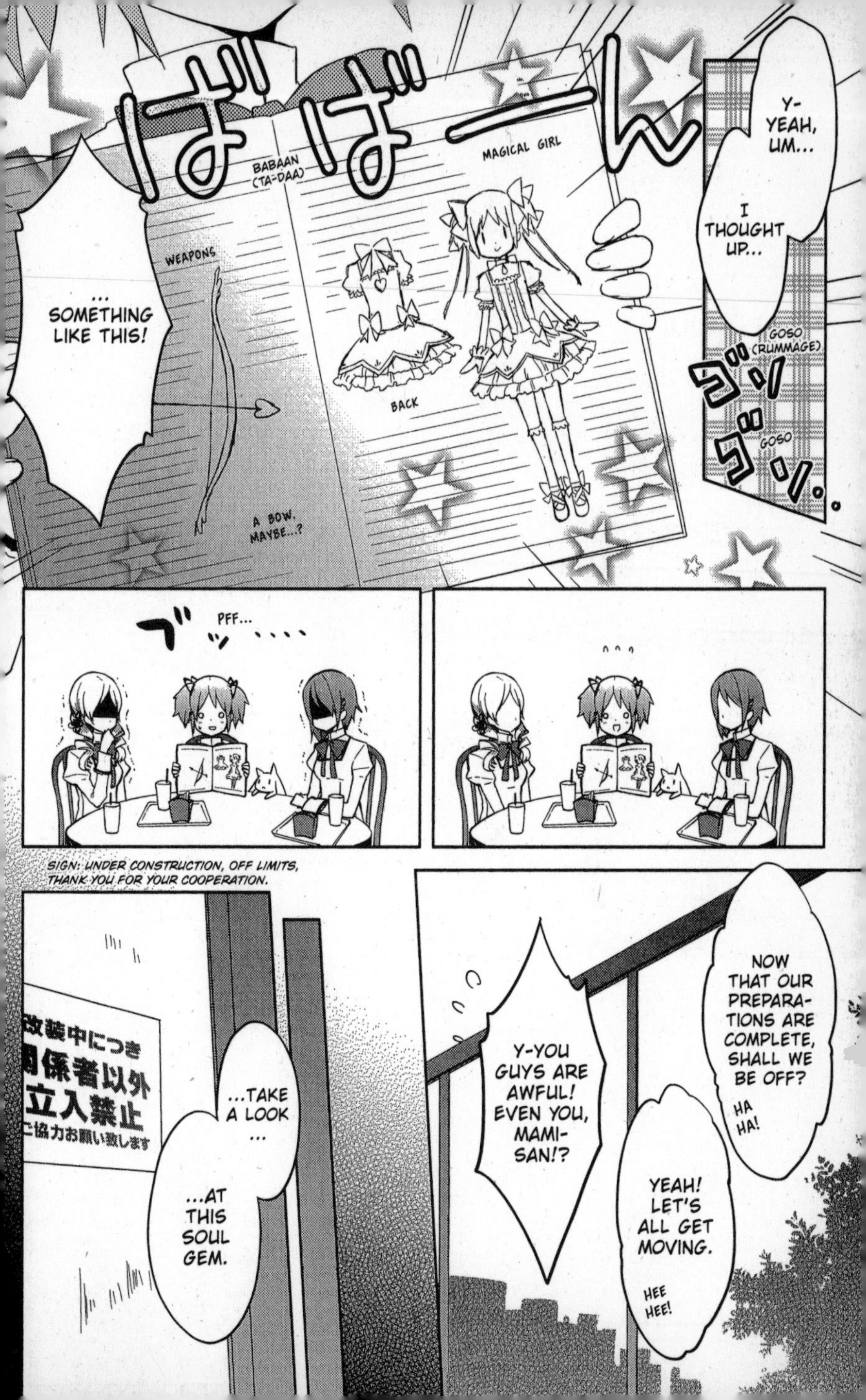
Y-YEAH, UM...
I THOUGHT UP...
GOSO (RUMMAGE)
GOSO
ばばーん
BABAAN (TA-DAA)
MAGICAL GIRL
BACK
WEAPONS
A BOW, MAYBE...?
... SOMETHING LIKE THIS!
ブッ
PFF...
NOW THAT OUR PREPARATIONS ARE COMPLETE, SHALL WE BE OFF?
HA HA!
YEAH! LET'S ALL GET MOVING.
HEE HEE!
Y-YOU GUYS ARE AWFUL! EVEN YOU, MAMI-SAN!?
改装中につき 関係者以外 立入禁止 ご協力お願い致します
SIGN: UNDER CONSTRUCTION, OFF LIMITS, THANK YOU FOR YOUR COOPERATION.
...TAKE A LOOK ...
...AT THIS SOUL GEM.

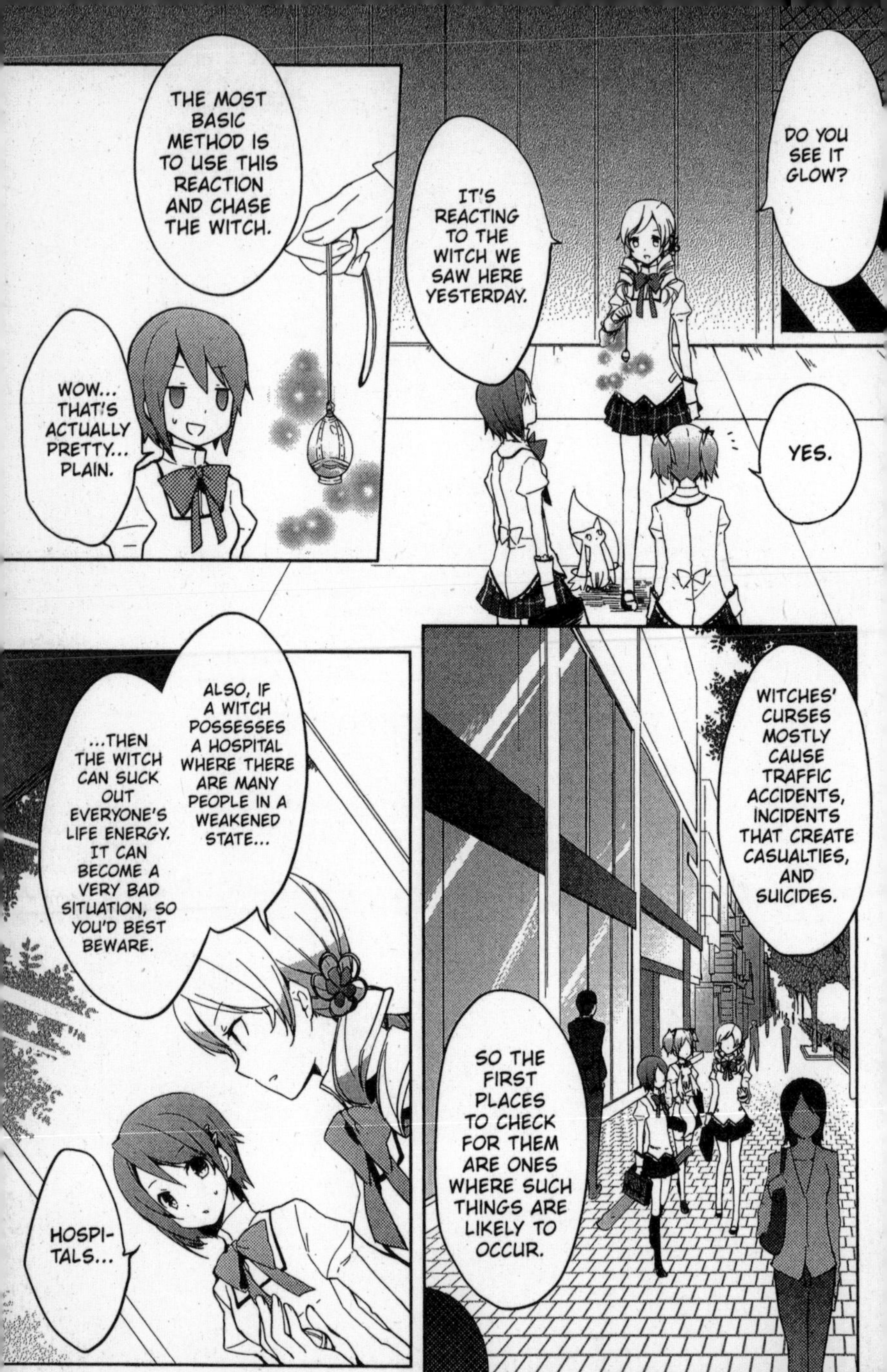
DO YOU SEE IT GLOW?
IT'S REACTING TO THE WITCH WE SAW HERE YESTERDAY.
YES.
THE MOST BASIC METHOD IS TO USE THIS REACTION AND CHASE THE WITCH.
WOW... THAT'S ACTUALLY PRETTY... PLAIN.
WITCHES' CURSES MOSTLY CAUSE TRAFFIC ACCIDENTS, INCIDENTS THAT CREATE CASUALTIES, AND SUICIDES.
SO THE FIRST PLACES TO CHECK FOR THEM ARE ONES WHERE SUCH THINGS ARE LIKELY TO OCCUR.
ALSO, IF A WITCH POSSESSES A HOSPITAL WHERE THERE ARE MANY PEOPLE IN A WEAKENED STATE...
...THEN THE WITCH CAN SUCK OUT EVERYONE'S LIFE ENERGY. IT CAN BECOME A VERY BAD SITUATION, SO YOU'D BEST BEWARE.
HOSPI-TALS...

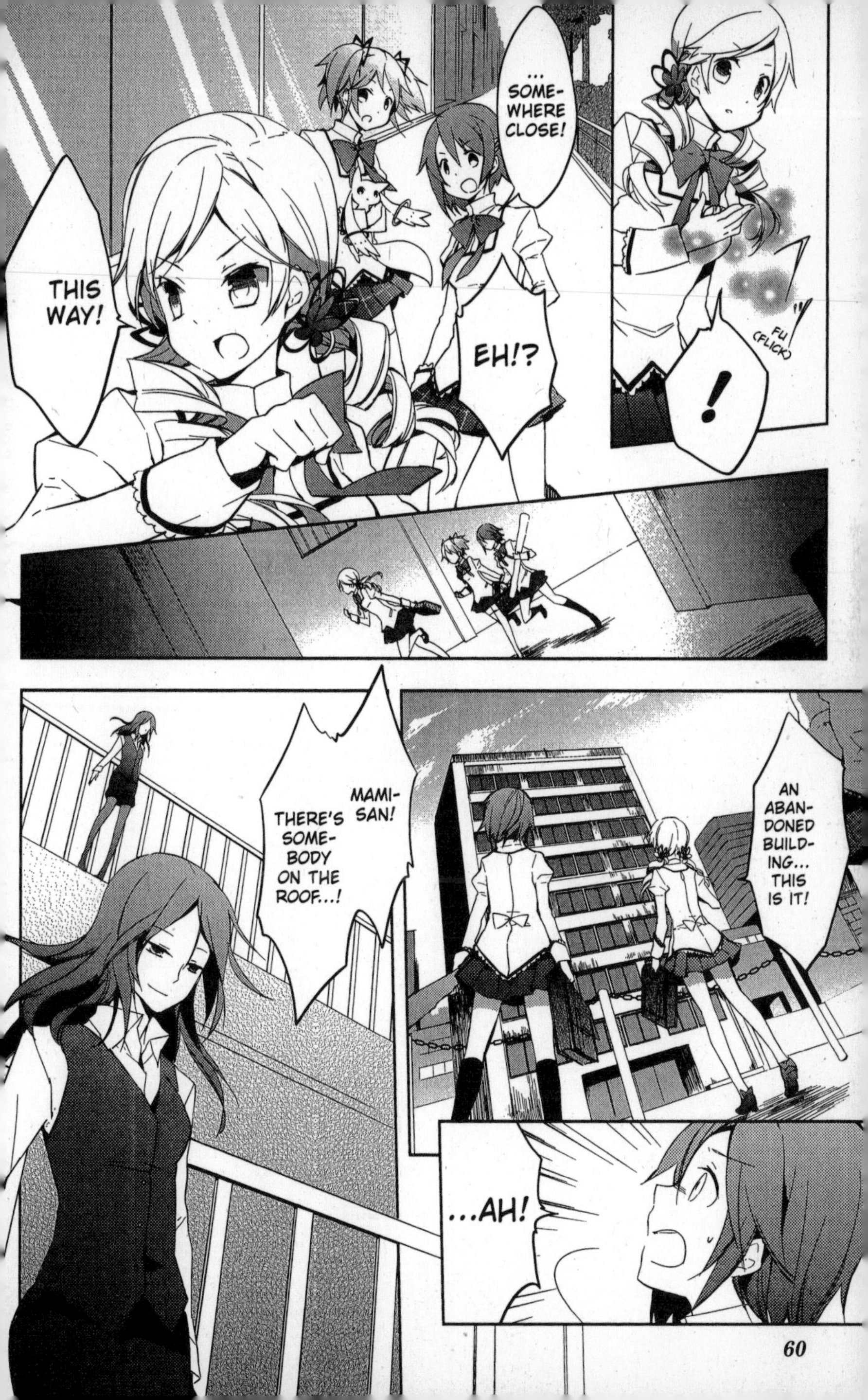
FU (FLICK)
!
... SOME-WHERE CLOSE!
EH!?
THIS WAY!
AN ABAN-DONED BUILD-ING... THIS IS IT!
...AH!
MAMI-SAN!
THERE'S SOME-BODY ON THE ROOF...!

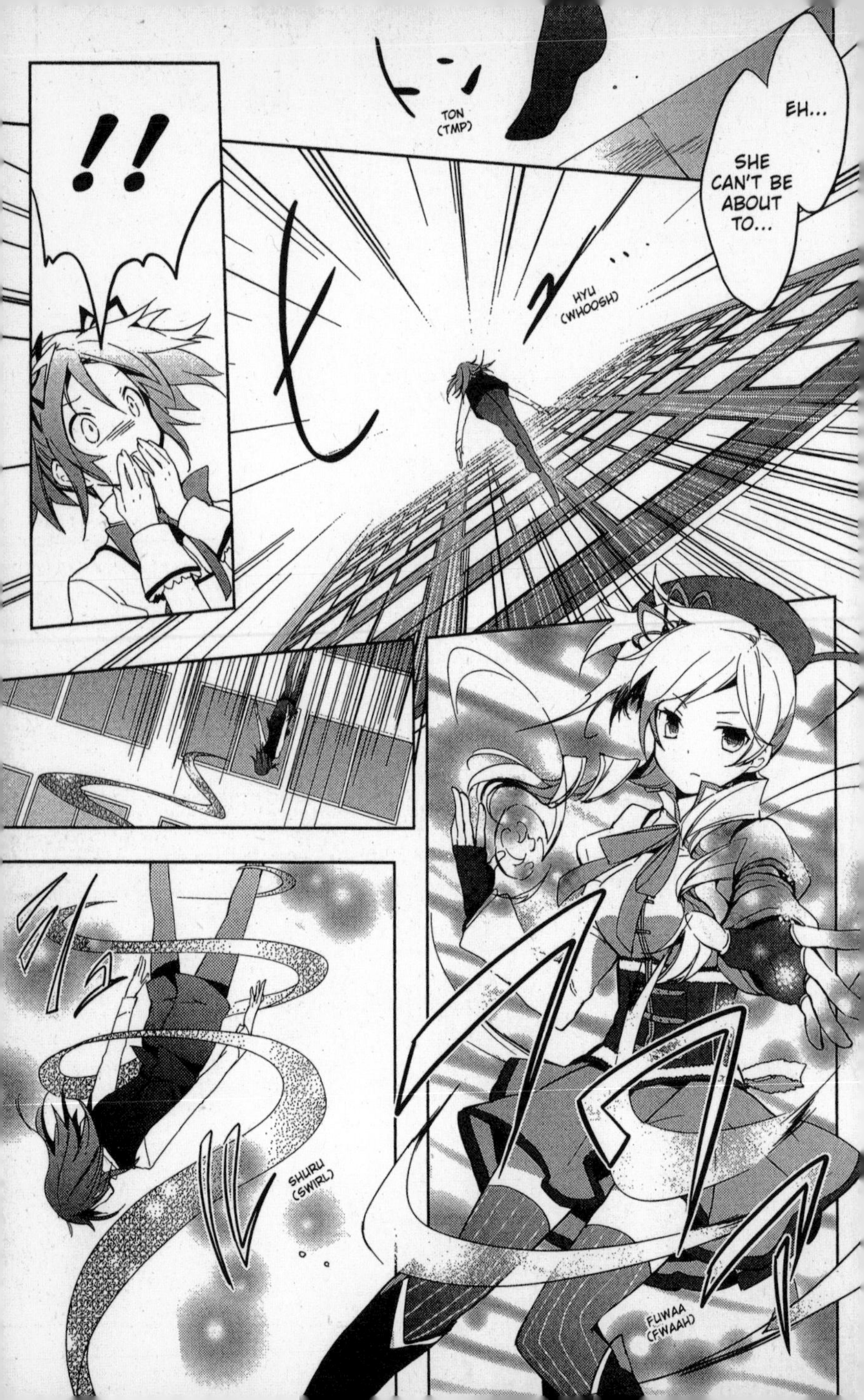
EH...
SHE CAN'T BE ABOUT TO...
TON (TMP)
HYU (WHOOSH)
!!
FUWAA (FWAAH)
SHURU (SWIRL)

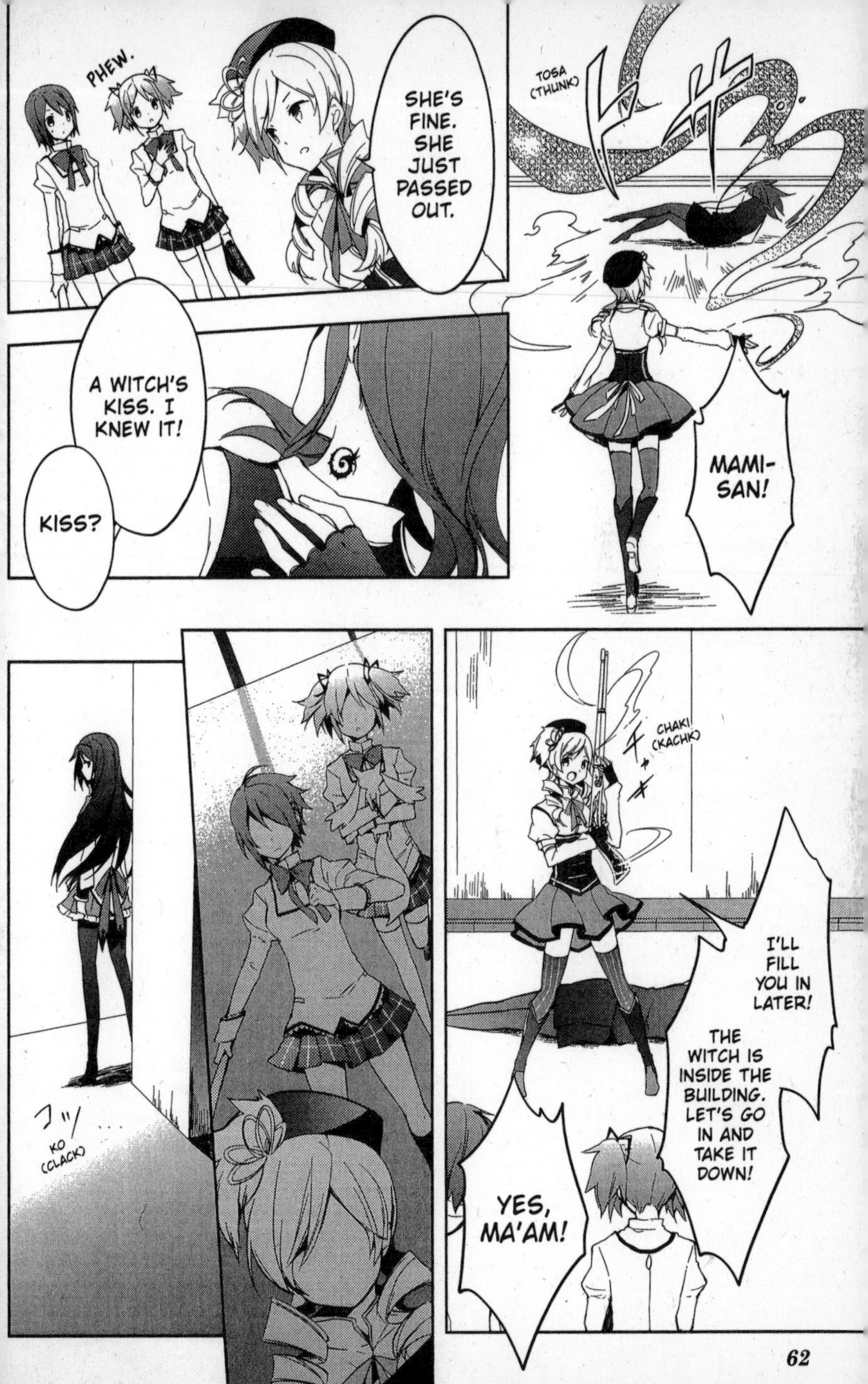
TOSA (THUNK)
MAMI-SAN!
SHE'S FINE. SHE JUST PASSED OUT.
PHEW.
A WITCH'S KISS. I KNEW IT!
KISS?
CHAKI (KACHK)
I'LL FILL YOU IN LATER!
THE WITCH IS INSIDE THE BUILDING. LET'S GO IN AND TAKE IT DOWN!
YES, MA'AM!
KO (CLACK)
...

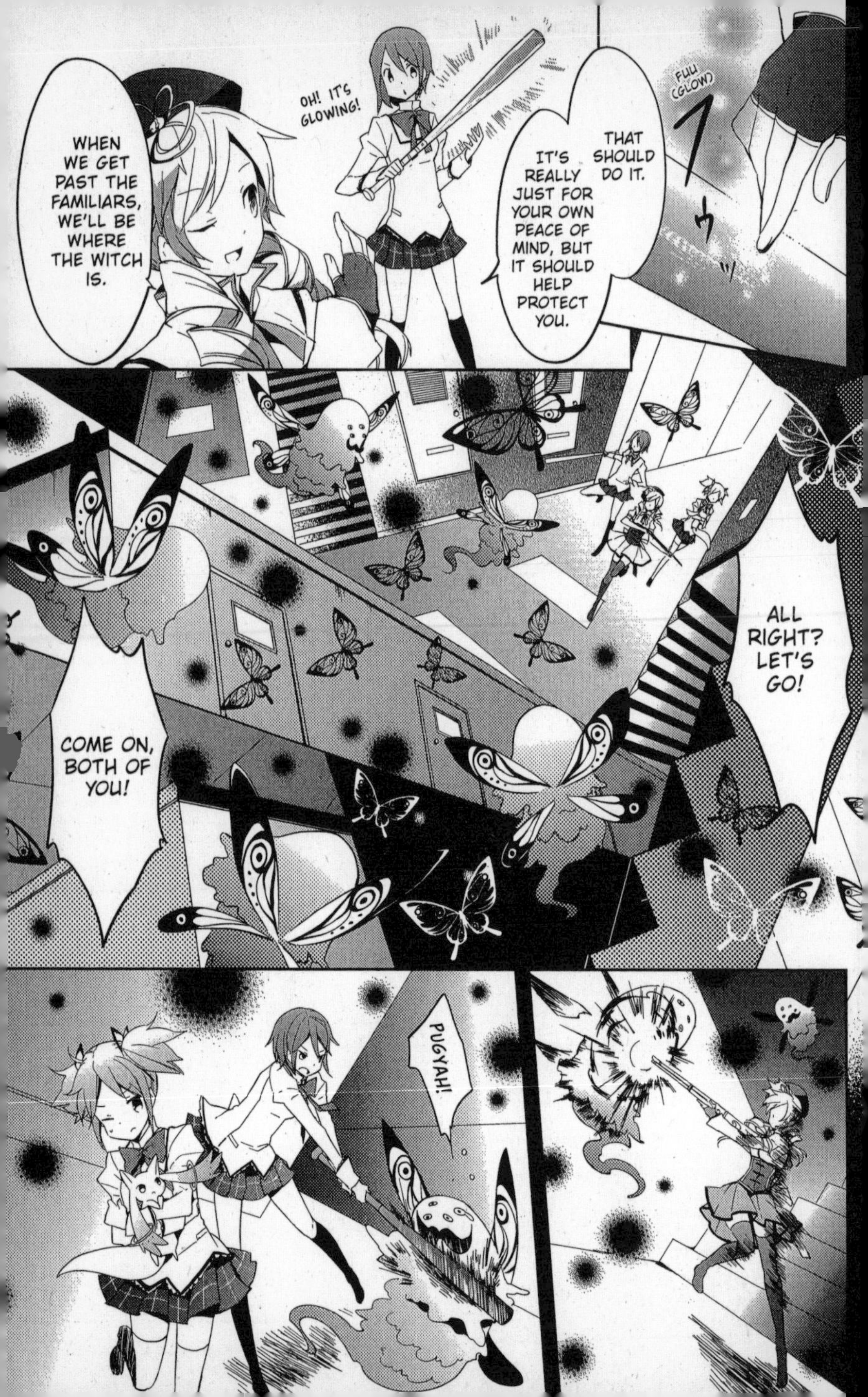
FUU (GLOW)
THAT SHOULD DO IT.
IT'S REALLY JUST FOR YOUR OWN PEACE OF MIND, BUT IT SHOULD HELP PROTECT YOU.
OH! IT'S GLOWING!
WHEN WE GET PAST THE FAMILIARS, WE'LL BE WHERE THE WITCH IS.
ALL RIGHT? LET'S GO!
COME ON, BOTH OF YOU!
PUGYAH!

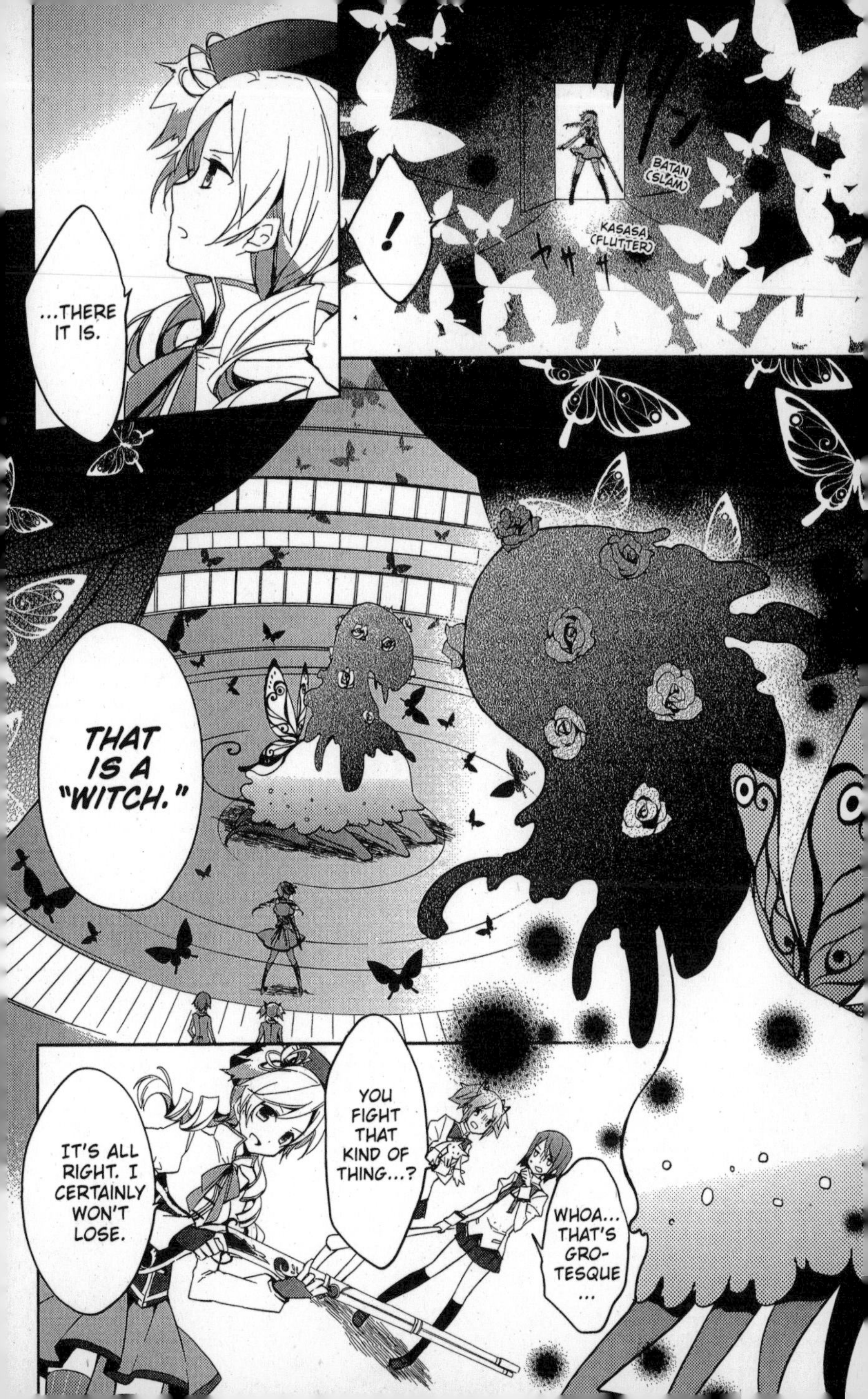
BATAN (SLAM)
KASASA (FLUTTER)
!
...THERE IT IS.
THAT IS A "WITCH."
WHOA... THAT'S GRO-TESQUE...
YOU FIGHT THAT KIND OF THING...?
IT'S ALL RIGHT. I CERTAINLY WON'T LOSE.

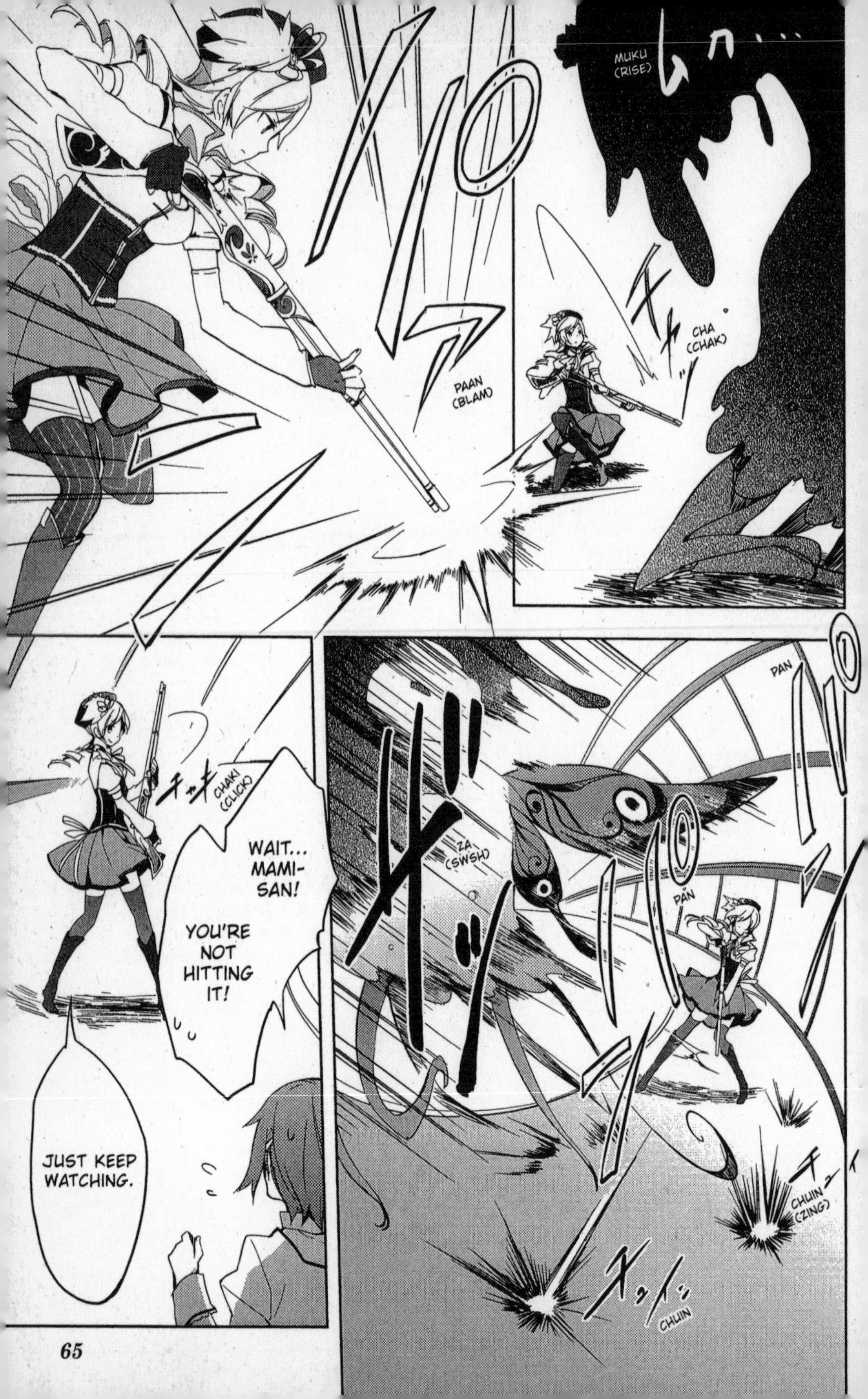
MUKU (RISE)
CHA (CHAK)
PAAN (BLAM)
PAN
ZA (SWSH)
PAN
CHUIN (ZING)
CHUIN
CHAKI (CLICK)
WAIT... MAMI-SAN!
YOU'RE NOT HITTING IT!
JUST KEEP WATCHING.

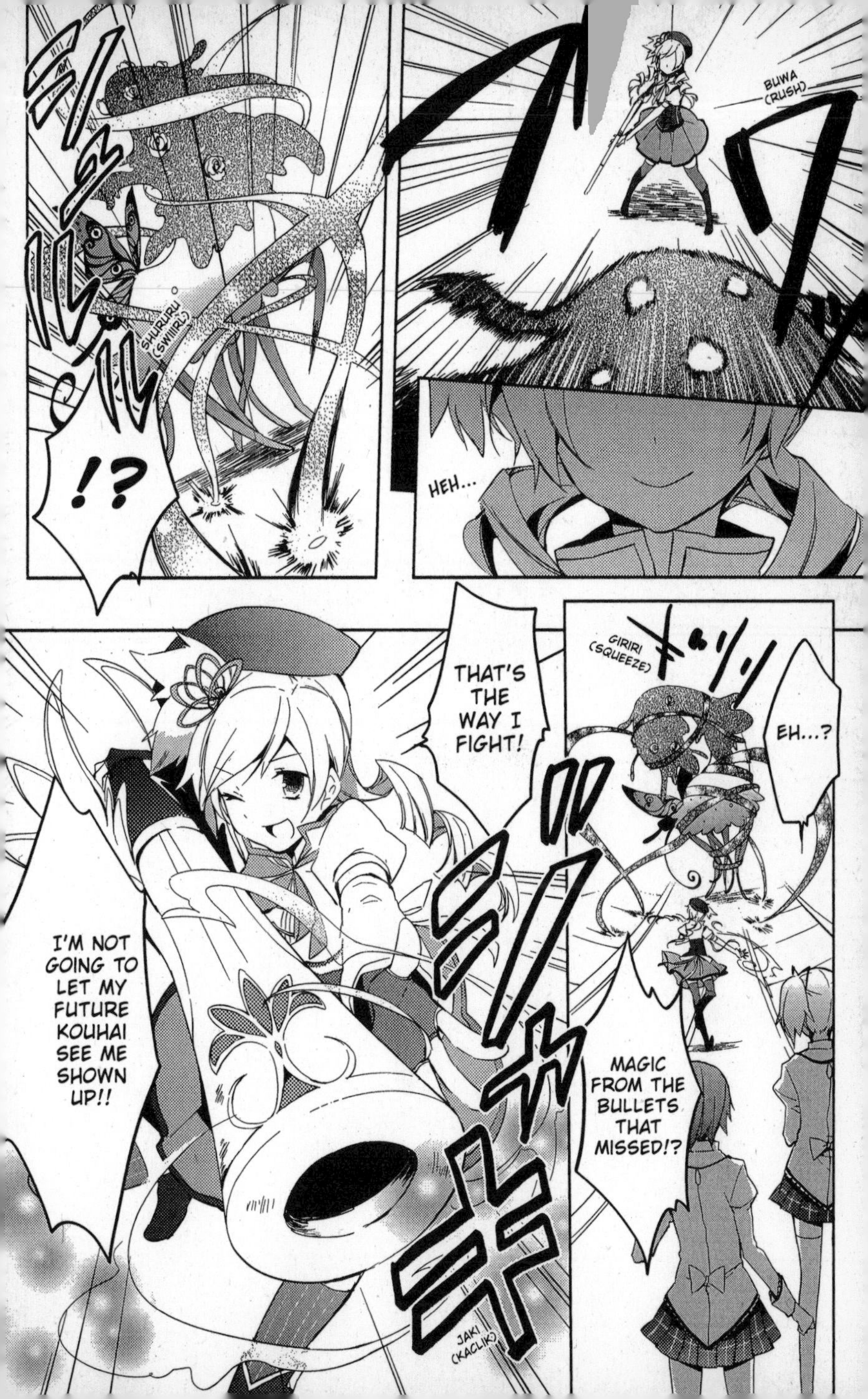
BUWA (RUSH)
HEH...
SHURURU (SWIIRL)
!?
GIRIRI (SQUEEZE)
EH...?
MAGIC FROM THE BULLETS THAT MISSED!?
THAT'S THE WAY I FIGHT!
I'M NOT GOING TO LET MY FUTURE KOUHAI SEE ME SHOWN UP!!
JAKI (KACLIK)

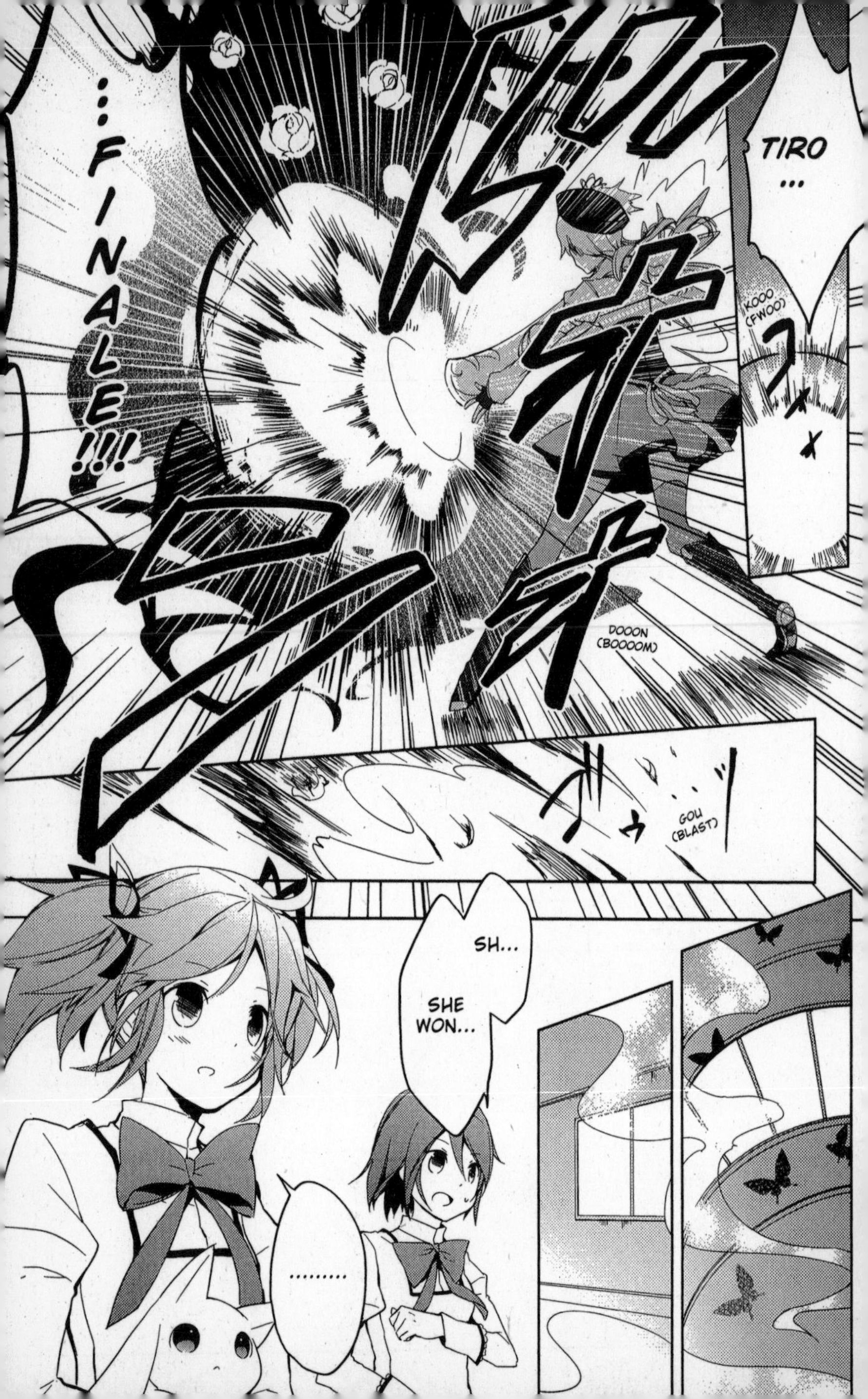
TIRO ...
KOOO (FWOO)
...FINALE!!!
DOOON (BOOOOM)
GOU (BLAST)
SH... SHE WON...
....

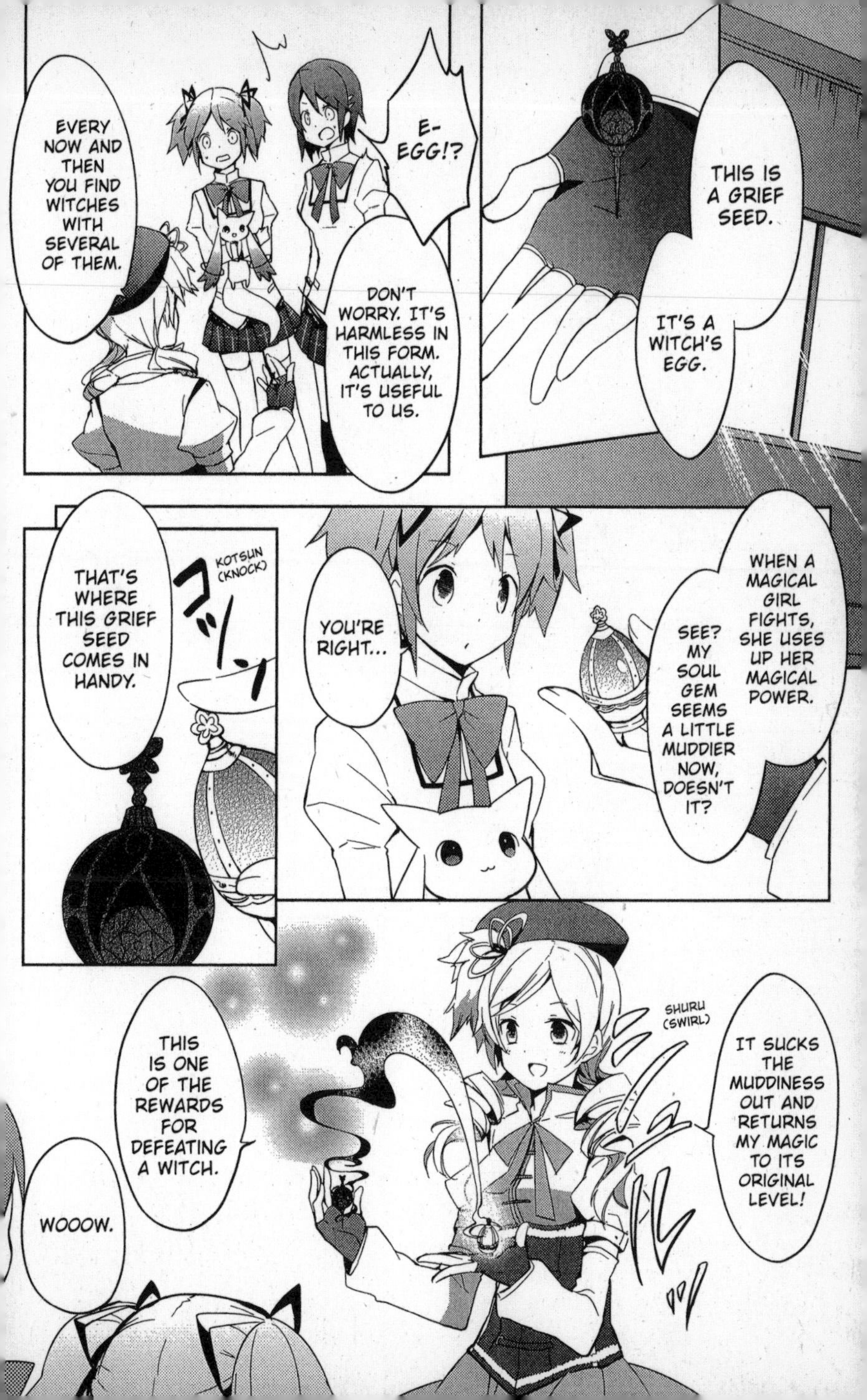
THIS IS A GRIEF SEED.
IT'S A WITCH'S EGG.
E-EGG!?
DON'T WORRY. IT'S HARMLESS IN THIS FORM. ACTUALLY, IT'S USEFUL TO US.
EVERY NOW AND THEN YOU FIND WITCHES WITH SEVERAL OF THEM.
WHEN A MAGICAL GIRL FIGHTS, SHE USES UP HER MAGICAL POWER.
SEE? MY SOUL GEM SEEMS A LITTLE MUDDIER NOW, DOESN'T IT?
YOU'RE RIGHT...
KOTSUN (KNOCK)
THAT'S WHERE THIS GRIEF SEED COMES IN HANDY.
SHURU (SWIRL)
IT SUCKS THE MUDDINESS OUT AND RETURNS MY MAGIC TO ITS ORIGINAL LEVEL!
THIS IS ONE OF THE REWARDS FOR DEFEATING A WITCH.
WOOOW.

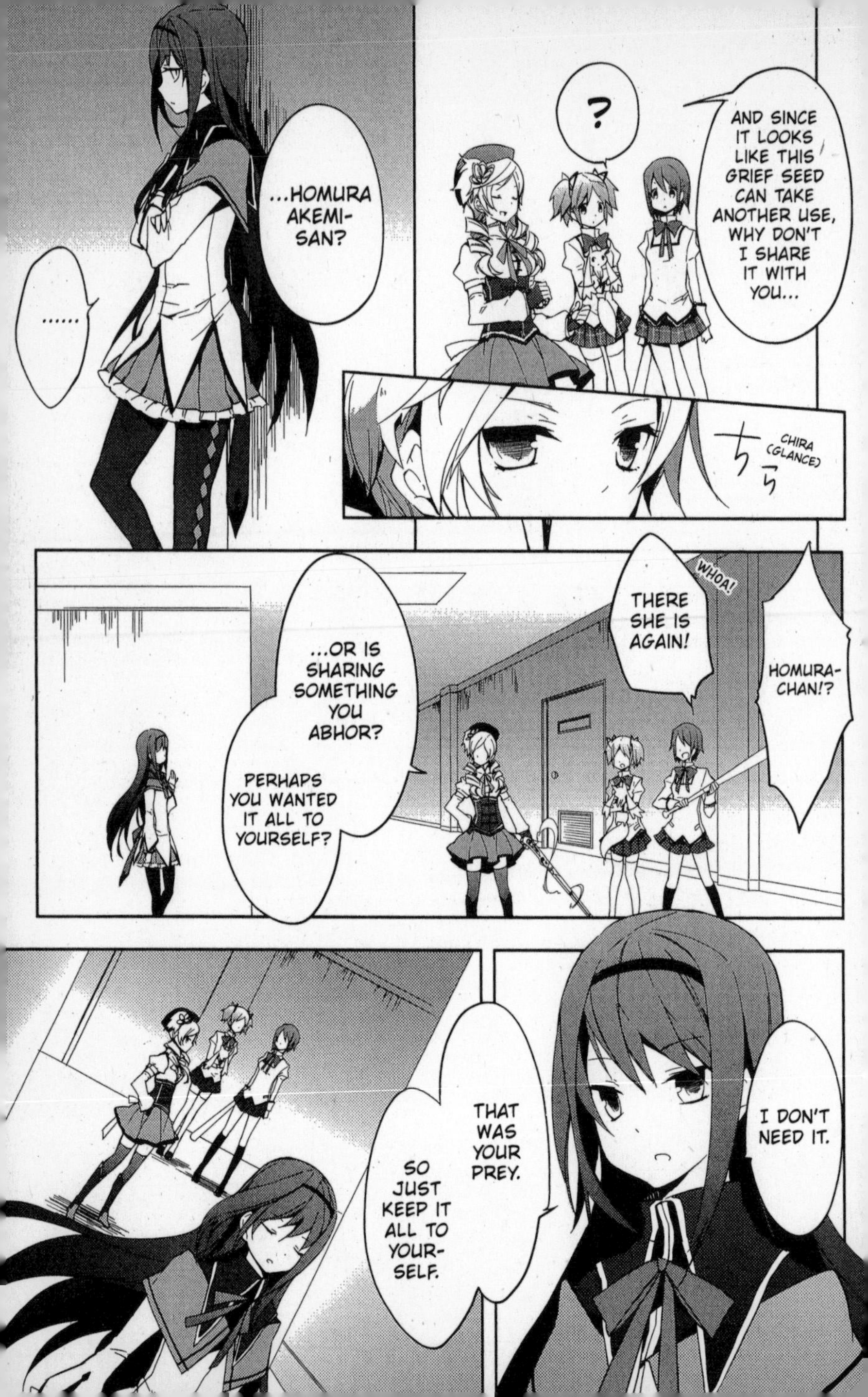
AND SINCE IT LOOKS LIKE THIS GRIEF SEED CAN TAKE ANOTHER USE, WHY DON'T I SHARE IT WITH YOU...
?
ちら
CHIRA (GLANCE)
...HOMURA AKEMI-SAN?
......
HOMURA-CHAN!?
WHOA!
THERE SHE IS AGAIN!
...OR IS SHARING SOMETHING YOU ABHOR?
PERHAPS YOU WANTED IT ALL TO YOURSELF?
I DON'T NEED IT.
THAT WAS YOUR PREY.
SO JUST KEEP IT ALL TO YOURSELF.

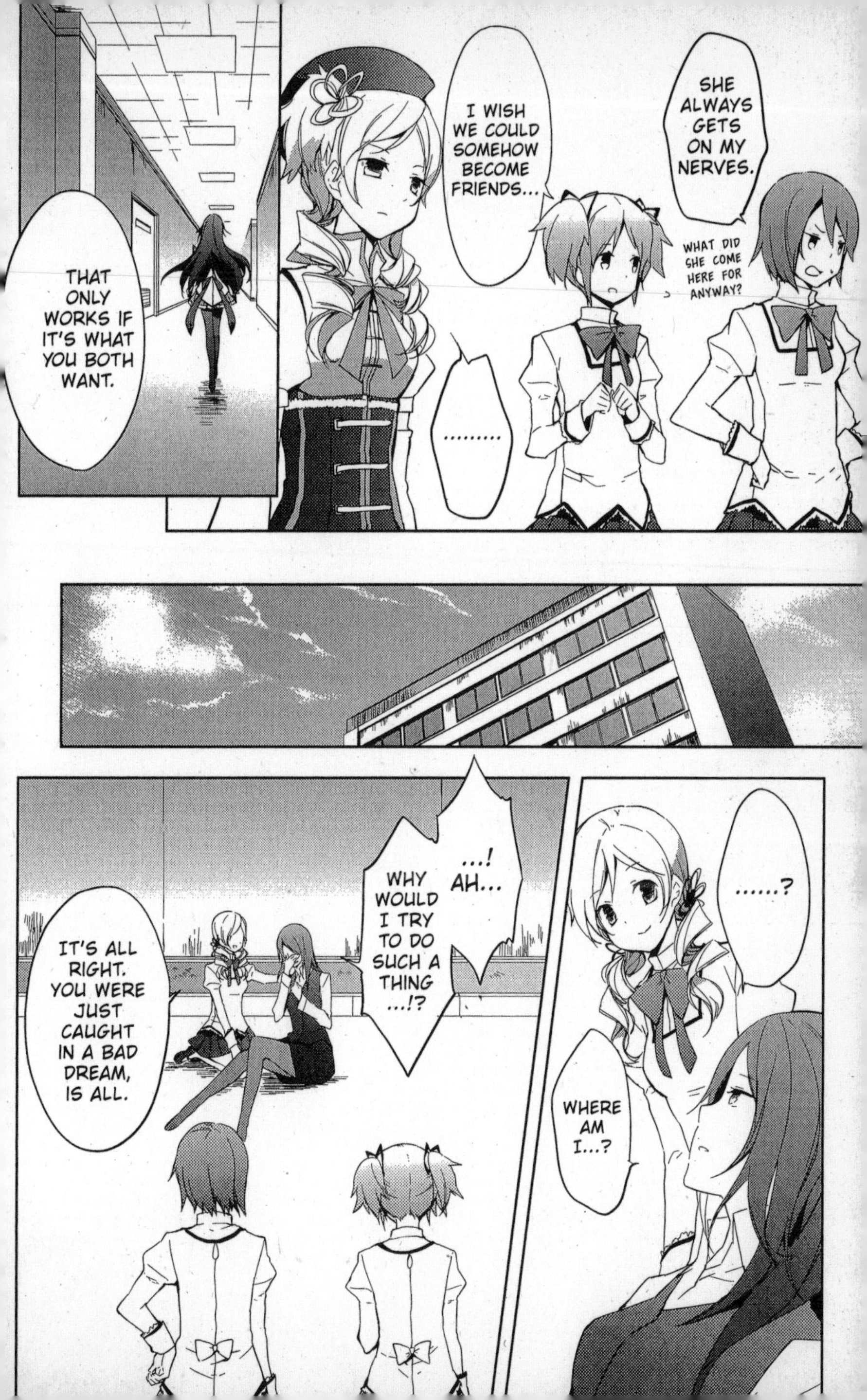
SHE ALWAYS GETS ON MY NERVES.
WHAT DID SHE COME HERE FOR ANYWAY?
I WISH WE COULD SOMEHOW BECOME FRIENDS...
....
THAT ONLY WORKS IF IT'S WHAT YOU BOTH WANT.
......?
WHERE AM I...?
...! AH...
WHY WOULD I TRY TO DO SUCH A THING ...!?
IT'S ALL RIGHT. YOU WERE JUST CAUGHT IN A BAD DREAM, IS ALL.

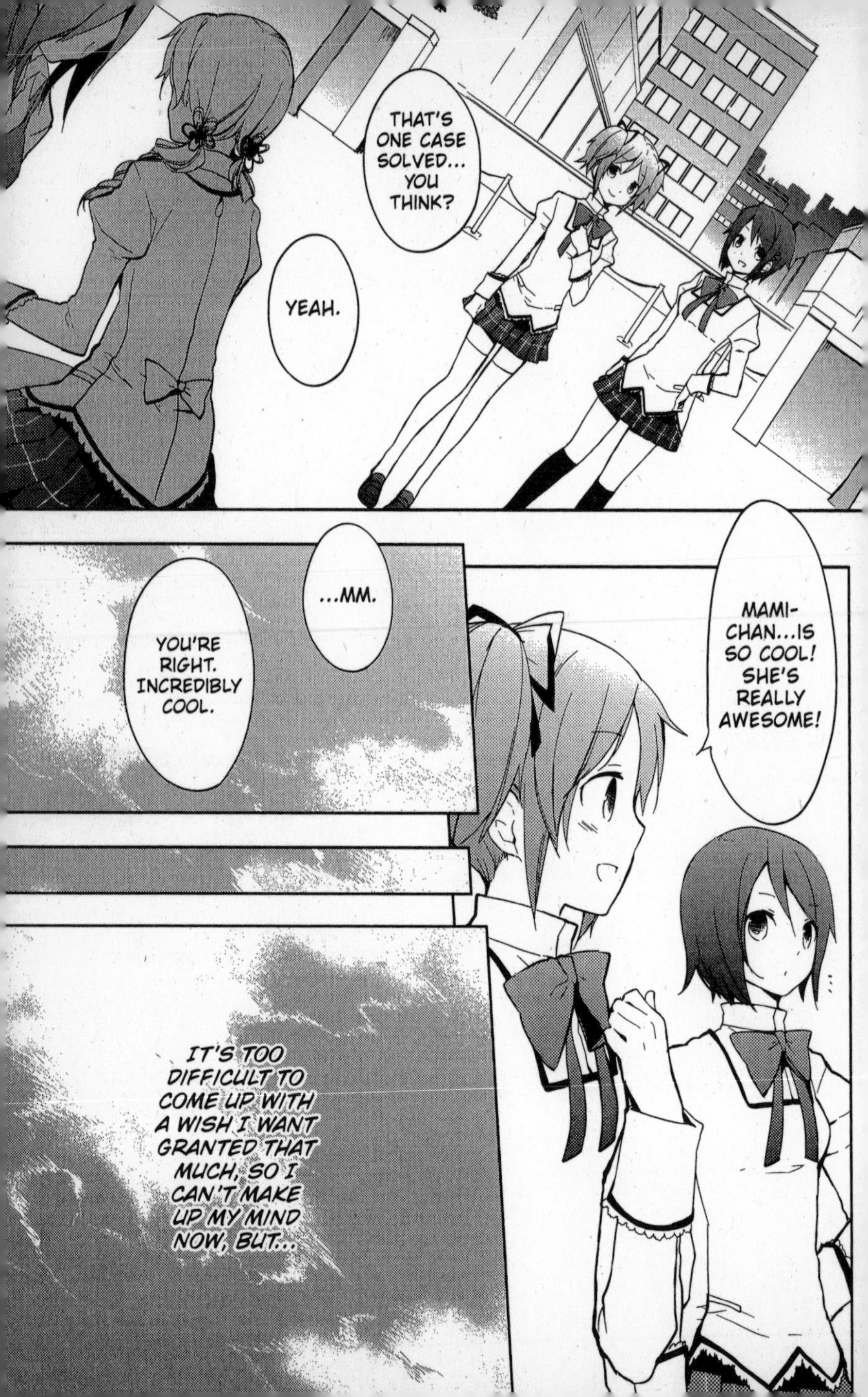
THAT'S ONE CASE SOLVED... YOU THINK?
YEAH.
MAMI-CHAN...IS SO COOL! SHE'S REALLY AWESOME!
...MM.
YOU'RE RIGHT. INCREDIBLY COOL.
IT'S TOO DIFFICULT TO COME UP WITH A WISH I WANT GRANTED THAT MUCH, SO I CAN'T MAKE UP MY MIND NOW, BUT...

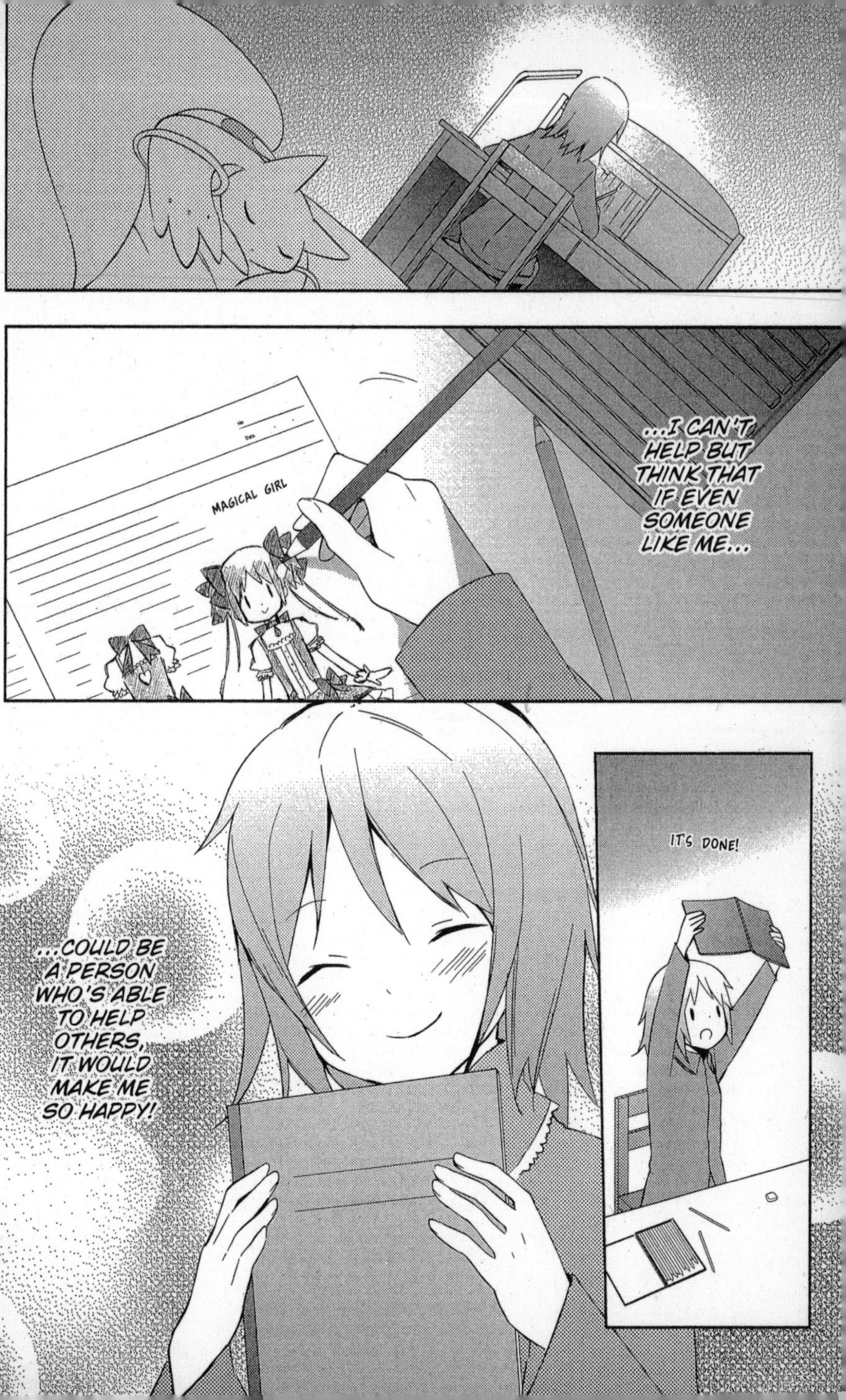
MAGICAL GIRL
...I CAN'T HELP BUT THINK THAT IF EVEN SOMEONE LIKE ME...
IT'S DONE!
...COULD BE A PERSON WHO'S ABLE TO HELP OTHERS, IT WOULD MAKE ME SO HAPPY!

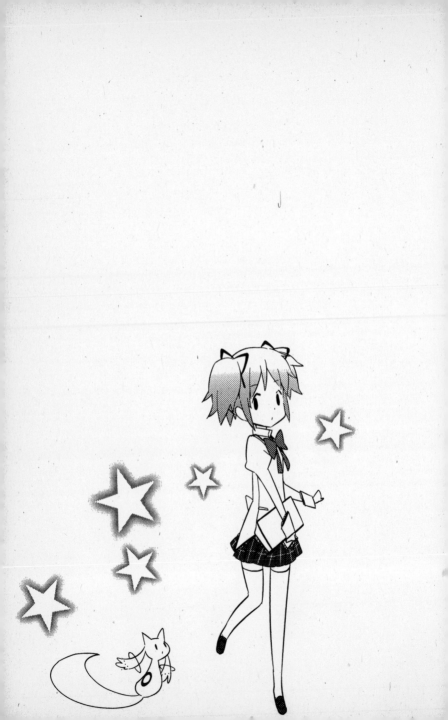

PUELLA MAGI
MADOKA★MAGICA

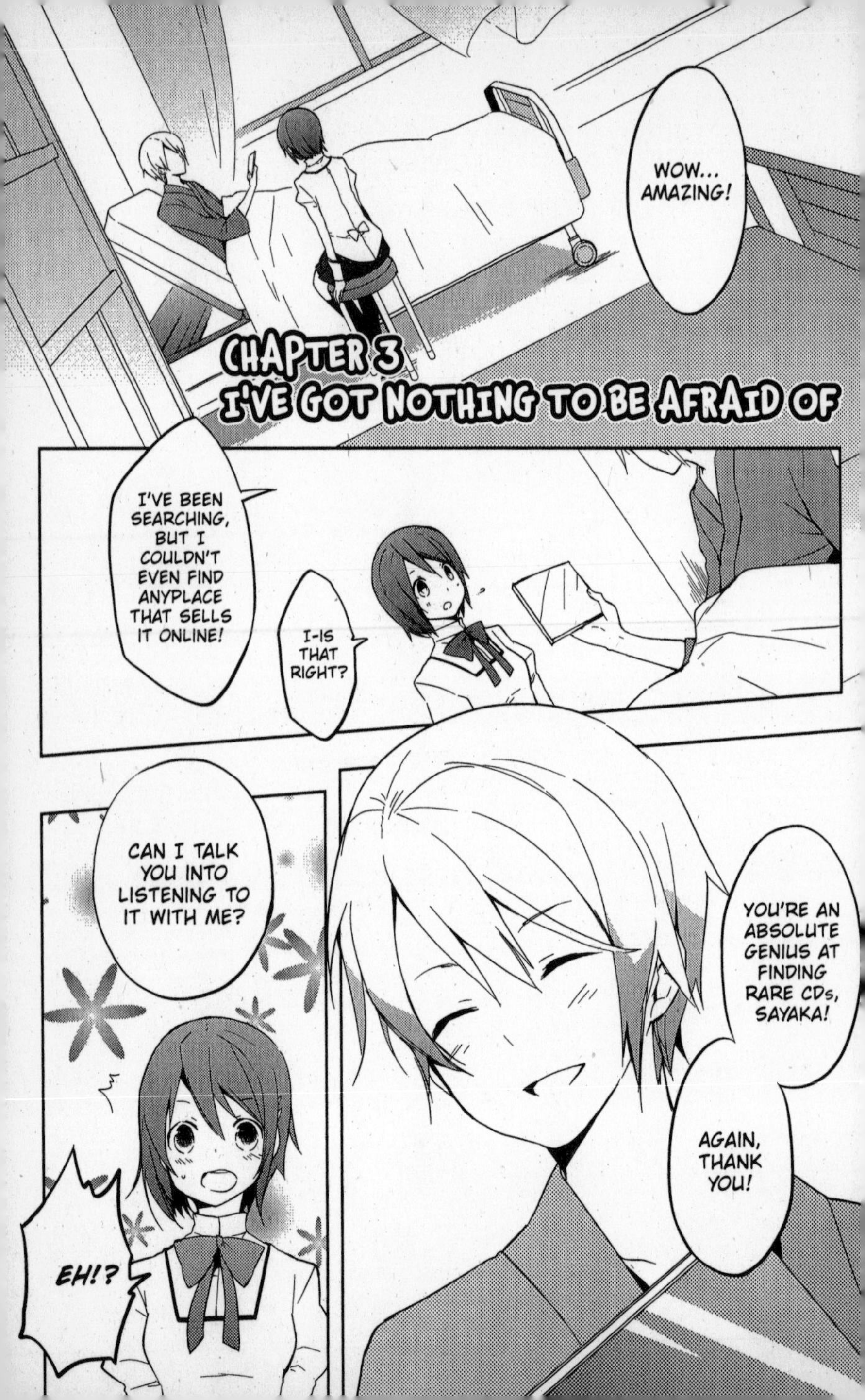
WOW... AMAZING!
CHAPTER 3
I'VE GOT NOTHING TO BE AFRAID OF
I'VE BEEN SEARCHING, BUT I COULDN'T EVEN FIND ANYPLACE THAT SELLS IT ONLINE!
I-IS THAT RIGHT?
YOU'RE AN ABSOLUTE GENIUS AT FINDING RARE CDs, SAYAKA!
AGAIN, THANK YOU!
CAN I TALK YOU INTO LISTENING TO IT WITH ME?
EH!?

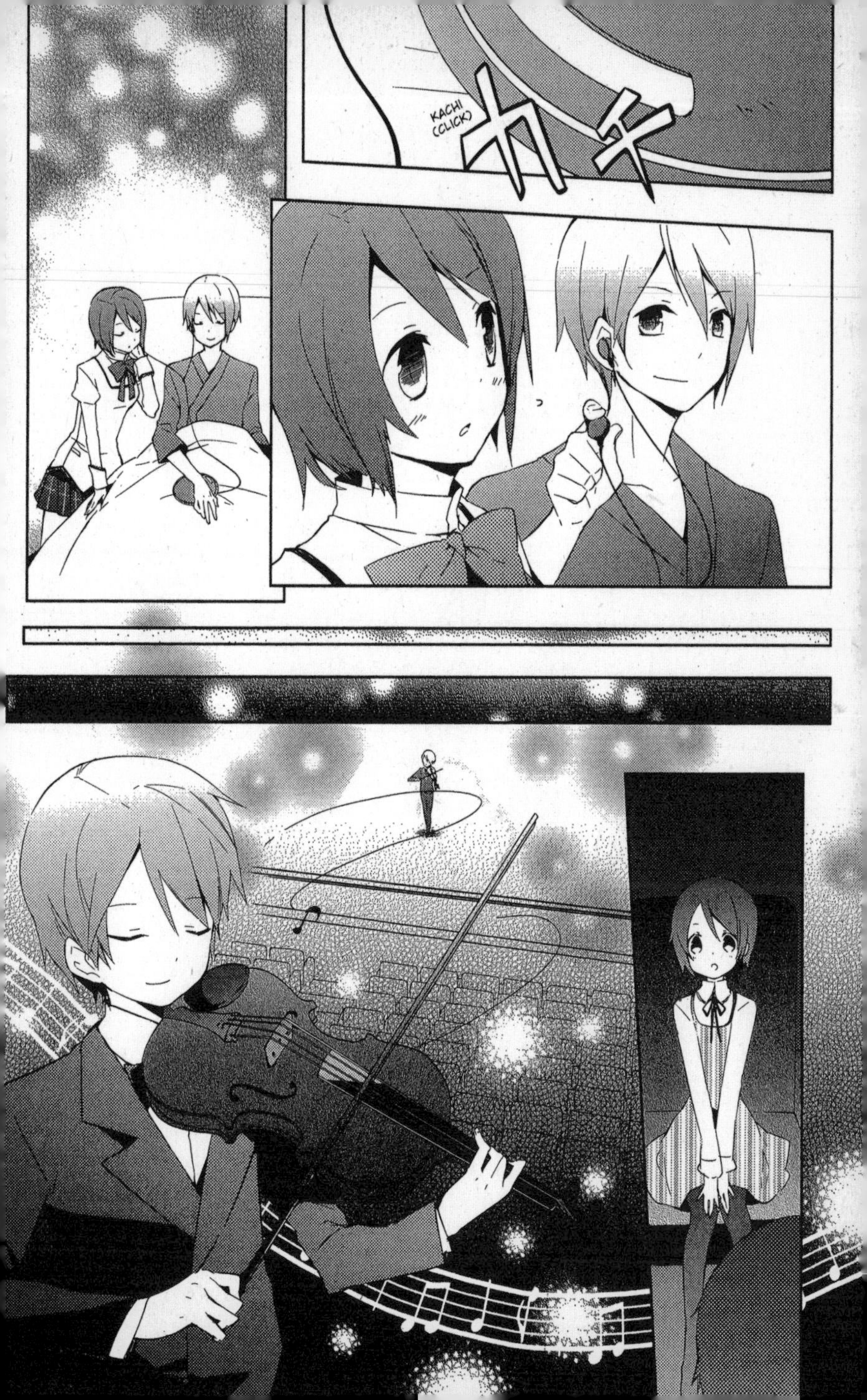
KACHI (CLICK)

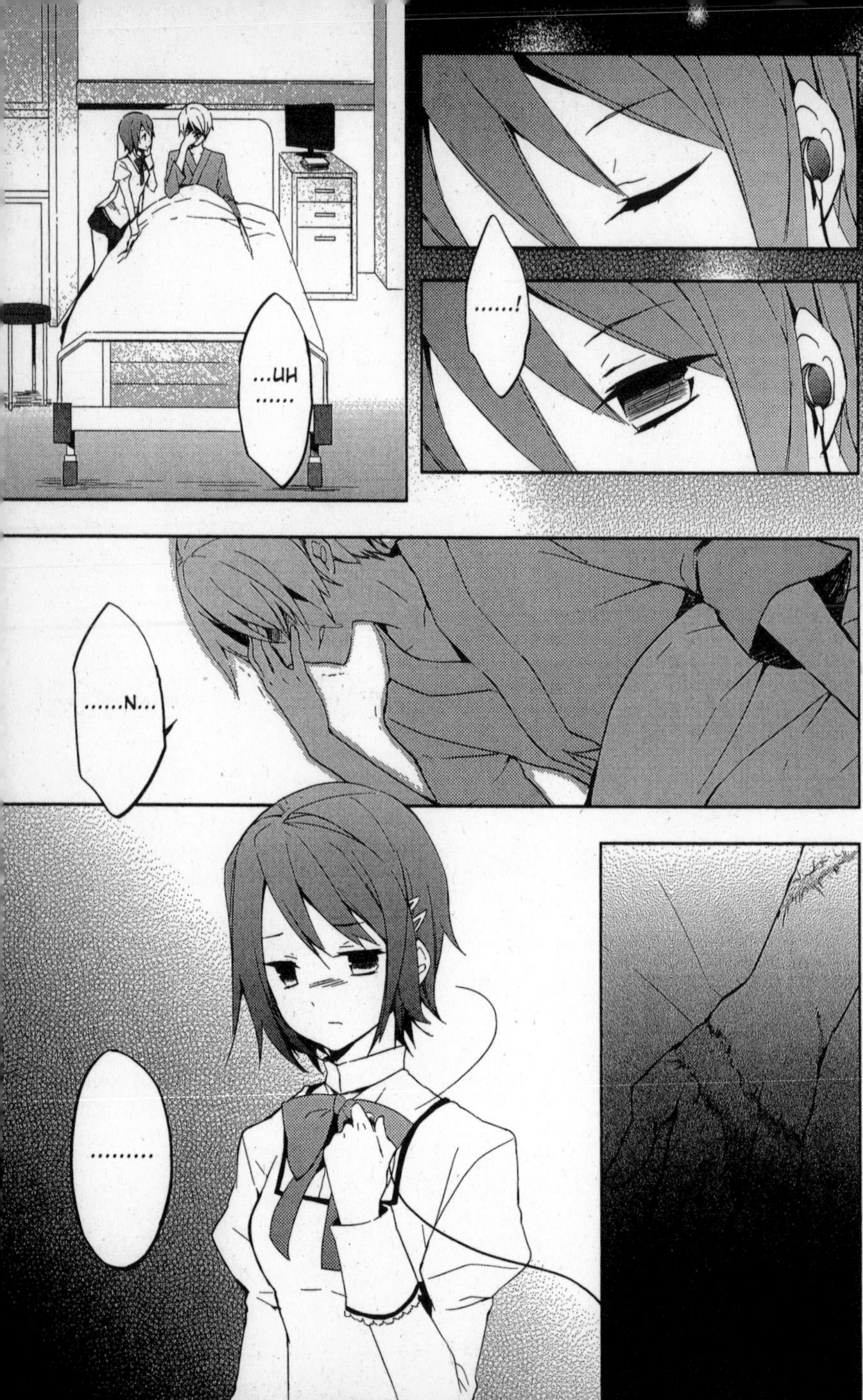
......!
...UH ......
......N...
....

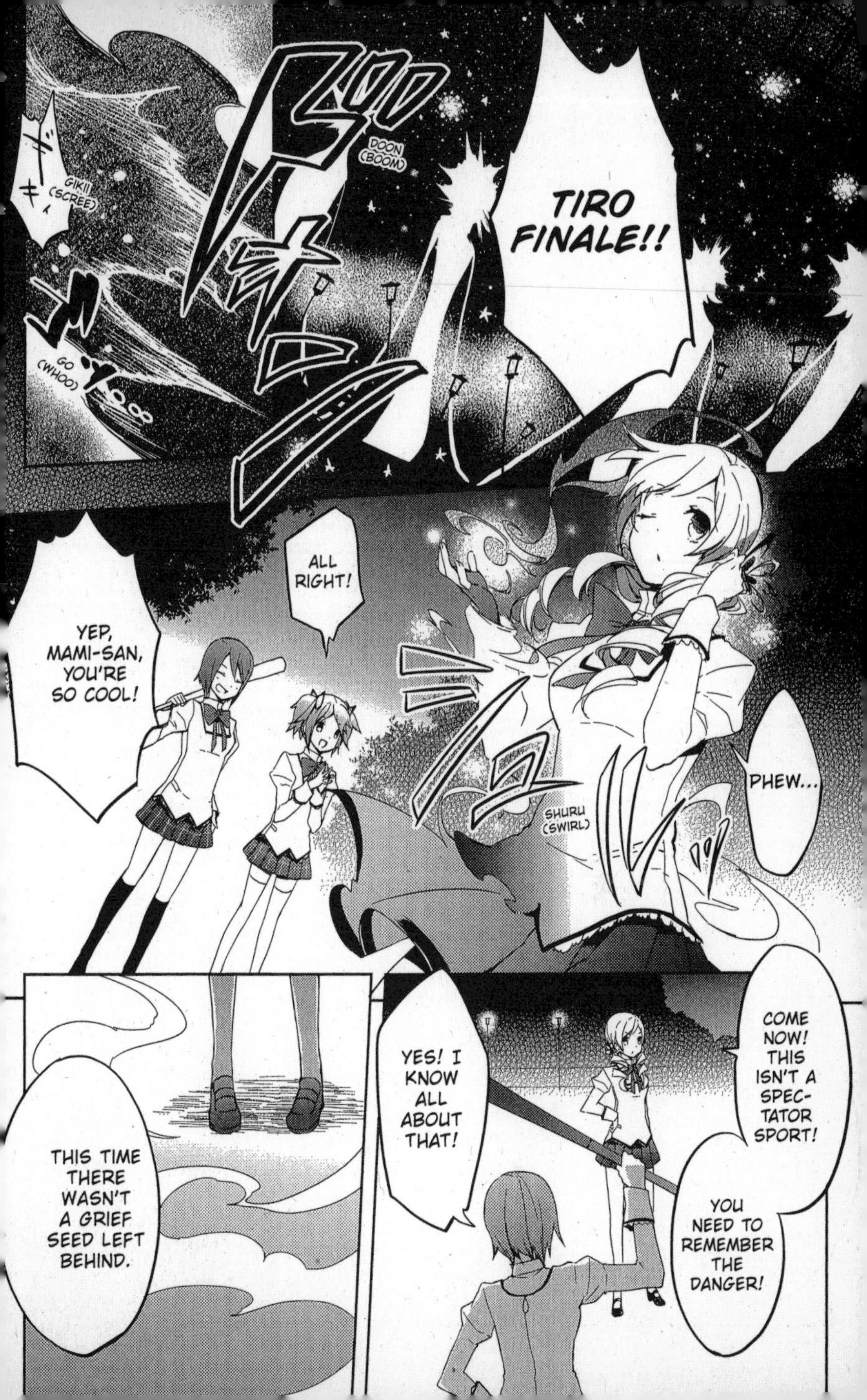
TIRO FINALE!!
DOON (BOOM)
GIKII (SCREE)
GO (WHOO)
PHEW...
SHURU (SWIRL)
ALL RIGHT!
YEP, MAMI-SAN, YOU'RE SO COOL!
COME NOW! THIS ISN'T A SPEC-TATOR SPORT!
YOU NEED TO REMEMBER THE DANGER!
YES! I KNOW ALL ABOUT THAT!
THIS TIME THERE WASN'T A GRIEF SEED LEFT BEHIND.

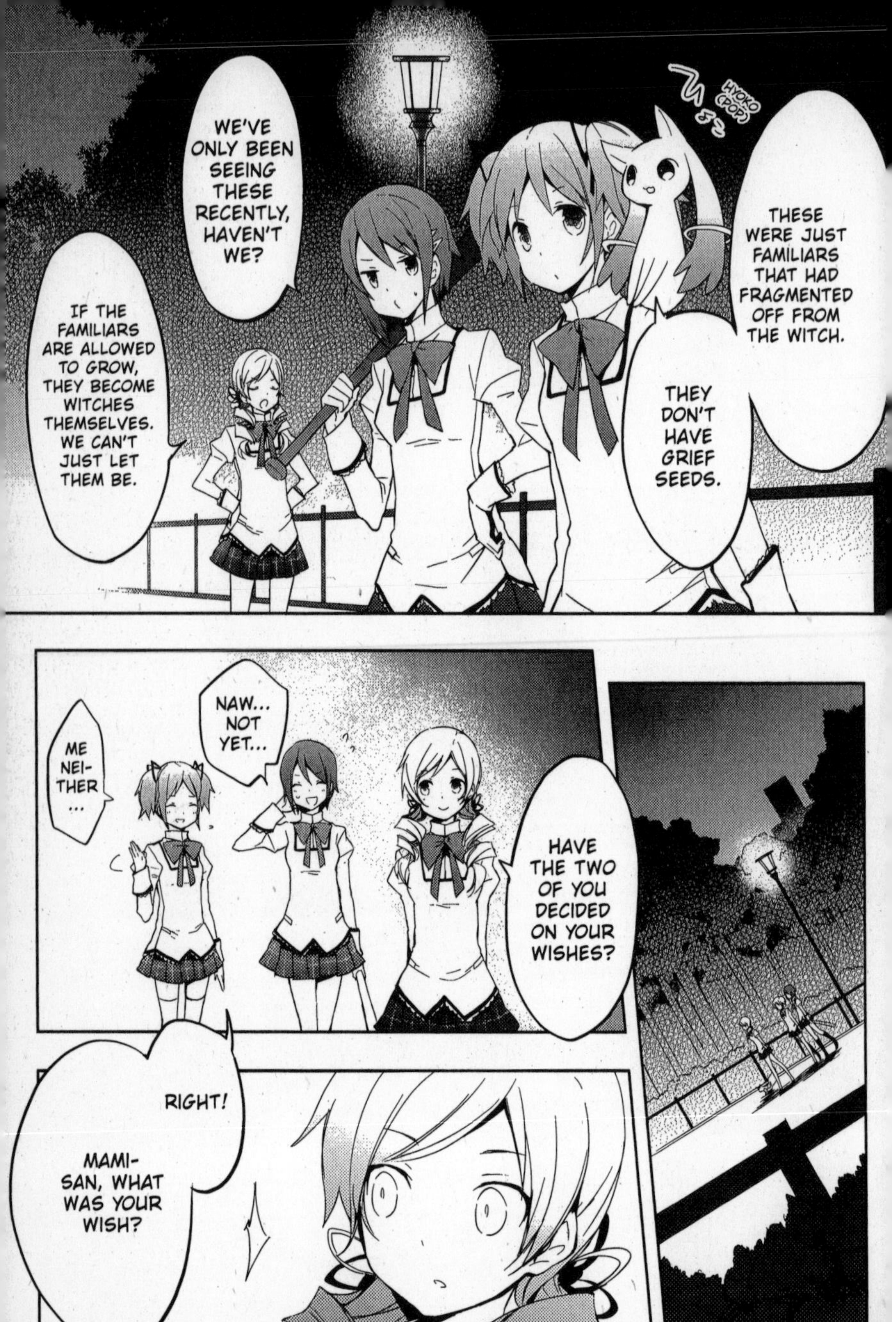
HYOKO (POP)
THESE WERE JUST FAMILIARS THAT HAD FRAGMENTED OFF FROM THE WITCH.
THEY DON'T HAVE GRIEF SEEDS.
WE'VE ONLY BEEN SEEING THESE RECENTLY, HAVEN'T WE?
IF THE FAMILIARS ARE ALLOWED TO GROW, THEY BECOME WITCHES THEMSELVES. WE CAN'T JUST LET THEM BE.
HAVE THE TWO OF YOU DECIDED ON YOUR WISHES?
NAW... NOT YET...
ME NEI-THER ...
RIGHT!
MAMI-SAN, WHAT WAS YOUR WISH?

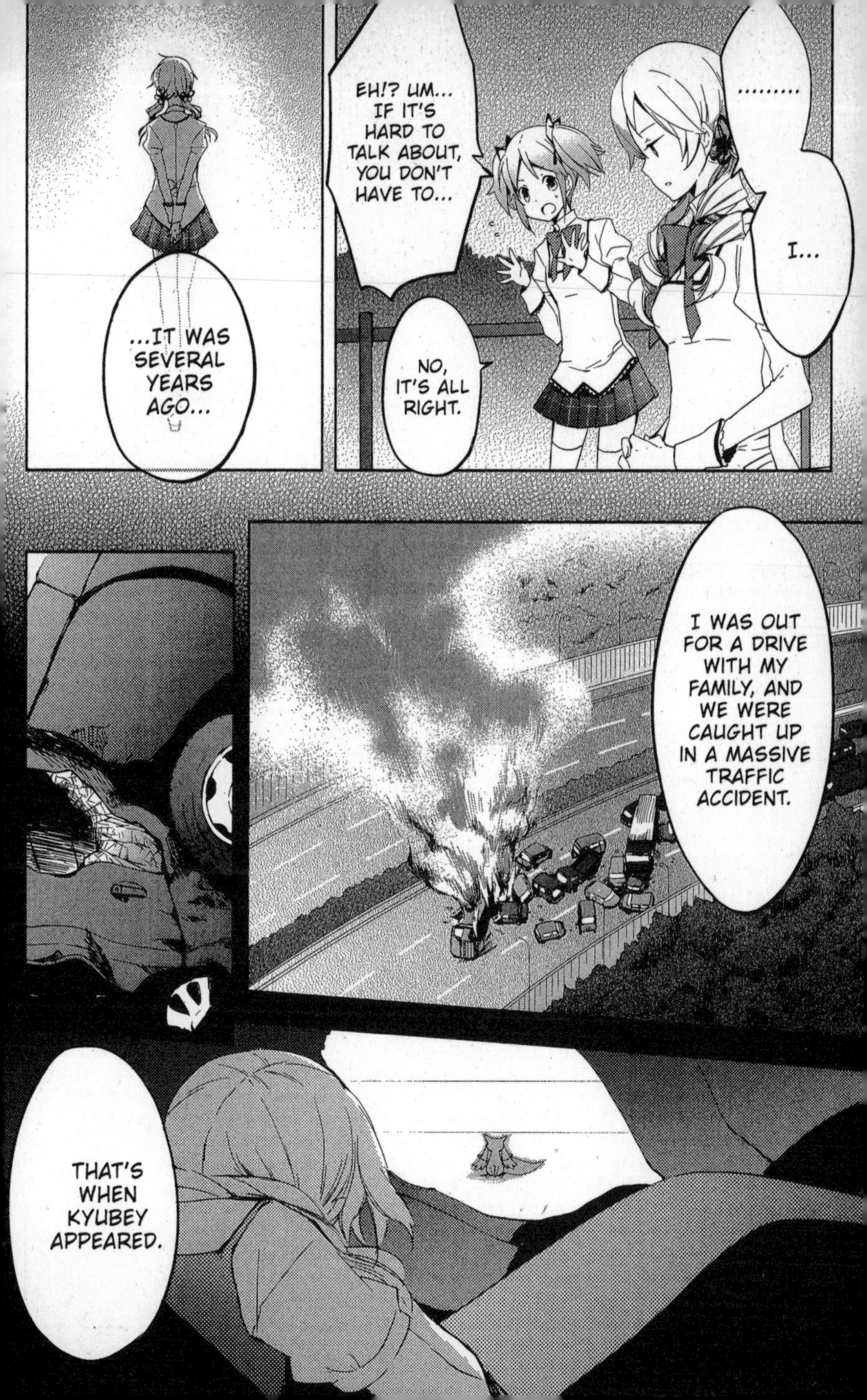
....
I...
EH!? UM... IF IT'S HARD TO TALK ABOUT, YOU DON'T HAVE TO...
NO, IT'S ALL RIGHT.
...IT WAS SEVERAL YEARS AGO...
I WAS OUT FOR A DRIVE WITH MY FAMILY, AND WE WERE CAUGHT UP IN A MASSIVE TRAFFIC ACCIDENT.
THAT'S WHEN KYUBEY APPEARED.

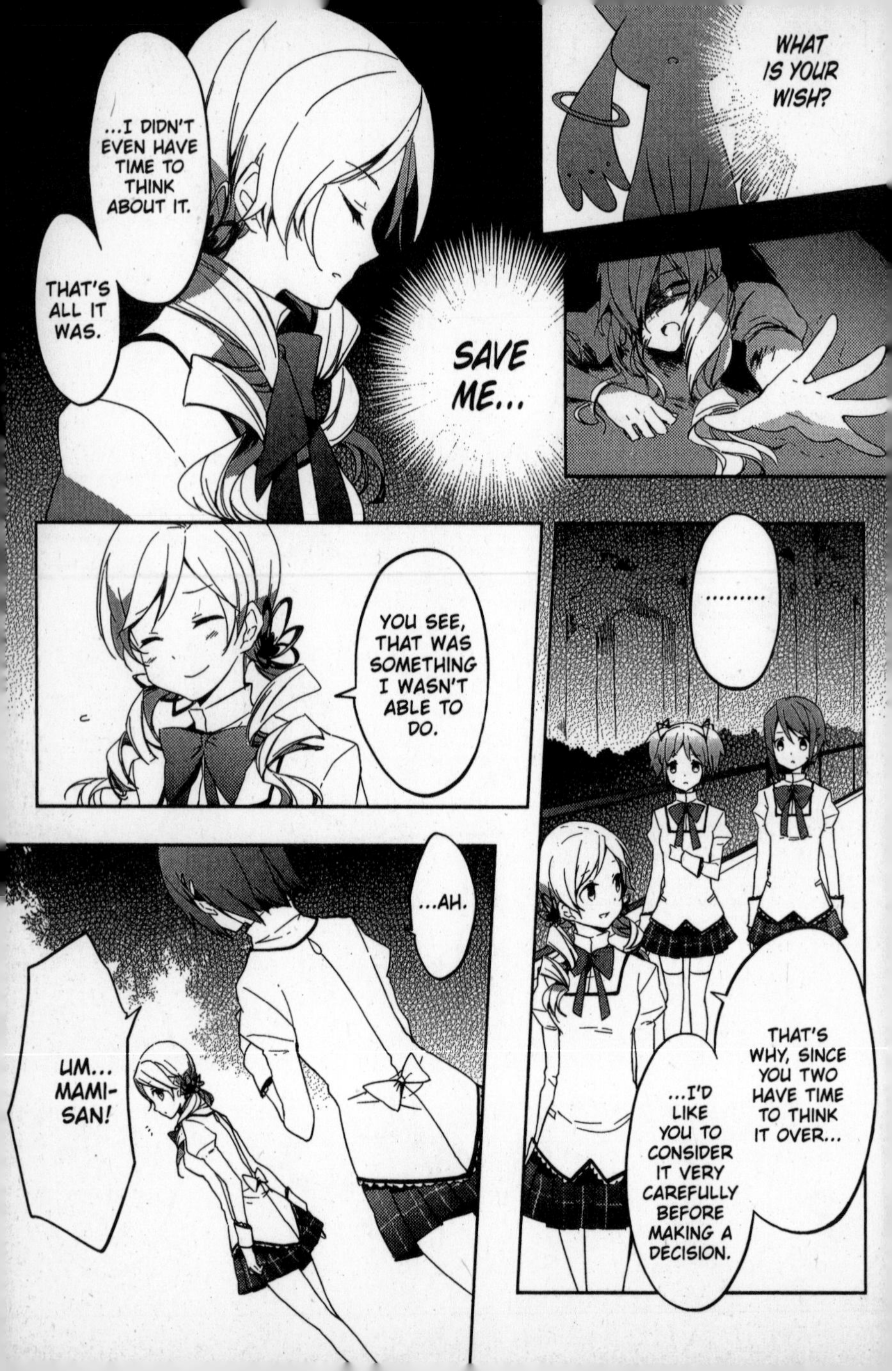
WHAT IS YOUR WISH?
SAVE ME...
...I DIDN'T EVEN HAVE TIME TO THINK ABOUT IT.
THAT'S ALL IT WAS.
....
THAT'S WHY, SINCE YOU TWO HAVE TIME TO THINK IT OVER...
...I'D LIKE YOU TO CONSIDER IT VERY CAREFULLY BEFORE MAKING A DECISION.
YOU SEE, THAT WAS SOMETHING I WASN'T ABLE TO DO.
...AH.
UM... MAMI-SAN!

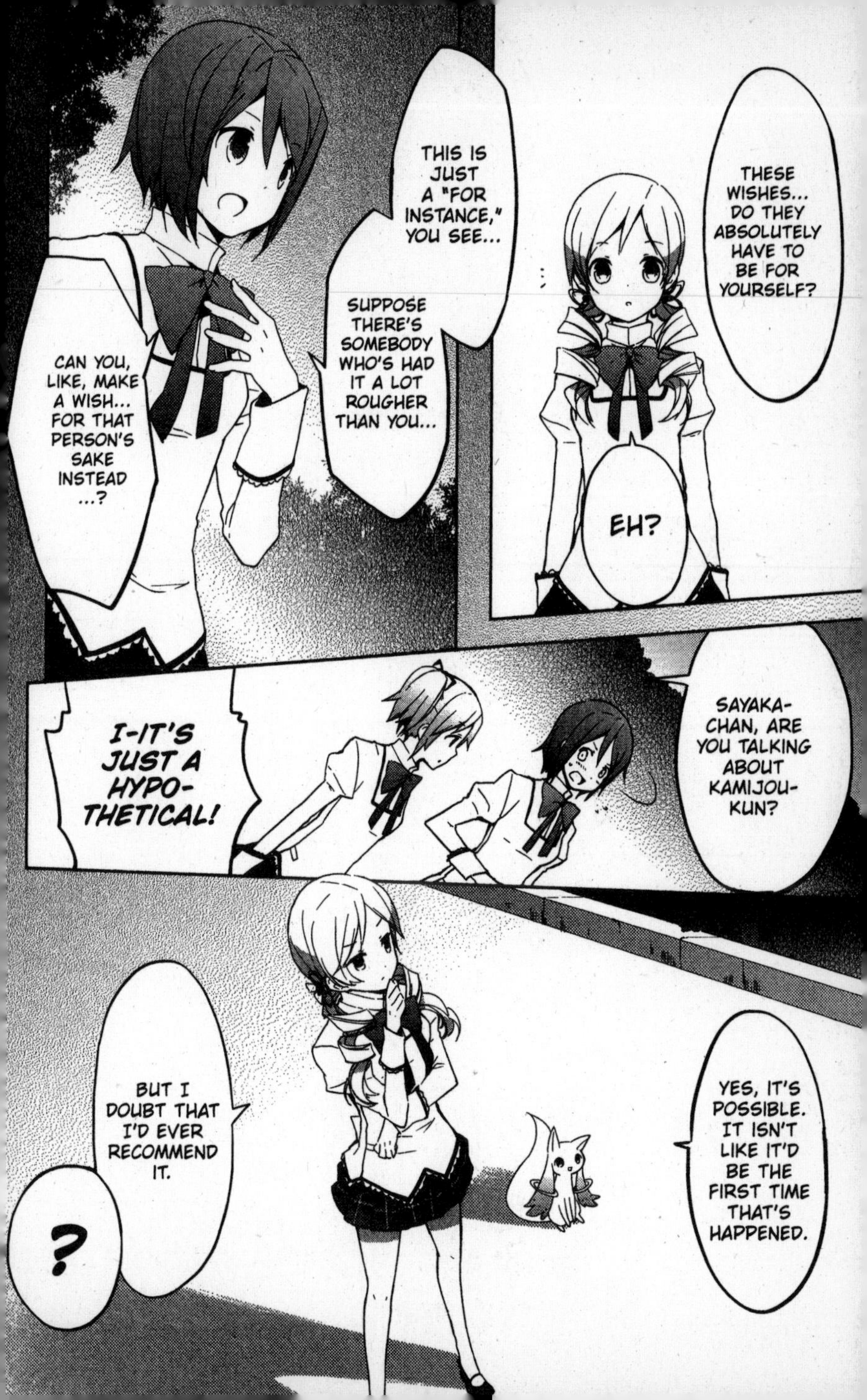
THESE WISHES... DO THEY ABSOLUTELY HAVE TO BE FOR YOURSELF?
EH?
THIS IS JUST A "FOR INSTANCE," YOU SEE...
SUPPOSE THERE'S SOMEBODY WHO'S HAD IT A LOT ROUGHER THAN YOU...
CAN YOU, LIKE, MAKE A WISH... FOR THAT PERSON'S SAKE INSTEAD ...?
SAYAKA-CHAN, ARE YOU TALKING ABOUT KAMIJOU-KUN?
I-IT'S JUST A HYPO-THETICAL!
YES, IT'S POSSIBLE. IT ISN'T LIKE IT'D BE THE FIRST TIME THAT'S HAPPENED.
BUT I DOUBT THAT I'D EVER RECOMMEND IT.
?

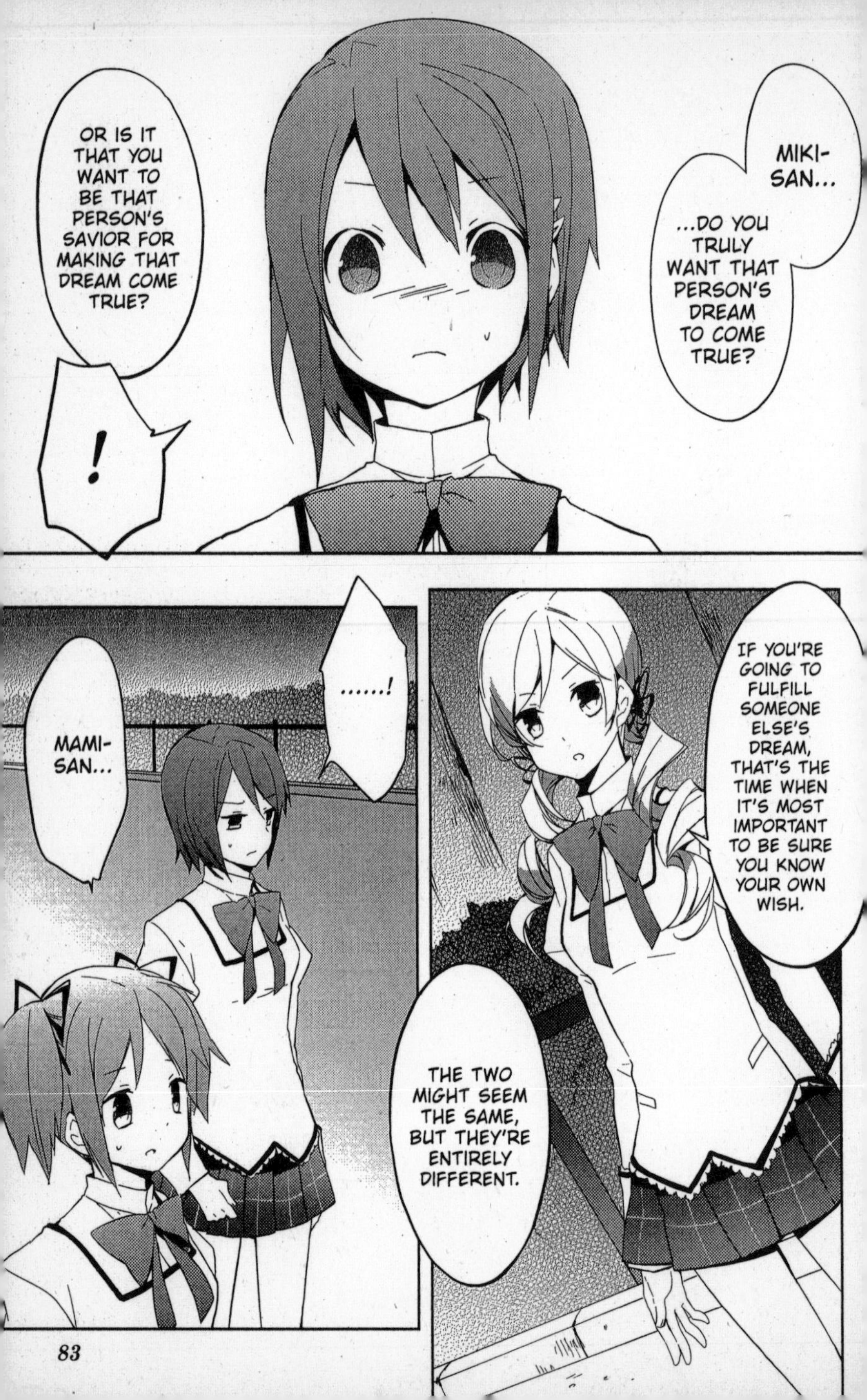
MIKI-SAN...
...DO YOU TRULY WANT THAT PERSON'S DREAM TO COME TRUE?
OR IS IT THAT YOU WANT TO BE THAT PERSON'S SAVIOR FOR MAKING THAT DREAM COME TRUE?
!
IF YOU'RE GOING TO FULFILL SOMEONE ELSE'S DREAM, THAT'S THE TIME WHEN IT'S MOST IMPORTANT TO BE SURE YOU KNOW YOUR OWN WISH.
THE TWO MIGHT SEEM THE SAME, BUT THEY'RE ENTIRELY DIFFERENT.
......!
MAMI-SAN...

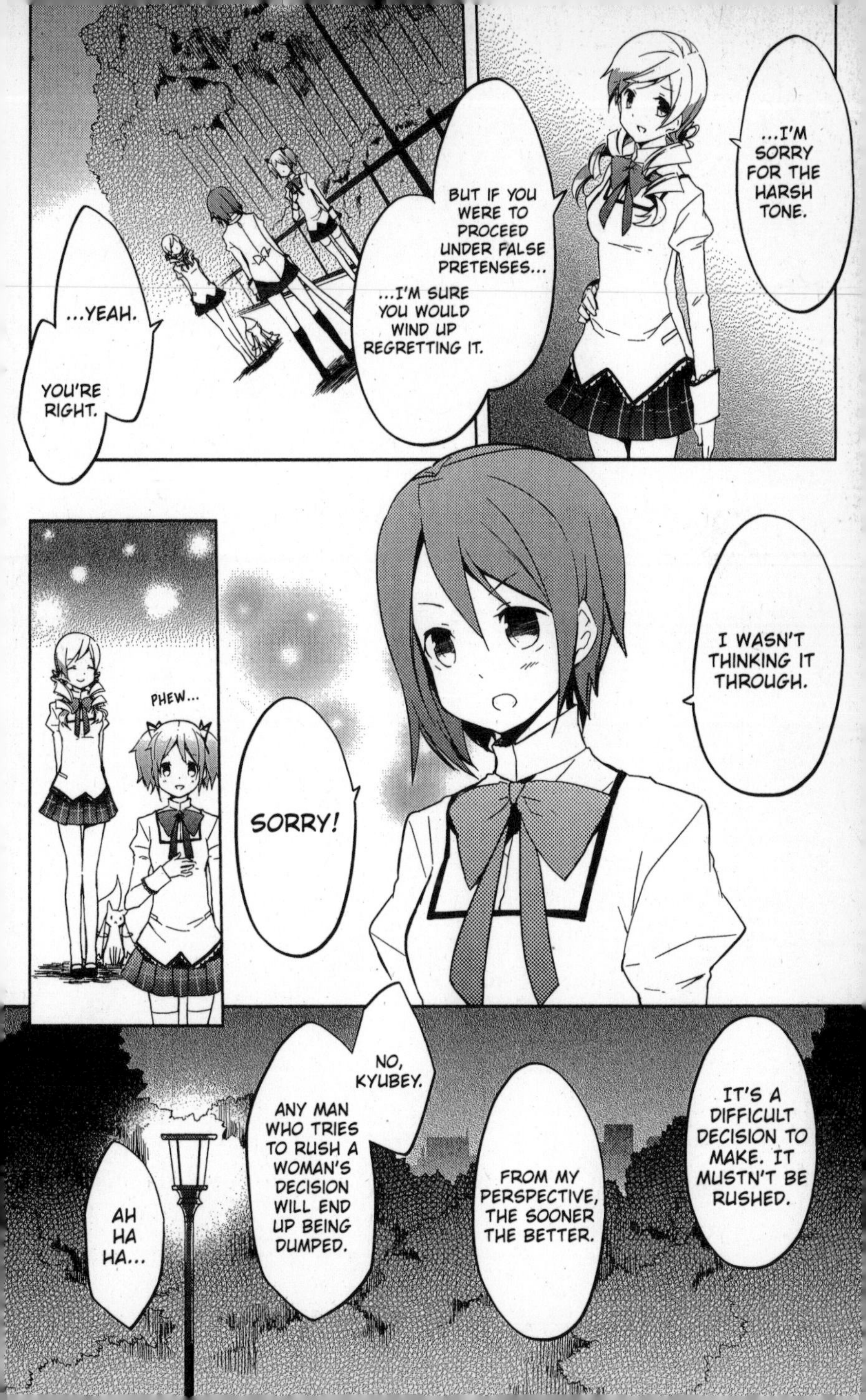
...I'M SORRY FOR THE HARSH TONE.
BUT IF YOU WERE TO PROCEED UNDER FALSE PRETENSES...
...I'M SURE YOU WOULD WIND UP REGRETTING IT.
...YEAH.
YOU'RE RIGHT.
I WASN'T THINKING IT THROUGH.
SORRY!
PHEW...
IT'S A DIFFICULT DECISION TO MAKE. IT MUSTN'T BE RUSHED.
FROM MY PERSPECTIVE, THE SOONER THE BETTER.
NO, KYUBEY.
ANY MAN WHO TRIES TO RUSH A WOMAN'S DECISION WILL END UP BEING DUMPED.
AH HA HA...

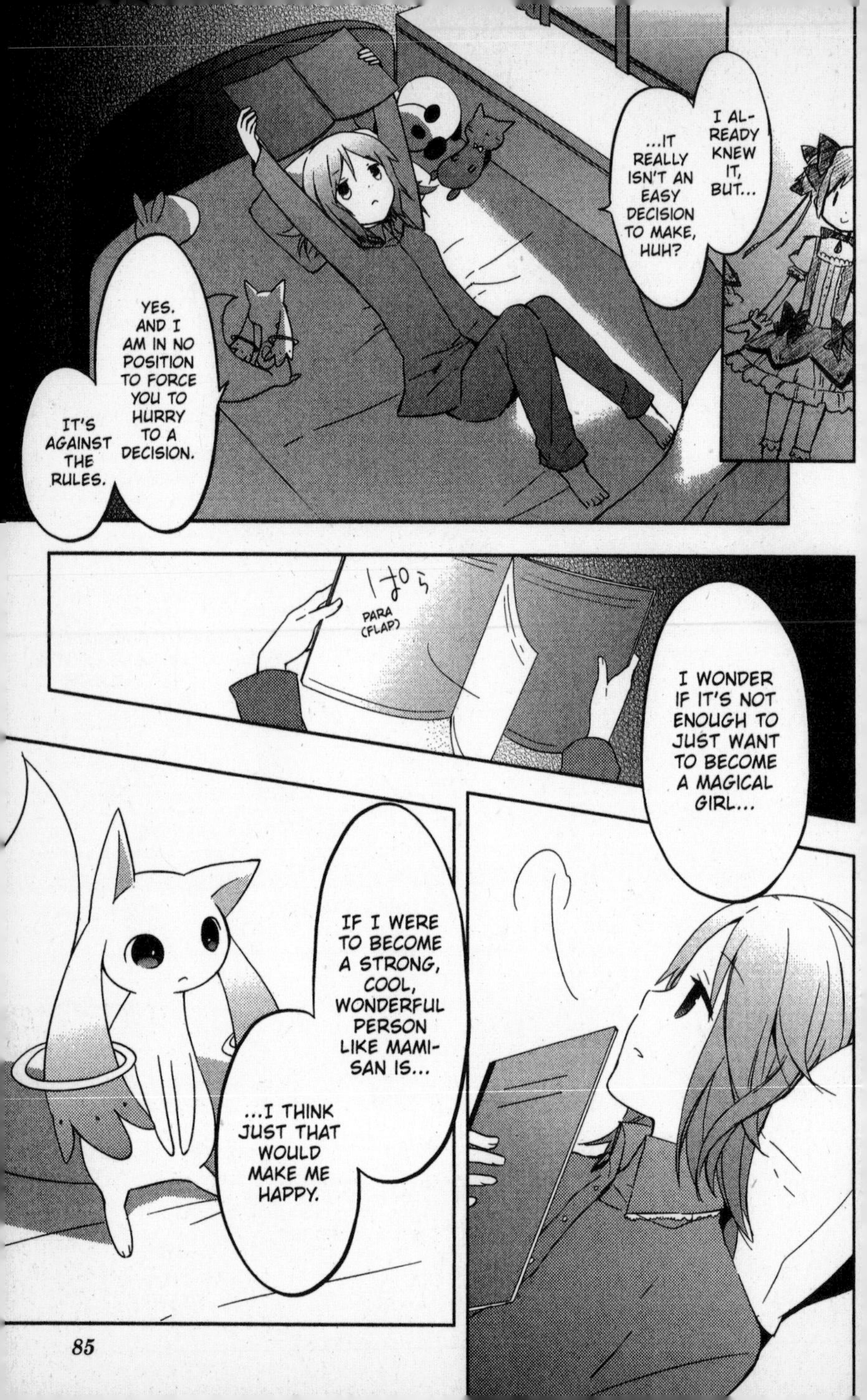
I AL-READY KNEW IT, BUT...
...IT REALLY ISN'T AN EASY DECISION TO MAKE, HUH?
YES. AND I AM IN NO POSITION TO FORCE YOU TO HURRY TO A DECISION.
IT'S AGAINST THE RULES.
I WONDER IF IT'S NOT ENOUGH TO JUST WANT TO BECOME A MAGICAL GIRL...
ぱら
PARA (FLAP)
IF I WERE TO BECOME A STRONG, COOL, WONDERFUL PERSON LIKE MAMI-SAN IS...
...I THINK JUST THAT WOULD MAKE ME HAPPY.

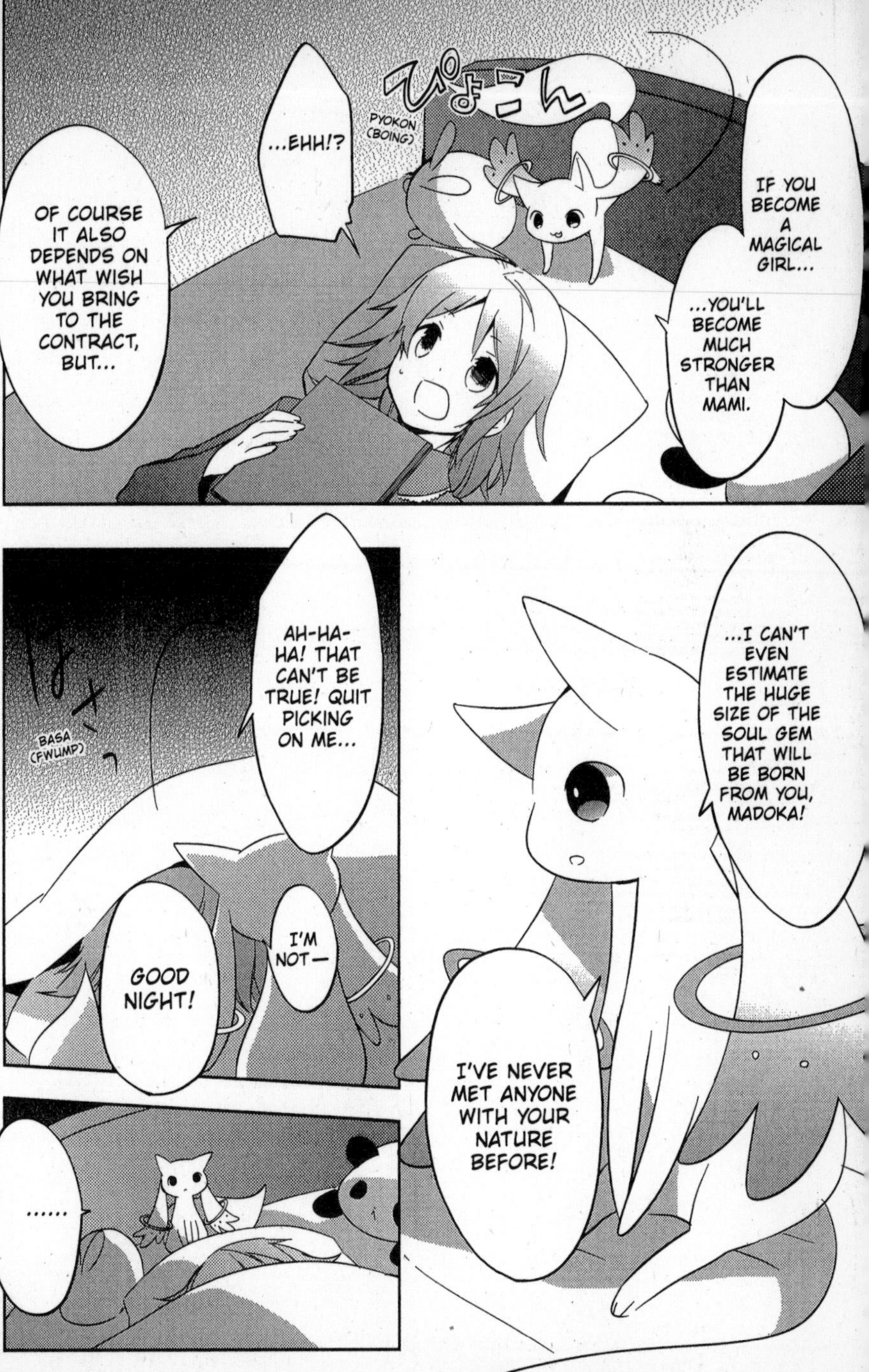
IF YOU BECOME A MAGICAL GIRL...
...YOU'LL BECOME MUCH STRONGER THAN MAMI.
ぴょこん
PYOKON (BOING)
...EHH!?
OF COURSE IT ALSO DEPENDS ON WHAT WISH YOU BRING TO THE CONTRACT, BUT...
...I CAN'T EVEN ESTIMATE THE HUGE SIZE OF THE SOUL GEM THAT WILL BE BORN FROM YOU, MADOKA!
I'VE NEVER MET ANYONE WITH YOUR NATURE BEFORE!
AH-HA-HA! THAT CAN'T BE TRUE! QUIT PICKING ON ME...
BASA (FWUMP)
I'M NOT—
GOOD NIGHT!
......

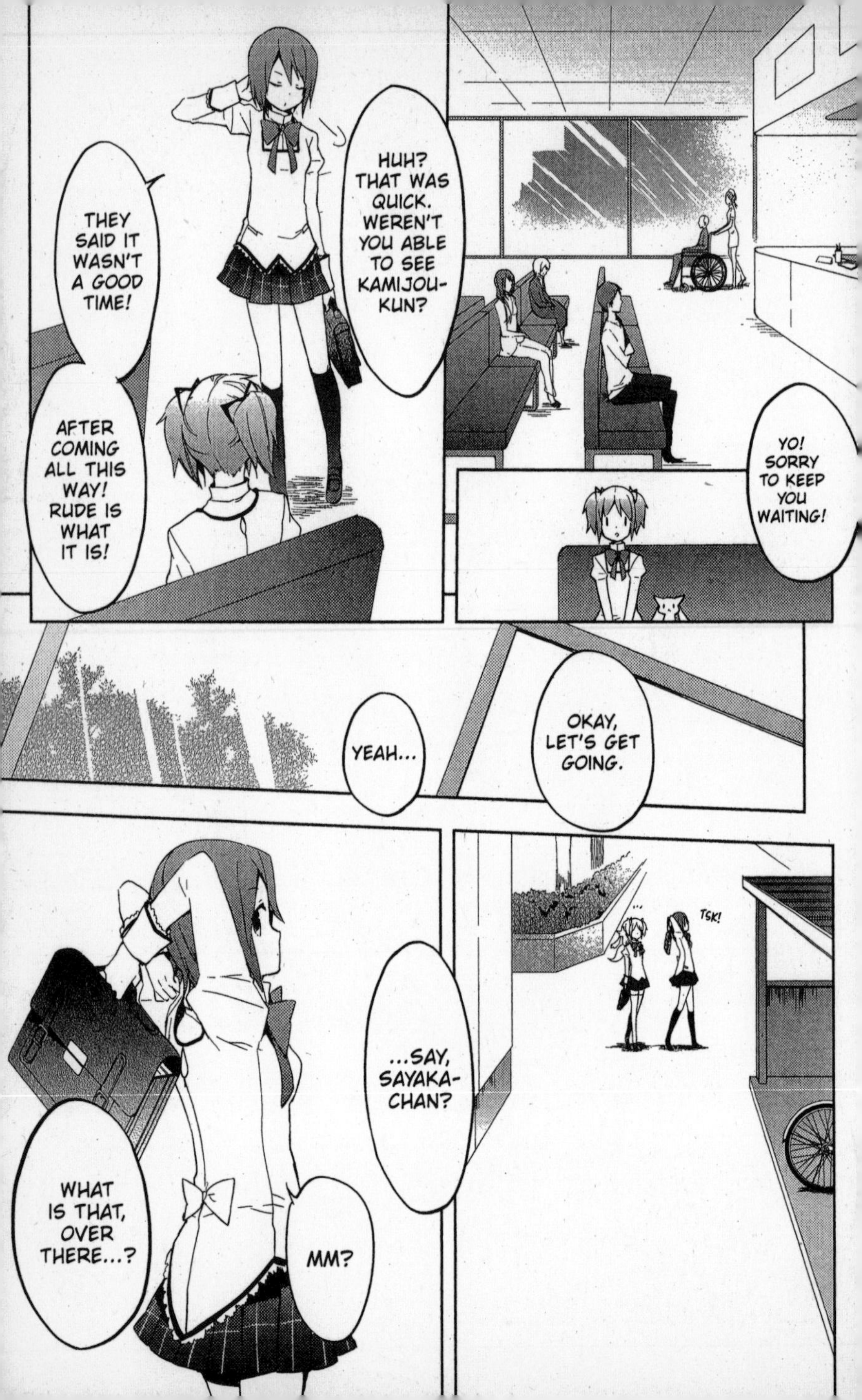
YO! SORRY TO KEEP YOU WAITING!
HUH? THAT WAS QUICK. WEREN'T YOU ABLE TO SEE KAMIJOU-KUN?
THEY SAID IT WASN'T A GOOD TIME!
AFTER COMING ALL THIS WAY! RUDE IS WHAT IT IS!
OKAY, LET'S GET GOING.
YEAH...
TSK!
...SAY, SAYAKA-CHAN?
MM?
WHAT IS THAT, OVER THERE...?

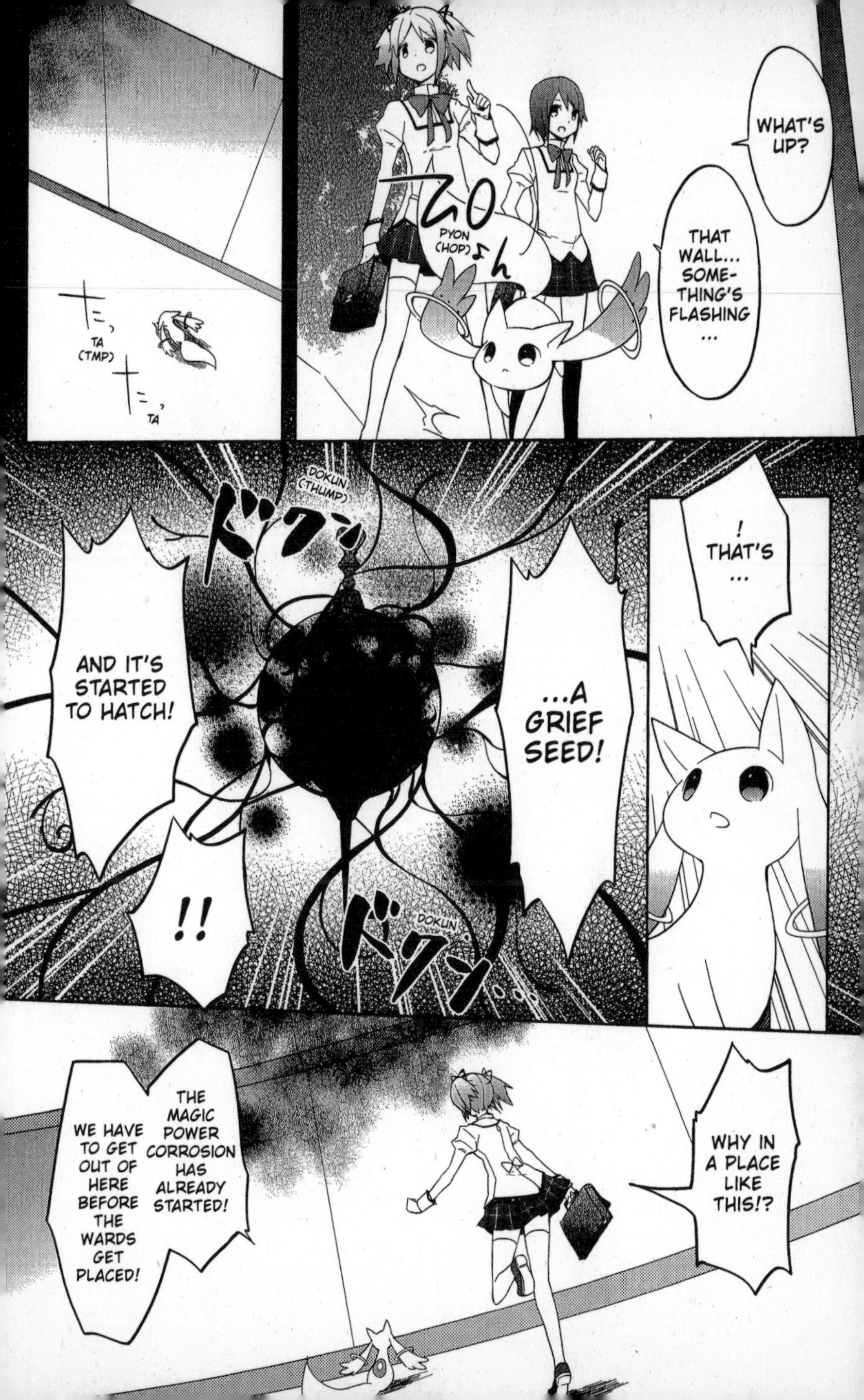
WHAT'S UP?
THAT WALL... SOMETHING'S FLASHING...
PYON (HOP)
TA (TMP)
TA
! THAT'S ...
DOKUN (THUMP)
...A GRIEF SEED!
AND IT'S STARTED TO HATCH!
!!
DOKUN
WHY IN A PLACE LIKE THIS!?
THE MAGIC POWER CORROSION HAS ALREADY STARTED!
WE HAVE TO GET OUT OF HERE BEFORE THE WARDS GET PLACED!

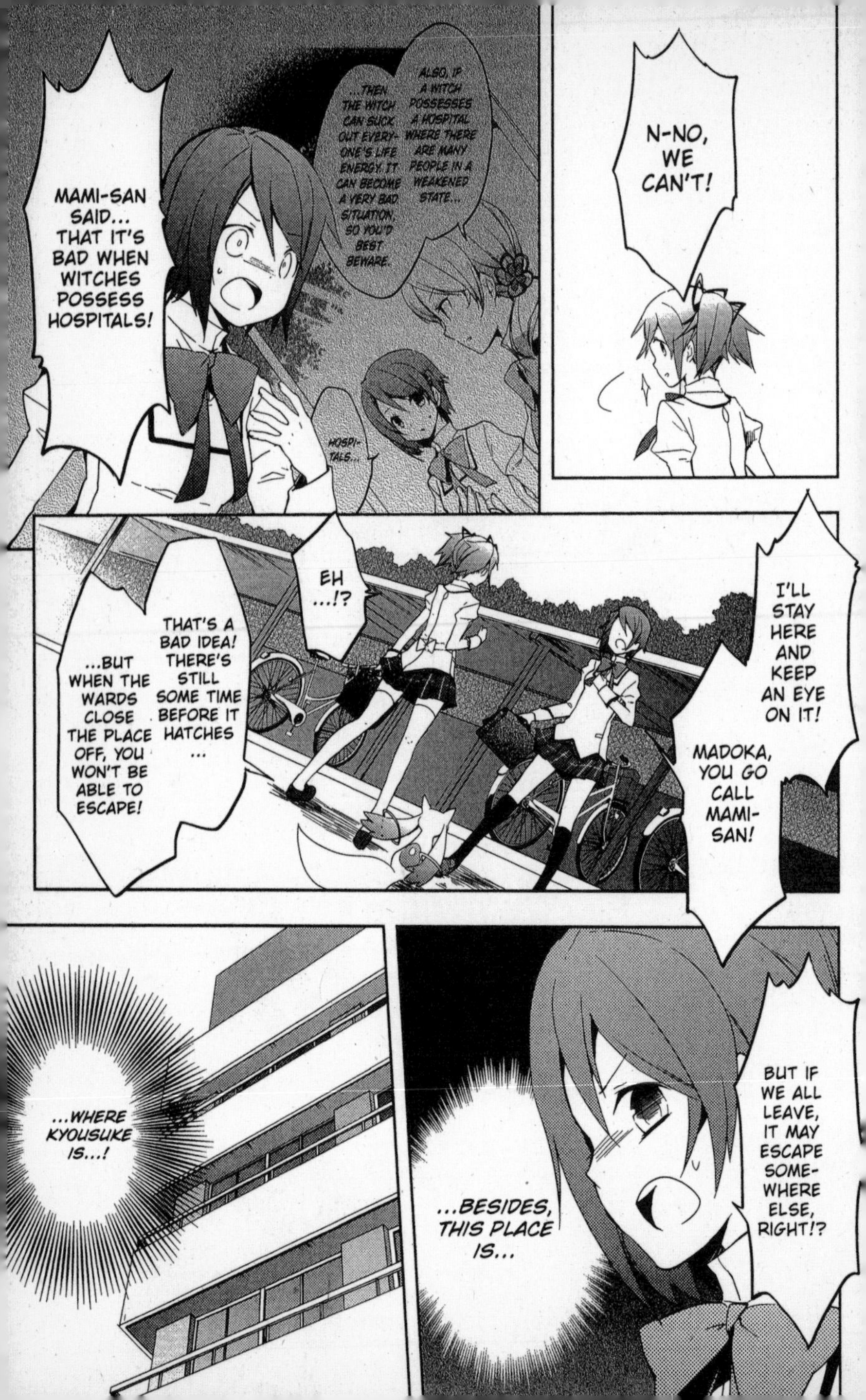
N-NO, WE CAN'T!
ALSO, IF A WITCH POSSESSES A HOSPITAL WHERE THERE ARE MANY PEOPLE IN A WEAKENED STATE...
...THEN THE WITCH CAN SUCK OUT EVERY-ONE'S LIFE ENERGY. IT CAN BECOME A VERY BAD SITUATION, SO YOU'D BEST BEWARE.
MAMI-SAN SAID... THAT IT'S BAD WHEN WITCHES POSSESS HOSPITALS!
HOSPI-TALS...
I'LL STAY HERE AND KEEP AN EYE ON IT!
MADOKA, YOU GO CALL MAMI-SAN!
EH ...!?
THAT'S A BAD IDEA! THERE'S STILL SOME TIME BEFORE IT HATCHES ...
...BUT WHEN THE WARDS CLOSE THE PLACE OFF, YOU WON'T BE ABLE TO ESCAPE!
BUT IF WE ALL LEAVE, IT MAY ESCAPE SOME-WHERE ELSE, RIGHT!?
...BESIDES, THIS PLACE IS...
...WHERE KYOUSUKE IS...!

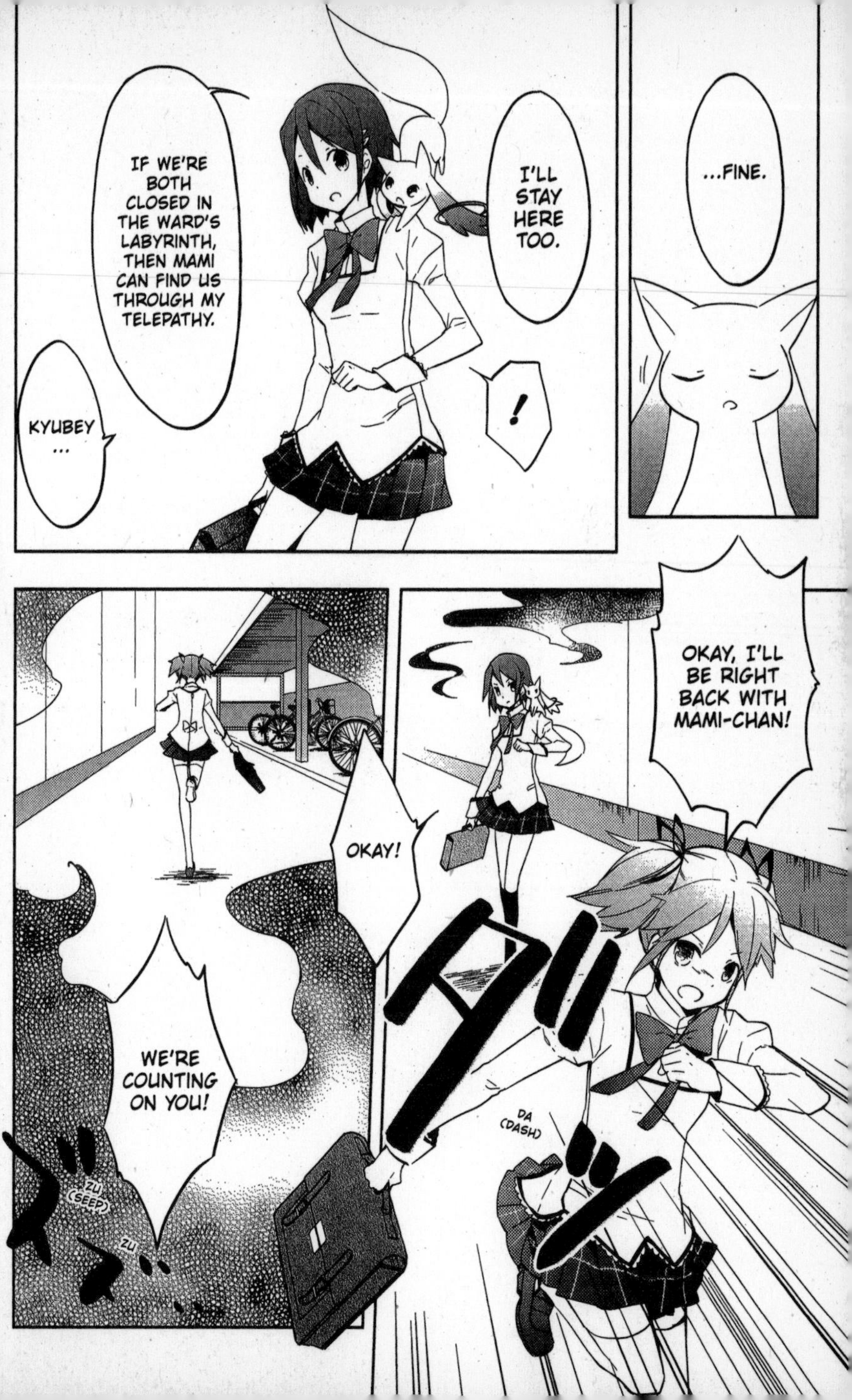
...FINE.
I'LL STAY HERE TOO.
IF WE'RE BOTH CLOSED IN THE WARD'S LABYRINTH, THEN MAMI CAN FIND US THROUGH MY TELEPATHY.
!
KYUBEY ...
OKAY, I'LL BE RIGHT BACK WITH MAMI-CHAN!
OKAY!
DA (DASH)
WE'RE COUNTING ON YOU!
ZU (SEEP)
ZU

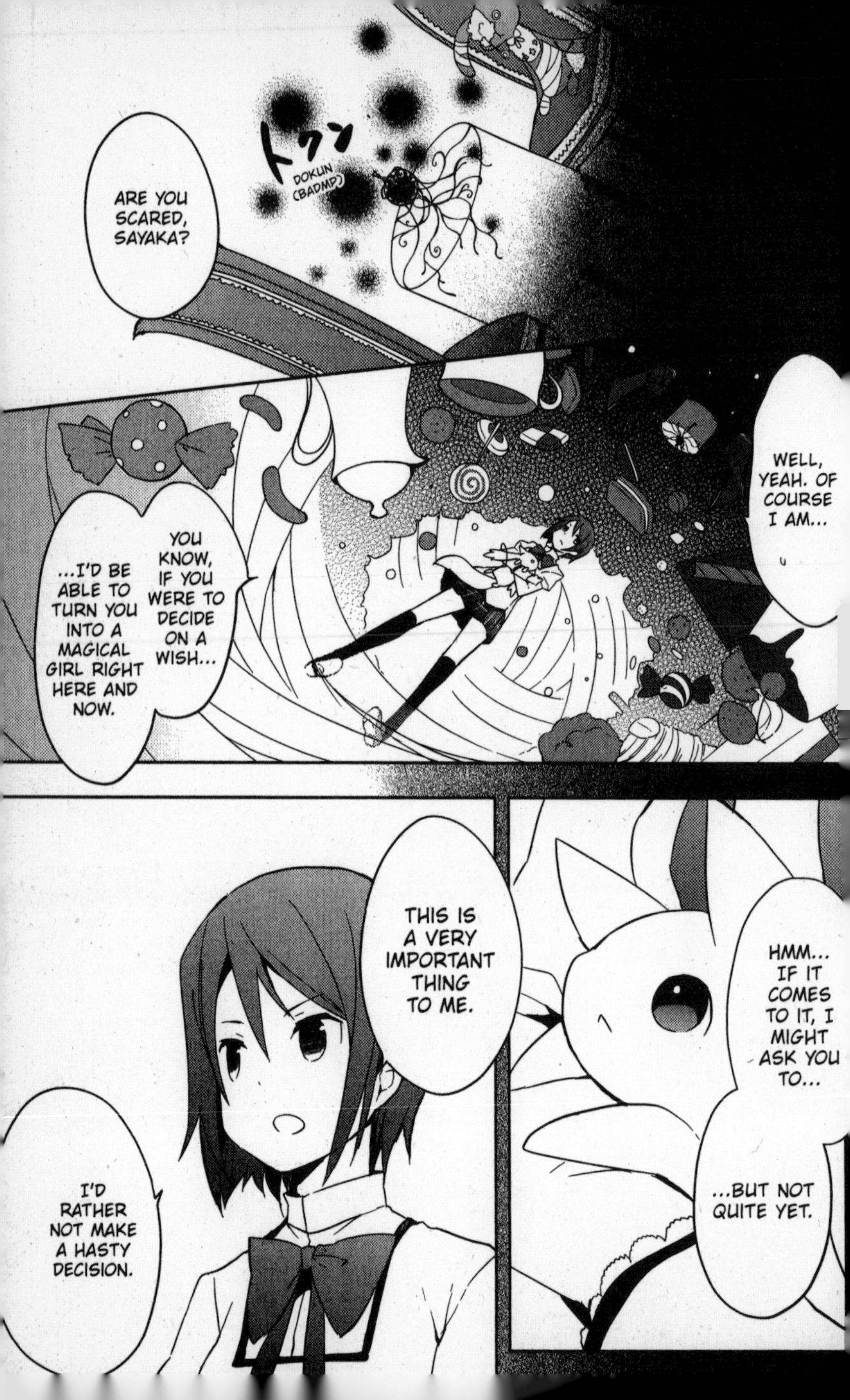
DOKUN (BADMP)
ARE YOU SCARED, SAYAKA?
WELL, YEAH. OF COURSE I AM...
YOU KNOW, IF YOU WERE TO DECIDE ON A WISH...
...I'D BE ABLE TO TURN YOU INTO A MAGICAL GIRL RIGHT HERE AND NOW.
HMM... IF IT COMES TO IT, I MIGHT ASK YOU TO...
...BUT NOT QUITE YET.
THIS IS A VERY IMPORTANT THING TO ME.
I'D RATHER NOT MAKE A HASTY DECISION.

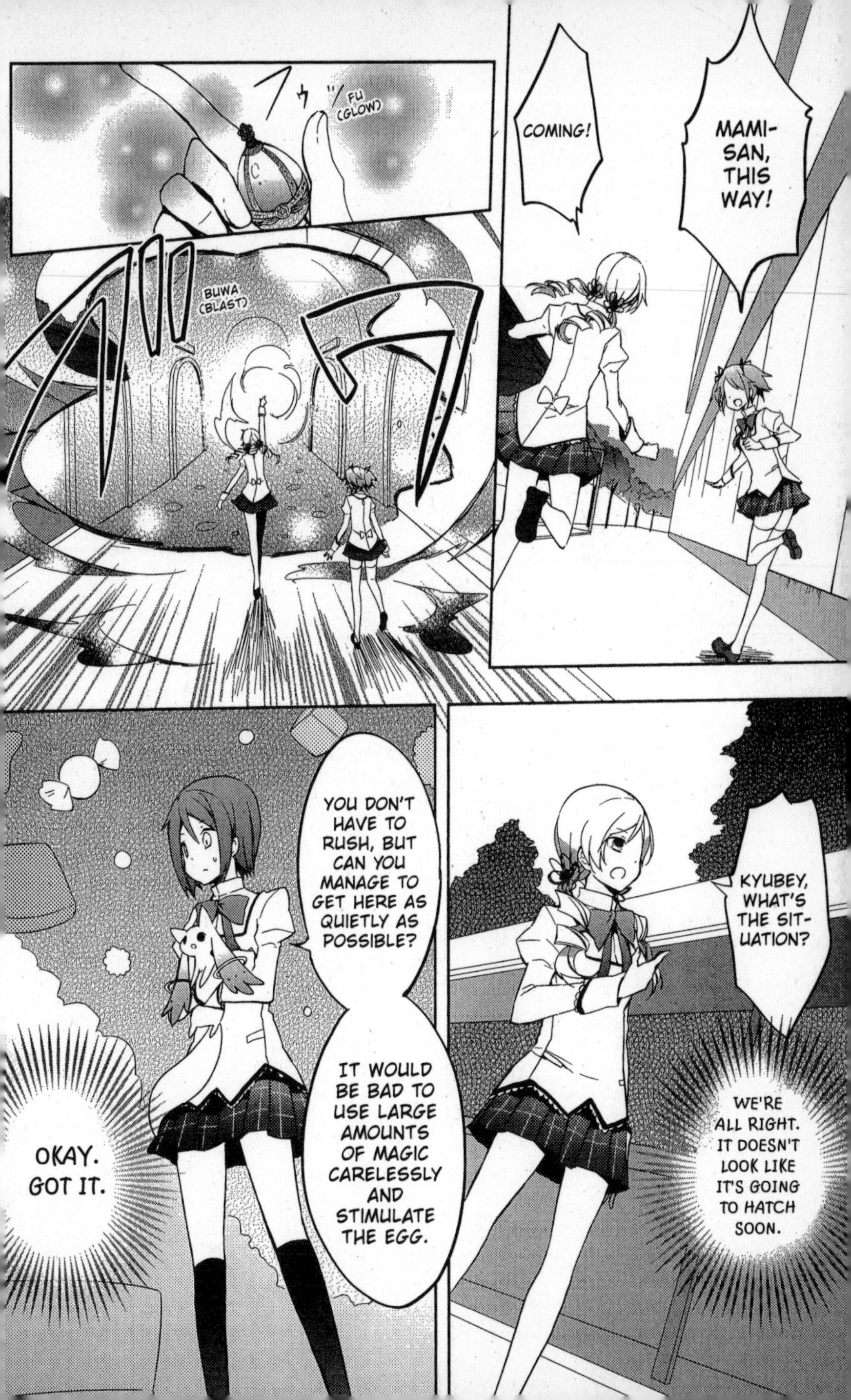
MAMI-SAN, THIS WAY!
COMING!
FU (GLOW)
BUWA (BLAST)
KYUBEY, WHAT'S THE SIT-UATION?
WE'RE ALL RIGHT. IT DOESN'T LOOK LIKE IT'S GOING TO HATCH SOON.
YOU DON'T HAVE TO RUSH, BUT CAN YOU MANAGE TO GET HERE AS QUIETLY AS POSSIBLE?
IT WOULD BE BAD TO USE LARGE AMOUNTS OF MAGIC CARELESSLY AND STIMULATE THE EGG.
OKAY. GOT IT.

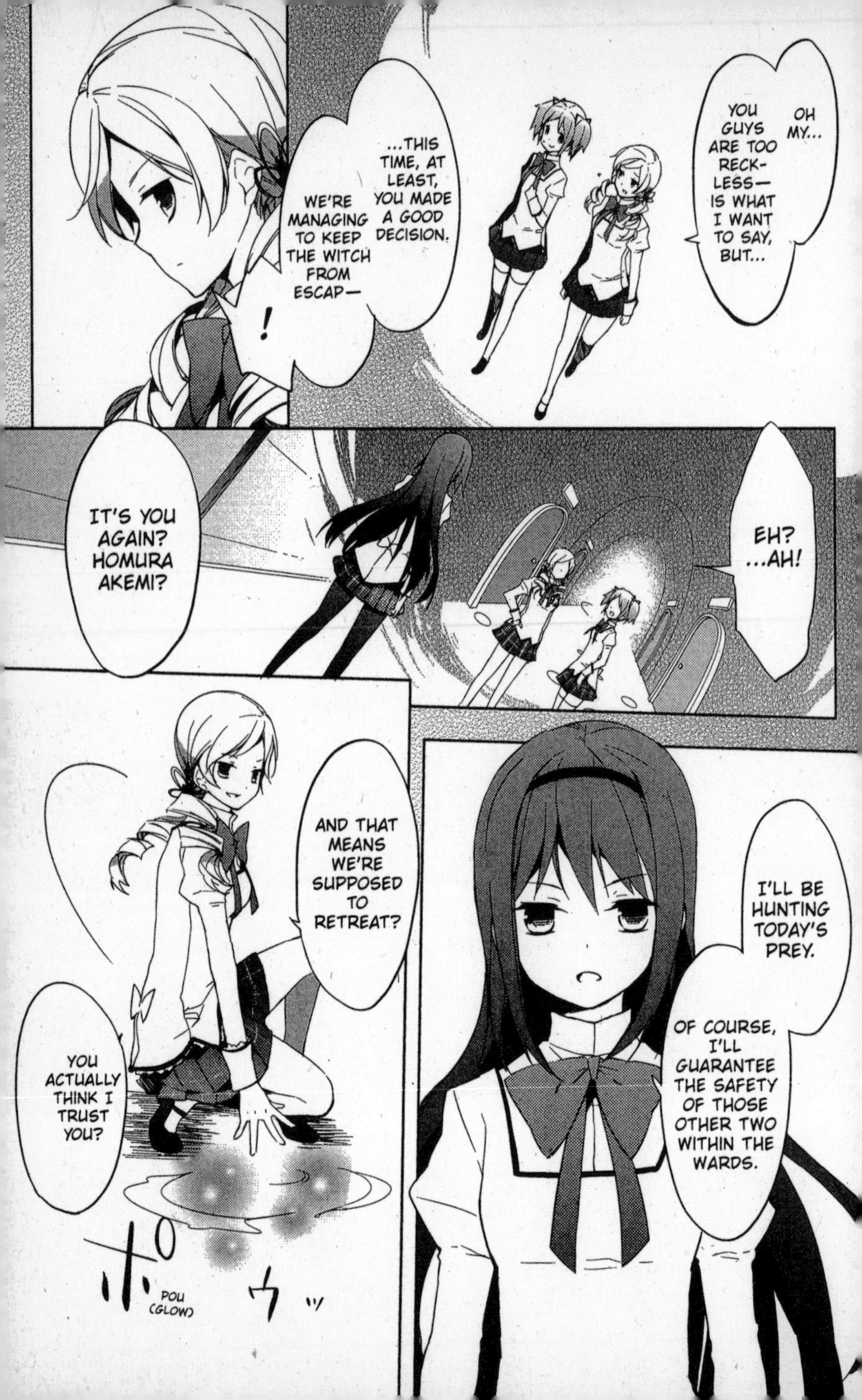
OH MY...
YOU GUYS ARE TOO RECK-LESS— IS WHAT I WANT TO SAY, BUT...
...THIS TIME, AT LEAST, YOU MADE A GOOD DECISION.
WE'RE MANAGING TO KEEP THE WITCH FROM ESCAP—
!
EH? ...AH!
IT'S YOU AGAIN? HOMURA AKEMI?
I'LL BE HUNTING TODAY'S PREY.
OF COURSE, I'LL GUARANTEE THE SAFETY OF THOSE OTHER TWO WITHIN THE WARDS.
AND THAT MEANS WE'RE SUPPOSED TO RETREAT?
YOU ACTUALLY THINK I TRUST YOU?
POU (GLOW)

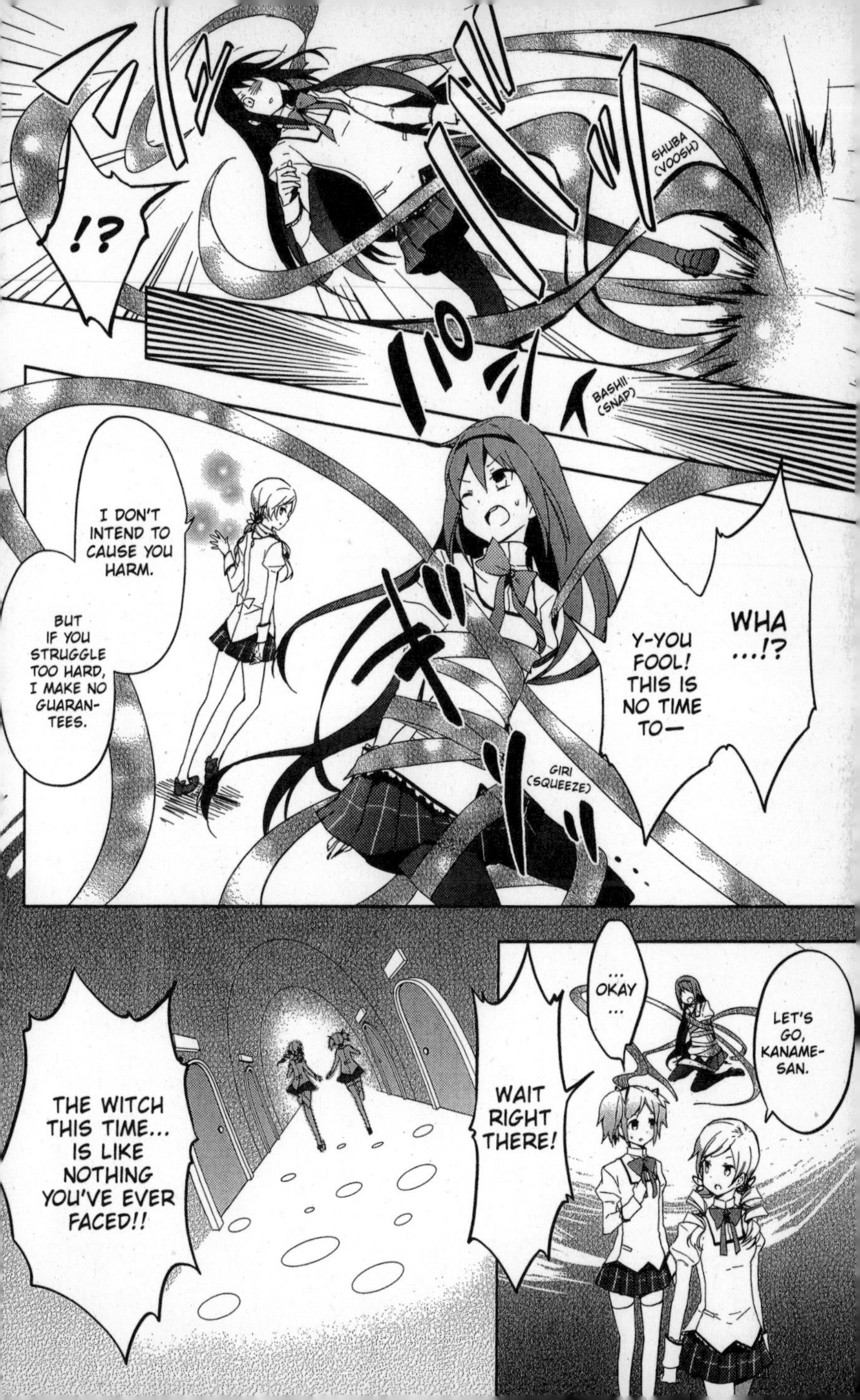
SHUBA (VOOSH)
!?
BASHII (SNAP)
WHA...!?
Y-YOU FOOL! THIS IS NO TIME TO—
GIRI (SQUEEZE)
I DON'T INTEND TO CAUSE YOU HARM.
BUT IF YOU STRUGGLE TOO HARD, I MAKE NO GUARANTEES.
LET'S GO, KANAME-SAN.
...OKAY...
WAIT RIGHT THERE!
THE WITCH THIS TIME... IS LIKE NOTHING YOU'VE EVER FACED!!

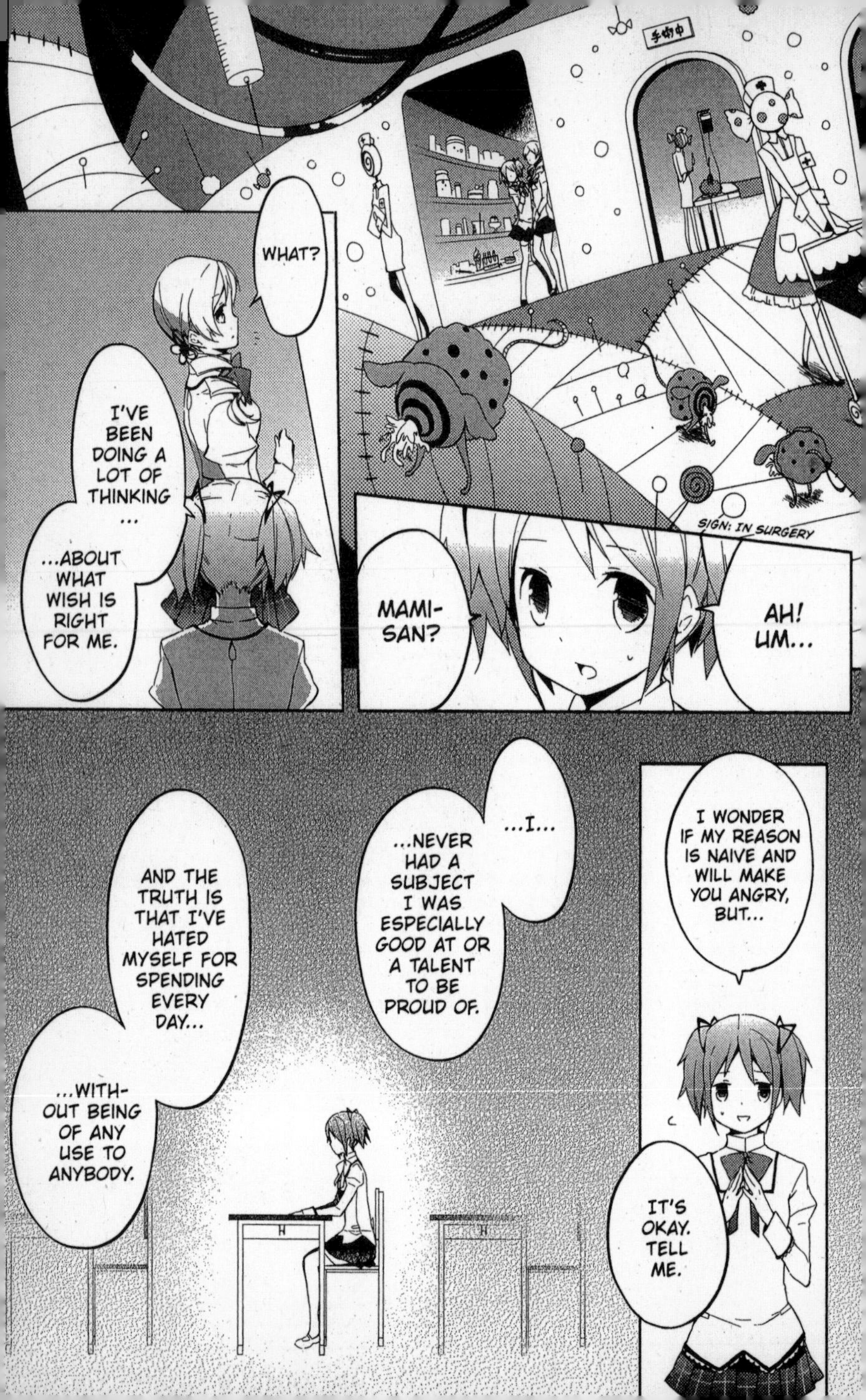
手術中
SIGN: IN SURGERY
AH! UM...
MAMI-SAN?
WHAT?
I'VE BEEN DOING A LOT OF THINKING ...
...ABOUT WHAT WISH IS RIGHT FOR ME.
I WONDER IF MY REASON IS NAIVE AND WILL MAKE YOU ANGRY, BUT...
IT'S OKAY. TELL ME.
...I...
...NEVER HAD A SUBJECT I WAS ESPECIALLY GOOD AT OR A TALENT TO BE PROUD OF.
AND THE TRUTH IS THAT I'VE HATED MYSELF FOR SPENDING EVERY DAY...
...WITH-OUT BEING OF ANY USE TO ANYBODY.

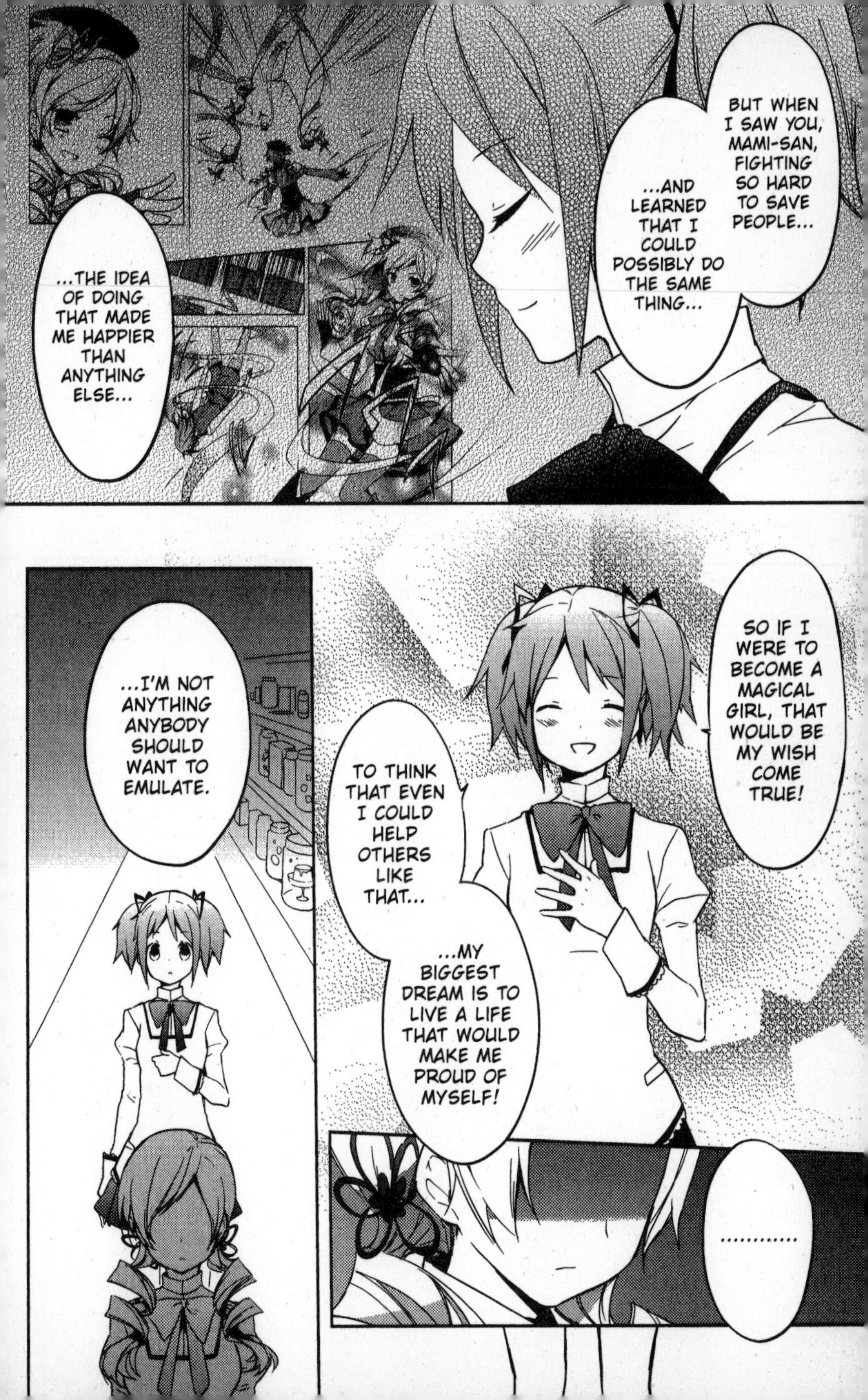
BUT WHEN I SAW YOU, MAMI-SAN, FIGHTING SO HARD TO SAVE PEOPLE...
...AND LEARNED THAT I COULD POSSIBLY DO THE SAME THING...
...THE IDEA OF DOING THAT MADE ME HAPPIER THAN ANYTHING ELSE...
SO IF I WERE TO BECOME A MAGICAL GIRL, THAT WOULD BE MY WISH COME TRUE!
TO THINK THAT EVEN I COULD HELP OTHERS LIKE THAT...
...MY BIGGEST DREAM IS TO LIVE A LIFE THAT WOULD MAKE ME PROUD OF MYSELF!
....
...I'M NOT ANYTHING ANYBODY SHOULD WANT TO EMULATE.

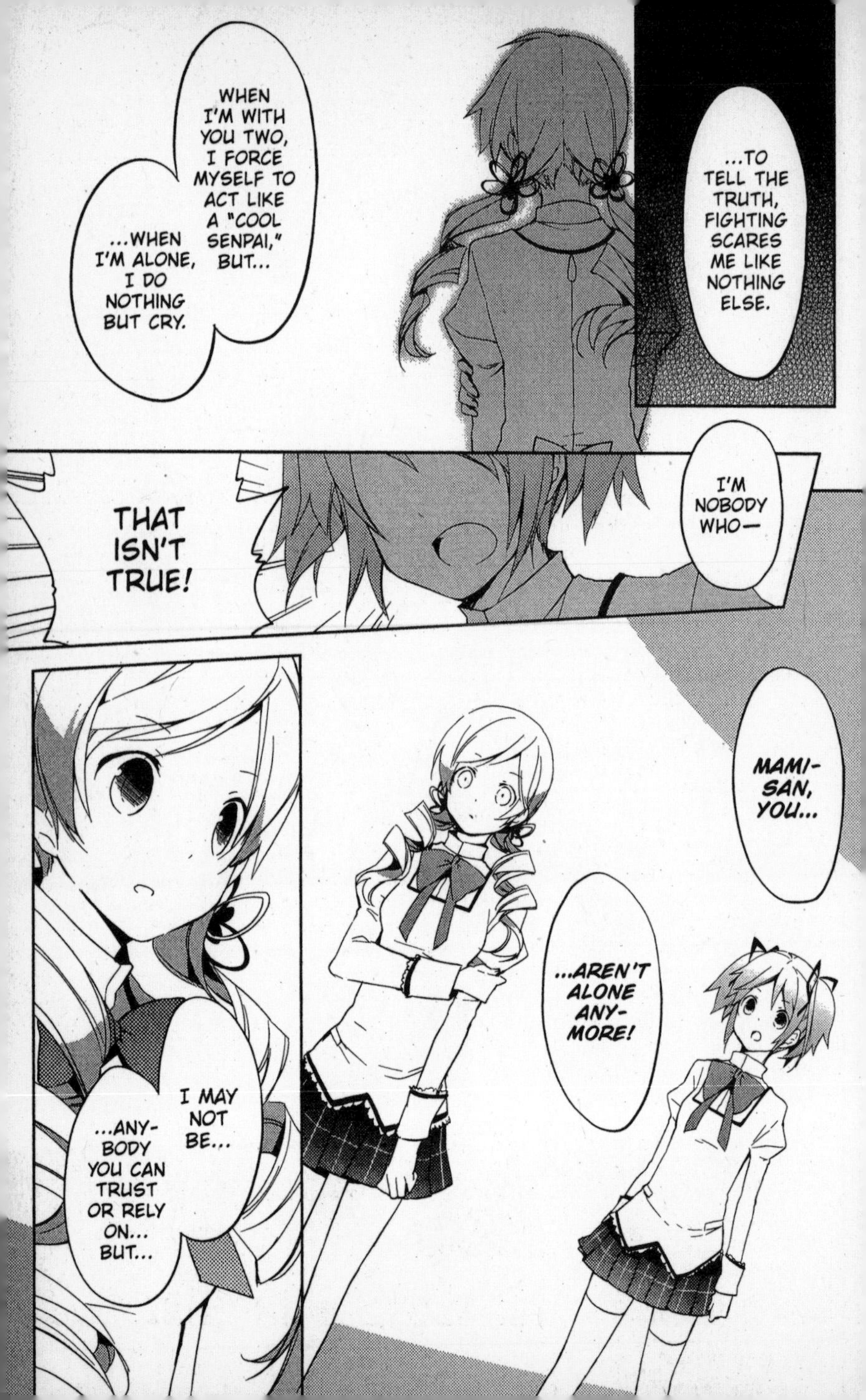
...TO TELL THE TRUTH, FIGHTING SCARES ME LIKE NOTHING ELSE.
WHEN I'M WITH YOU TWO, I FORCE MYSELF TO ACT LIKE A "COOL SENPAI," BUT...
...WHEN I'M ALONE, I DO NOTHING BUT CRY.
I'M NOBODY WHO—
THAT ISN'T TRUE!
MAMI-SAN, YOU...
...AREN'T ALONE ANY-MORE!
I MAY NOT BE...
...ANY-BODY YOU CAN TRUST OR RELY ON... BUT...

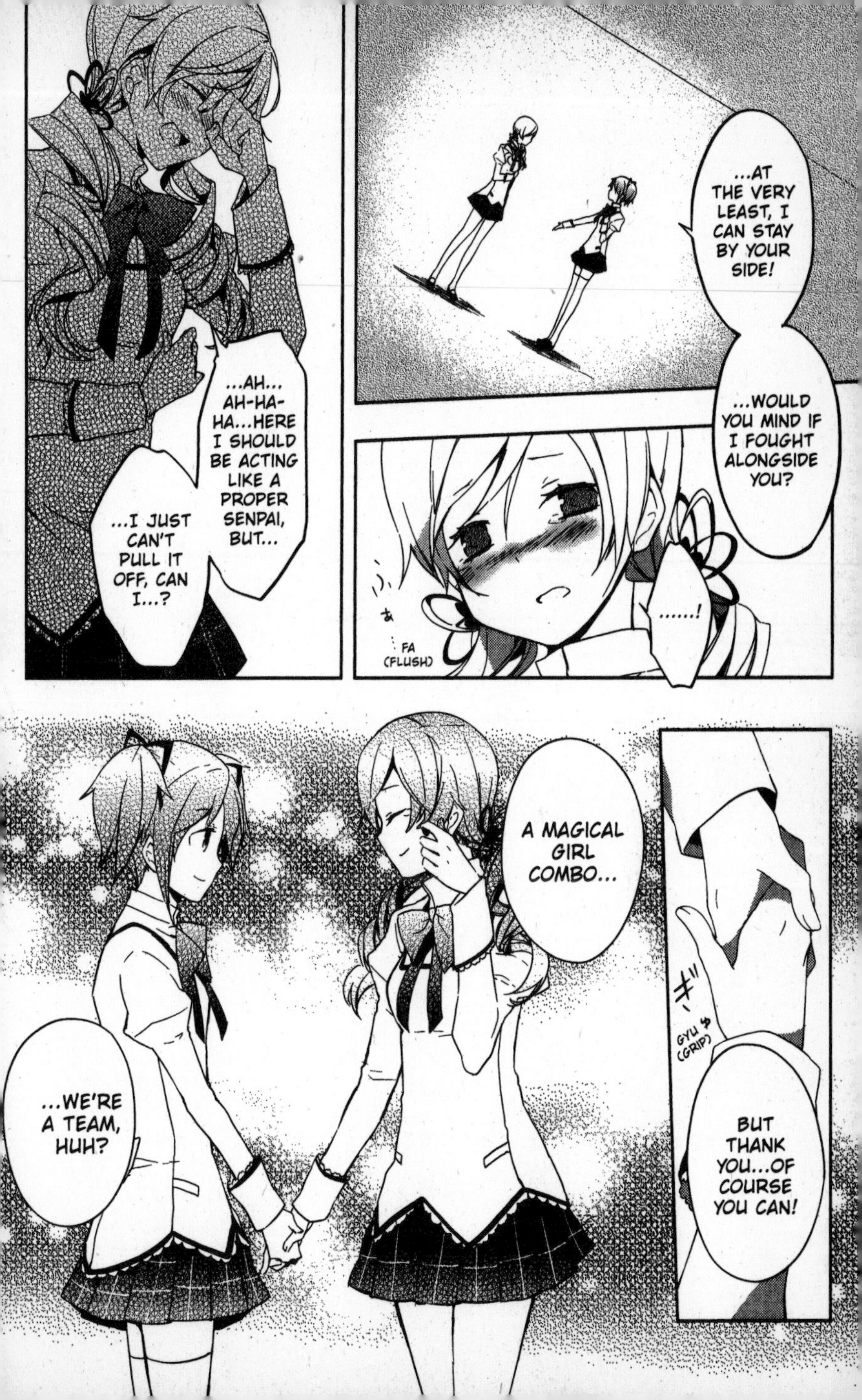
...AT THE VERY LEAST, I CAN STAY BY YOUR SIDE!
...WOULD YOU MIND IF I FOUGHT ALONGSIDE YOU?
......!
FA (FLUSH)
...AH... AH-HA-HA...HERE I SHOULD BE ACTING LIKE A PROPER SENPAI, BUT...
...I JUST CAN'T PULL IT OFF, CAN I...?
GYU (GRIP)
BUT THANK YOU...OF COURSE YOU CAN!
A MAGICAL GIRL COMBO...
...WE'RE A TEAM, HUH?

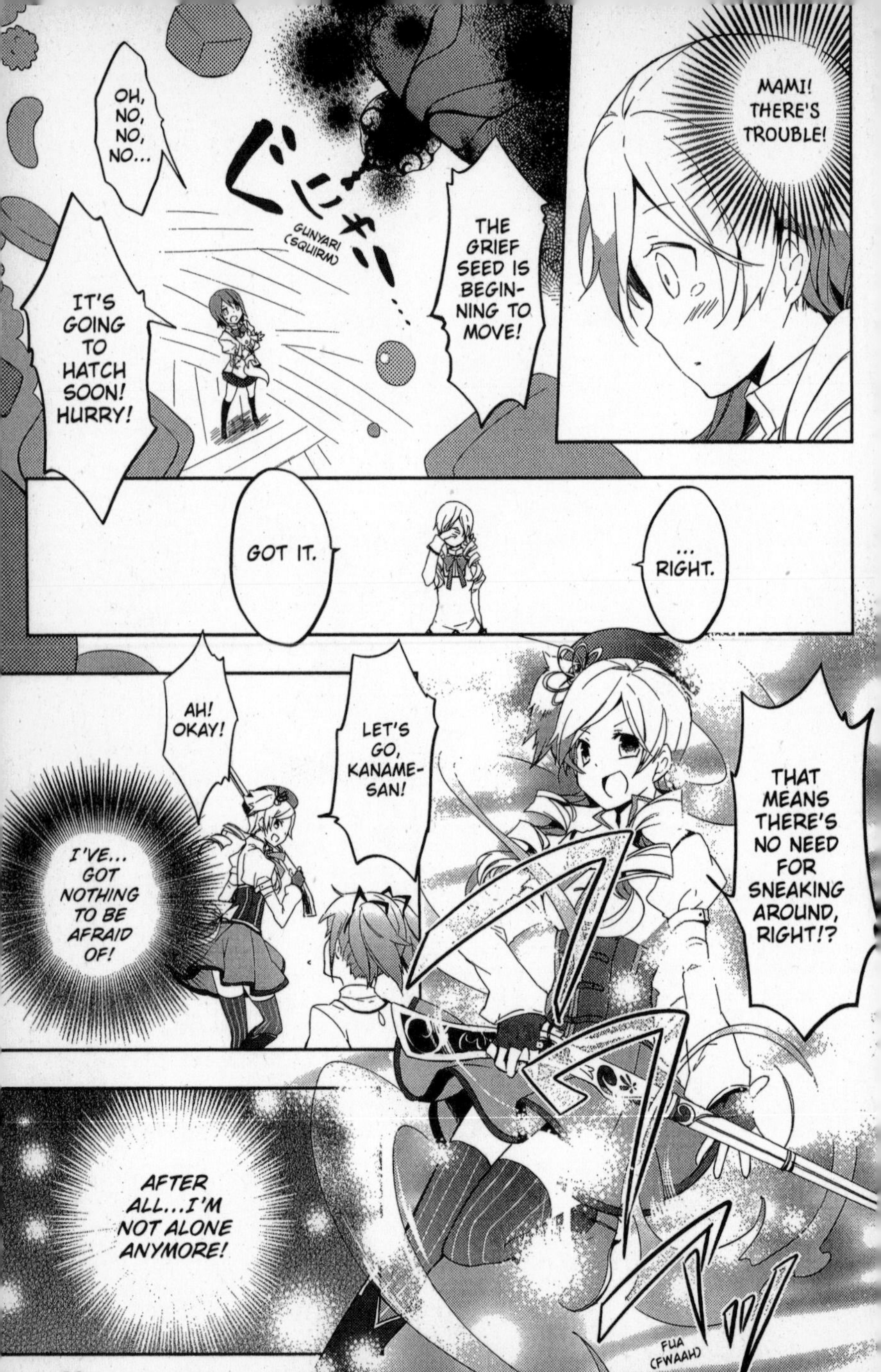
MAMI! THERE'S TROUBLE!
THE GRIEF SEED IS BEGIN-NING TO MOVE!
GUNYARI (SQUIRM)
OH, NO, NO, NO...
IT'S GOING TO HATCH SOON! HURRY!
... RIGHT.
GOT IT.
THAT MEANS THERE'S NO NEED FOR SNEAKING AROUND, RIGHT!?
LET'S GO, KANAME-SAN!
AH! OKAY!
I'VE... GOT NOTHING TO BE AFRAID OF!
AFTER ALL...I'M NOT ALONE ANYMORE!
FUA (FWAAH)

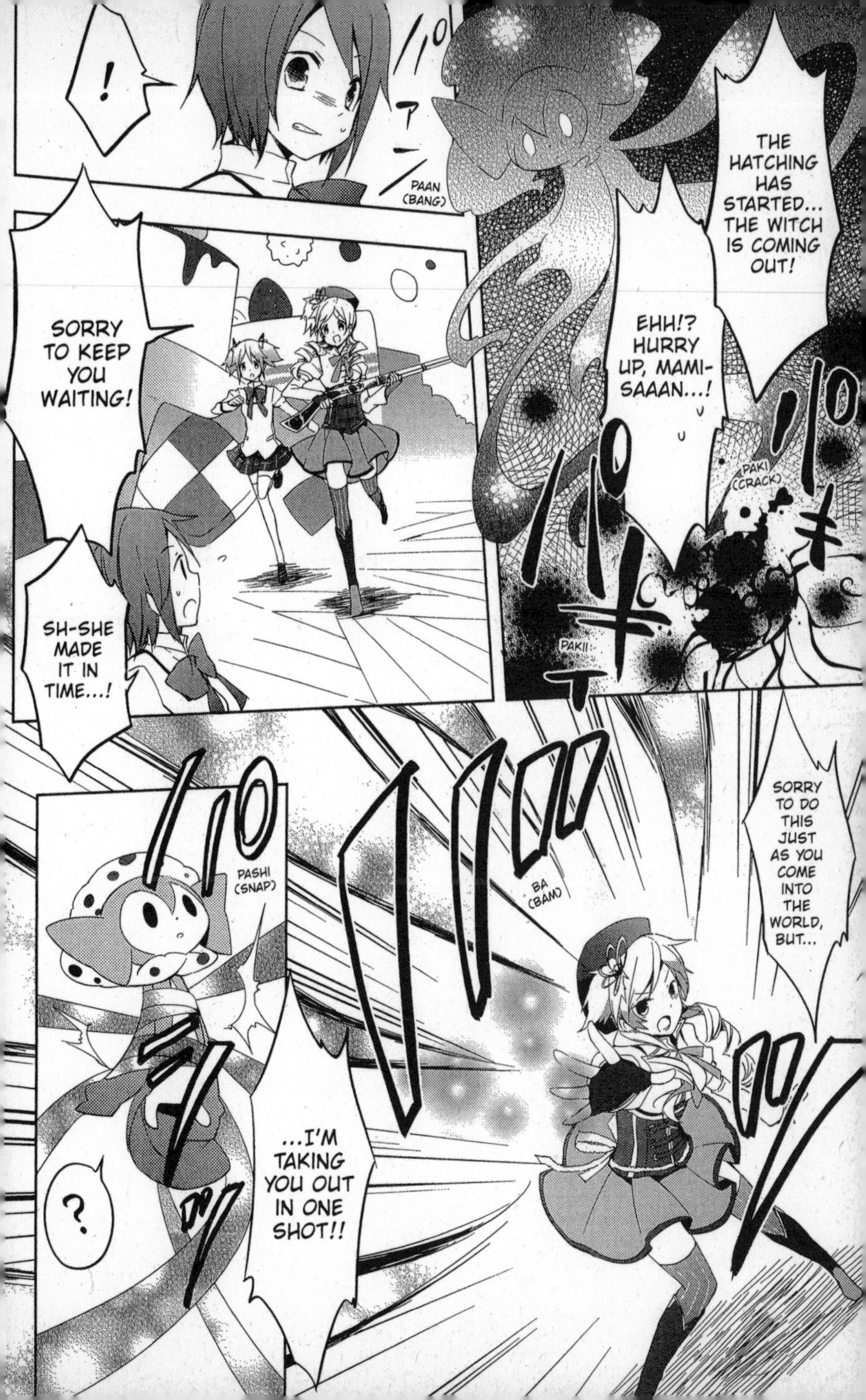
THE HATCHING HAS STARTED... THE WITCH IS COMING OUT!
EHH!? HURRY UP, MAMI-SAAAN...!
PAKI (CRACK)
PAKII
!
PAAN (BANG)
SORRY TO KEEP YOU WAITING!
SH-SHE MADE IT IN TIME...!
SORRY TO DO THIS JUST AS YOU COME INTO THE WORLD, BUT...
BA (BAM)
...I'M TAKING YOU OUT IN ONE SHOT!!
PASHI (SNAP)
?

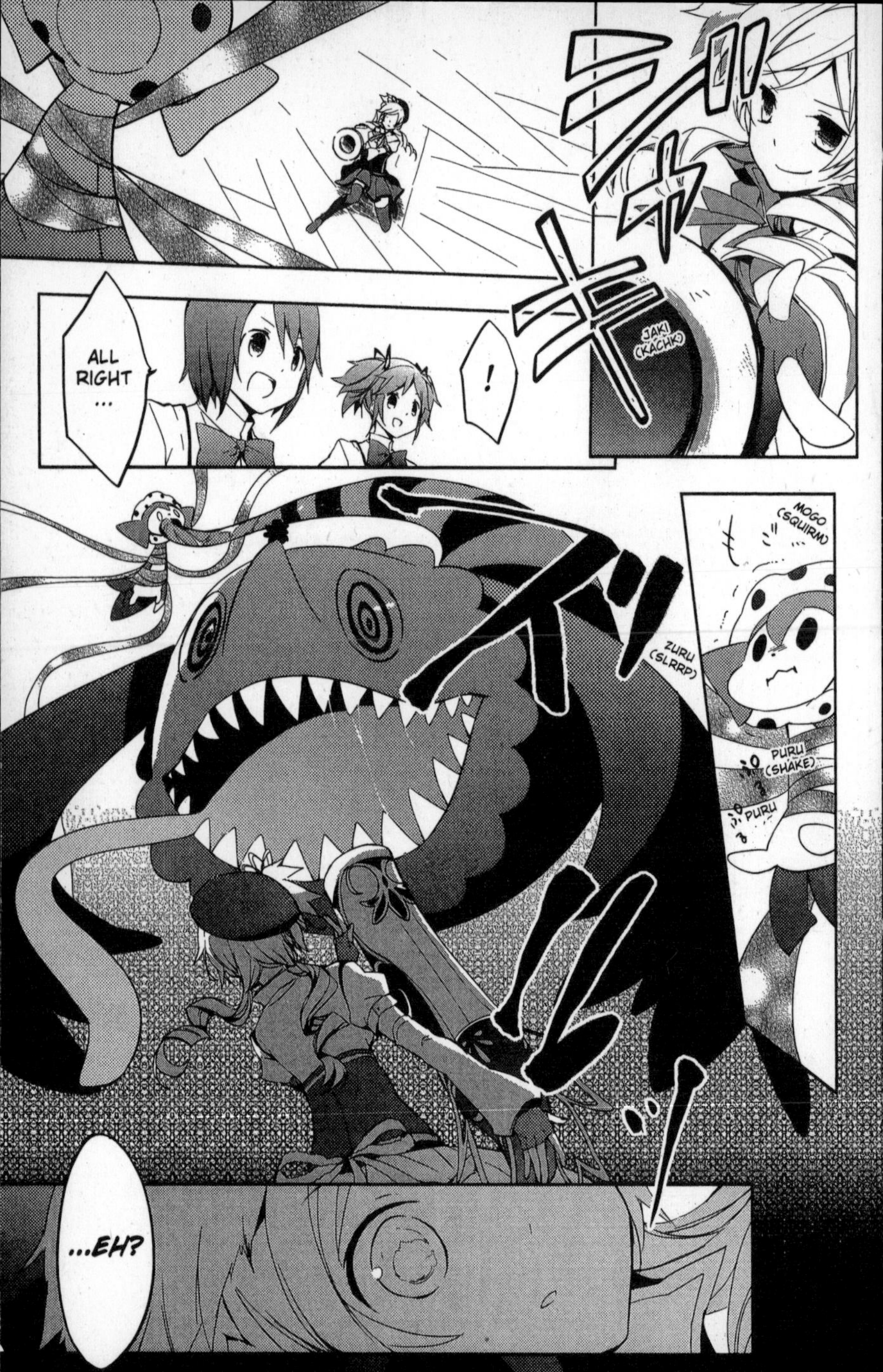
JAKI (KACHK)
ALL RIGHT ...
!
MOGO (SQUIRM)
ZURU (SLRRP)
PURU (SHAKE)
PURU
...EH?

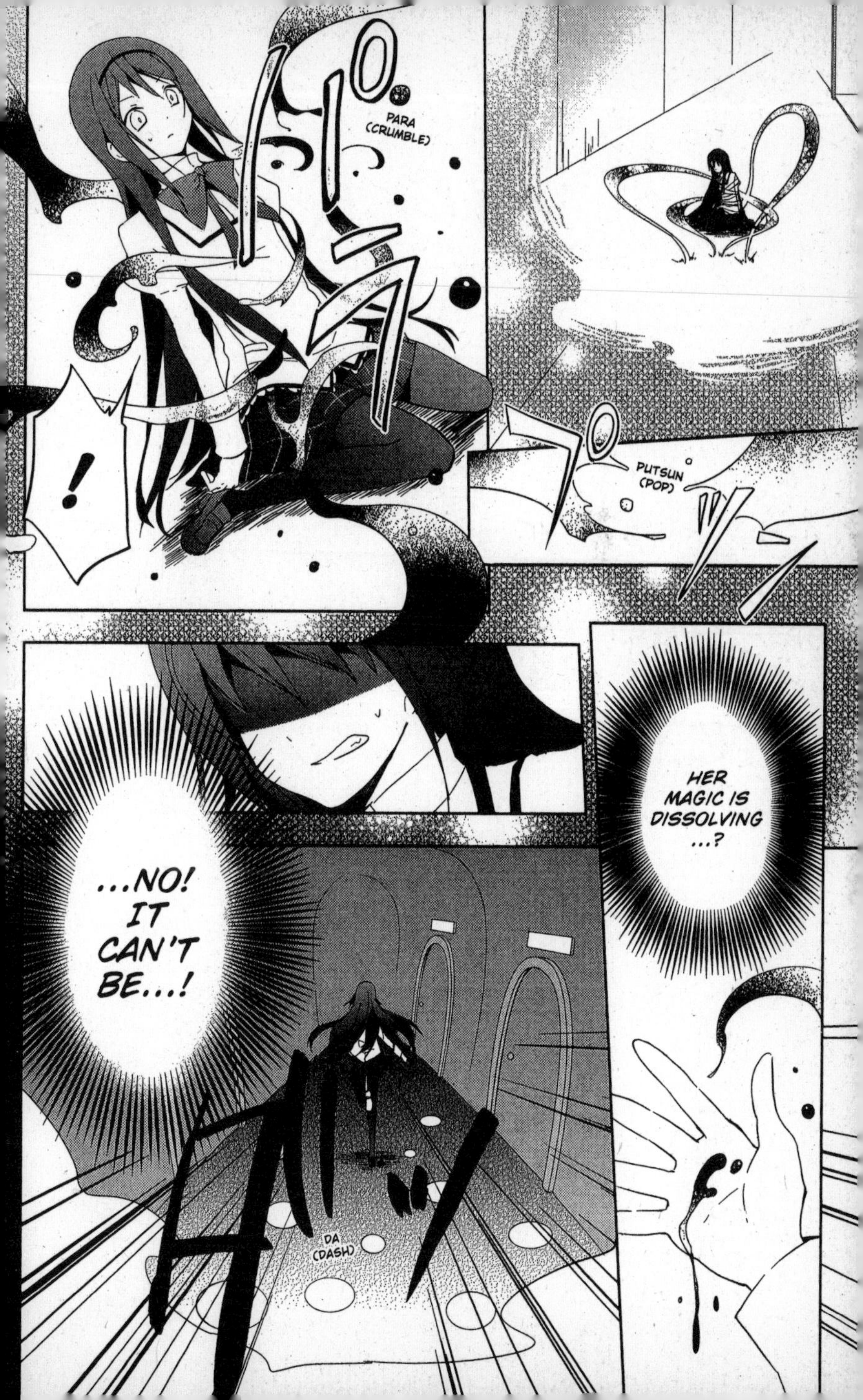
PUTSUN (POP)
PARA (CRUMBLE)
!
HER MAGIC IS DISSOLVING ...?
...NO! IT CAN'T BE...!
DA (DASH)

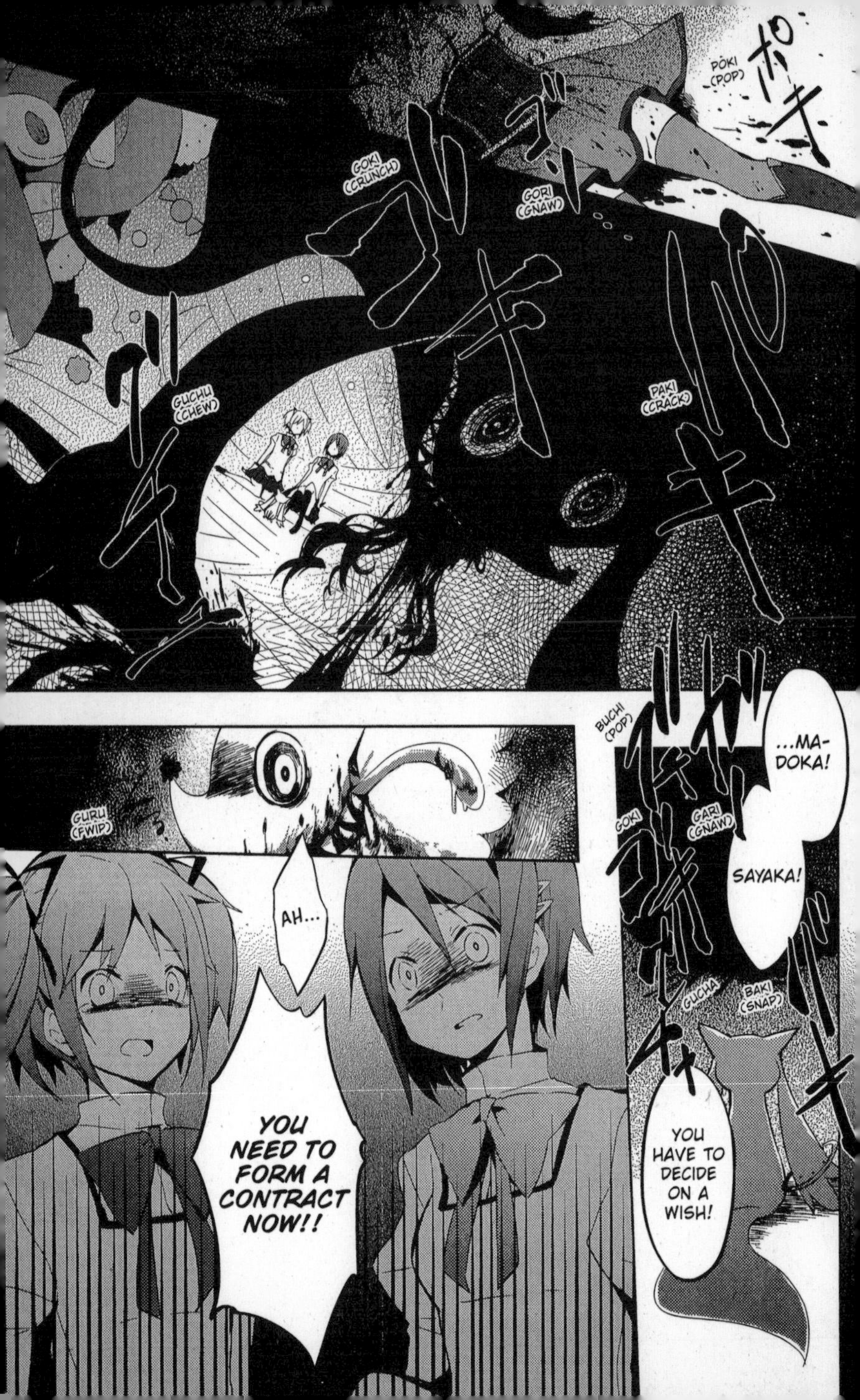
PŌKI (POP)
GORI (GNAW)
GOKI (CRUNCH)
PAKI (CRACK)
GUCHU (CHEW)
BUCHI (POP)
...MA-DOKA!
GARI (GNAW)
GOKI
SAYAKA!
BAKI (SNAP)
GUCHA
YOU HAVE TO DECIDE ON A WISH!
GURU (FWIP)
AH...
YOU NEED TO FORM A CONTRACT NOW!!

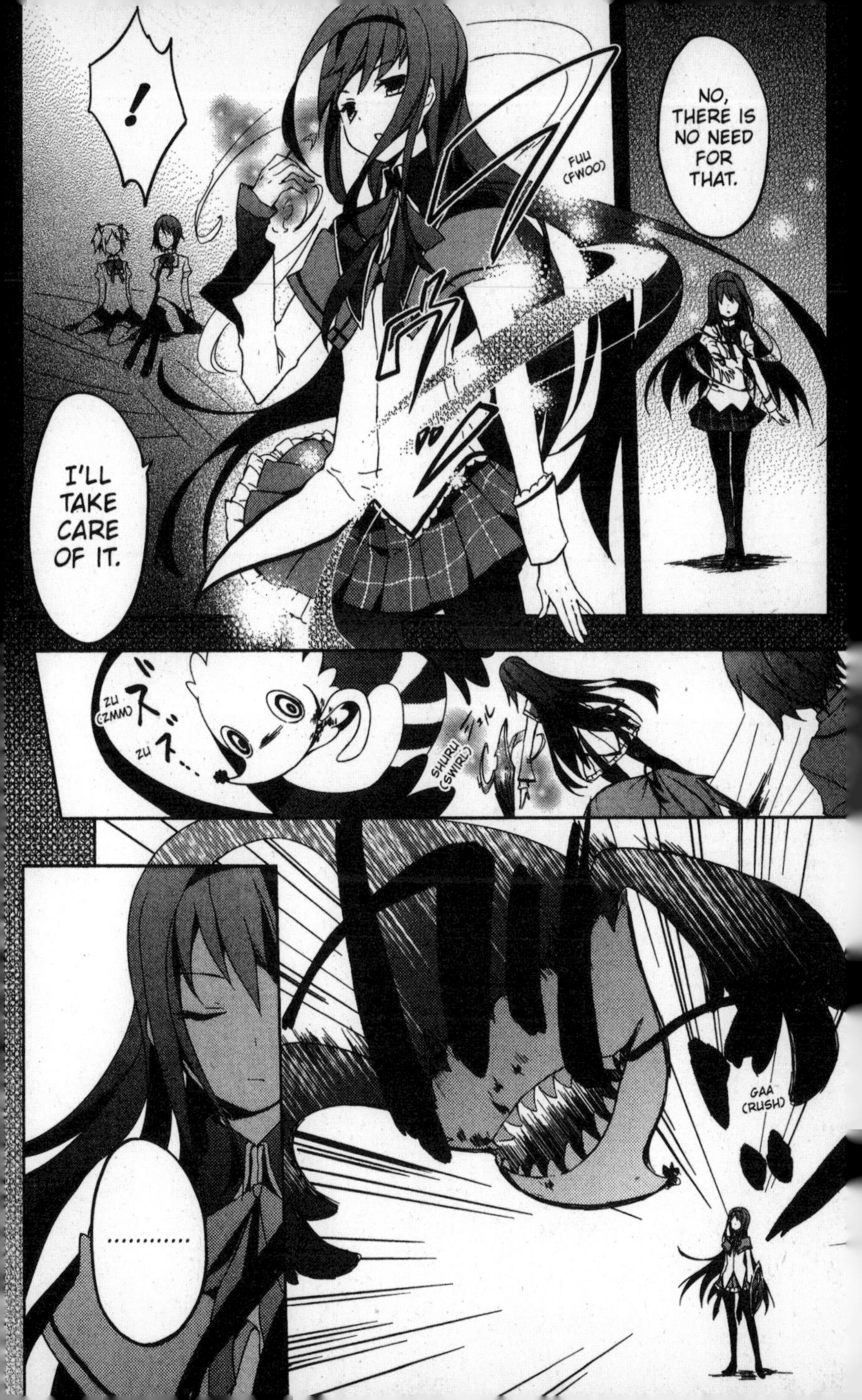
NO, THERE IS NO NEED FOR THAT.
FUU (FWOO)
!
I'LL TAKE CARE OF IT.
SHURU (SWIRL)
ZU (ZMM)
ZU...
GAA (RUSH)
....

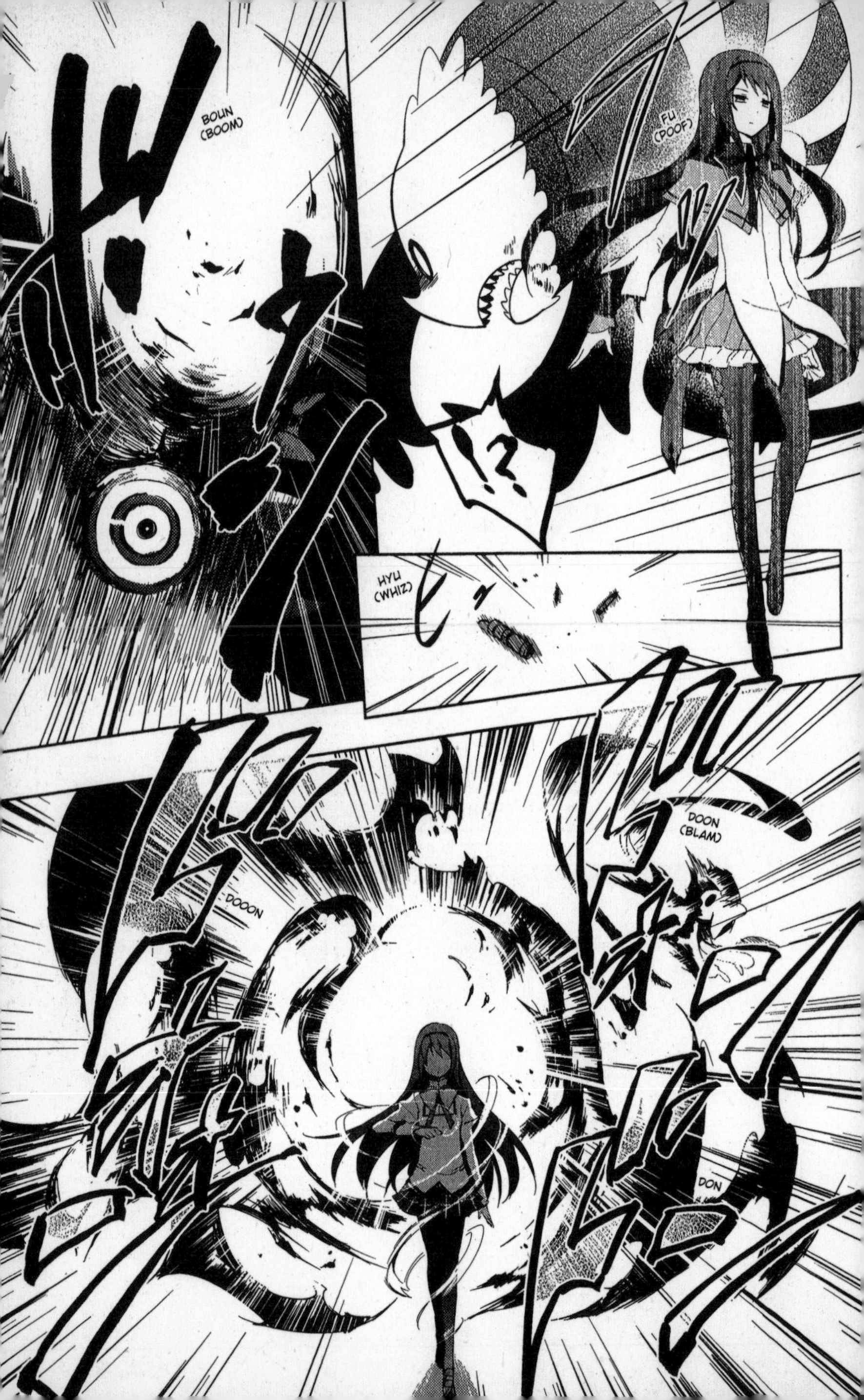
FU (POOF)
!?
BOUN (BOOM)
HYU (WHIZ)
DOON (BLAM)
DOOON
DON

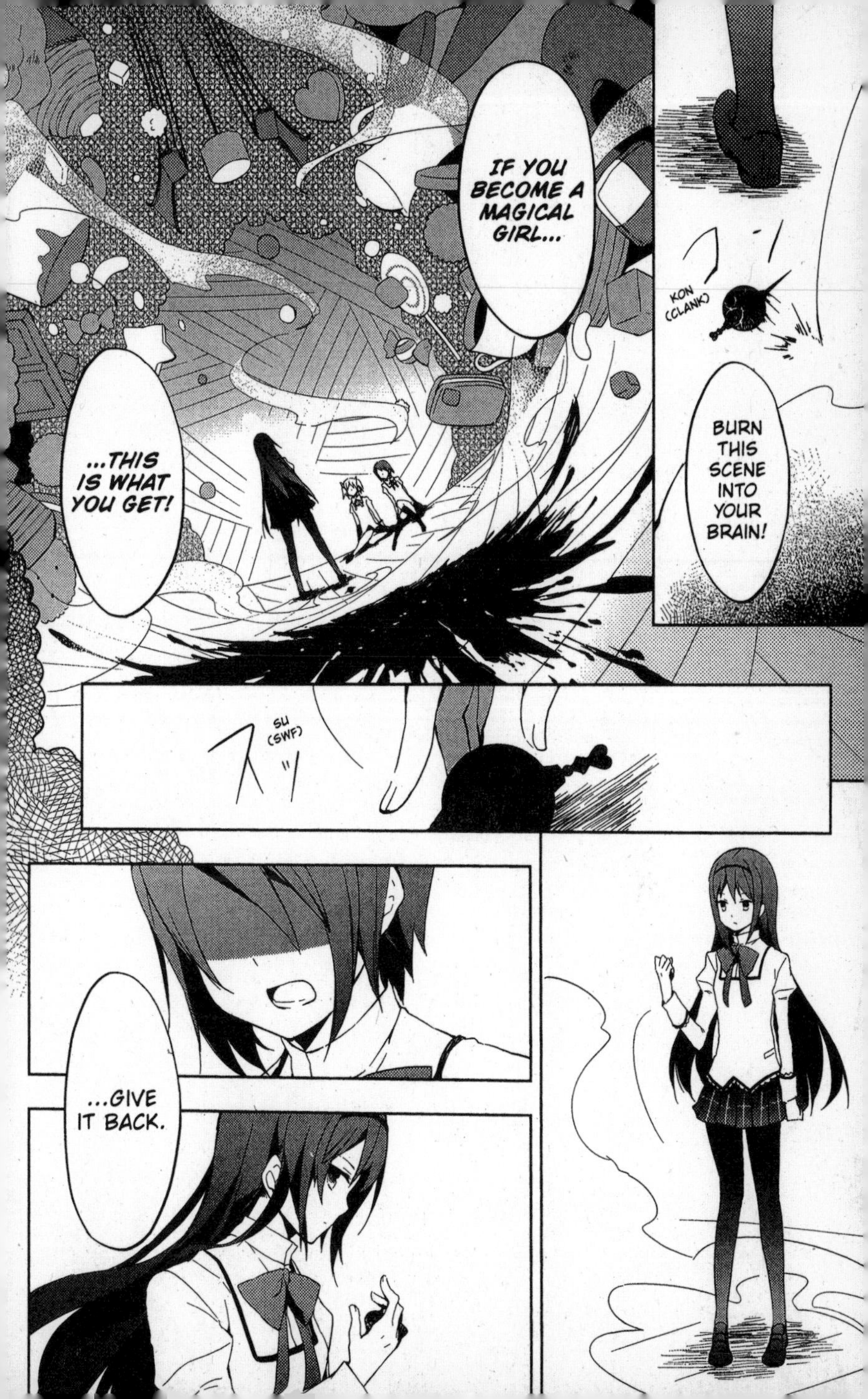
KON (CLANK)
BURN THIS SCENE INTO YOUR BRAIN!
IF YOU BECOME A MAGICAL GIRL...
...THIS IS WHAT YOU GET!
SU (SWF)
...GIVE IT BACK.

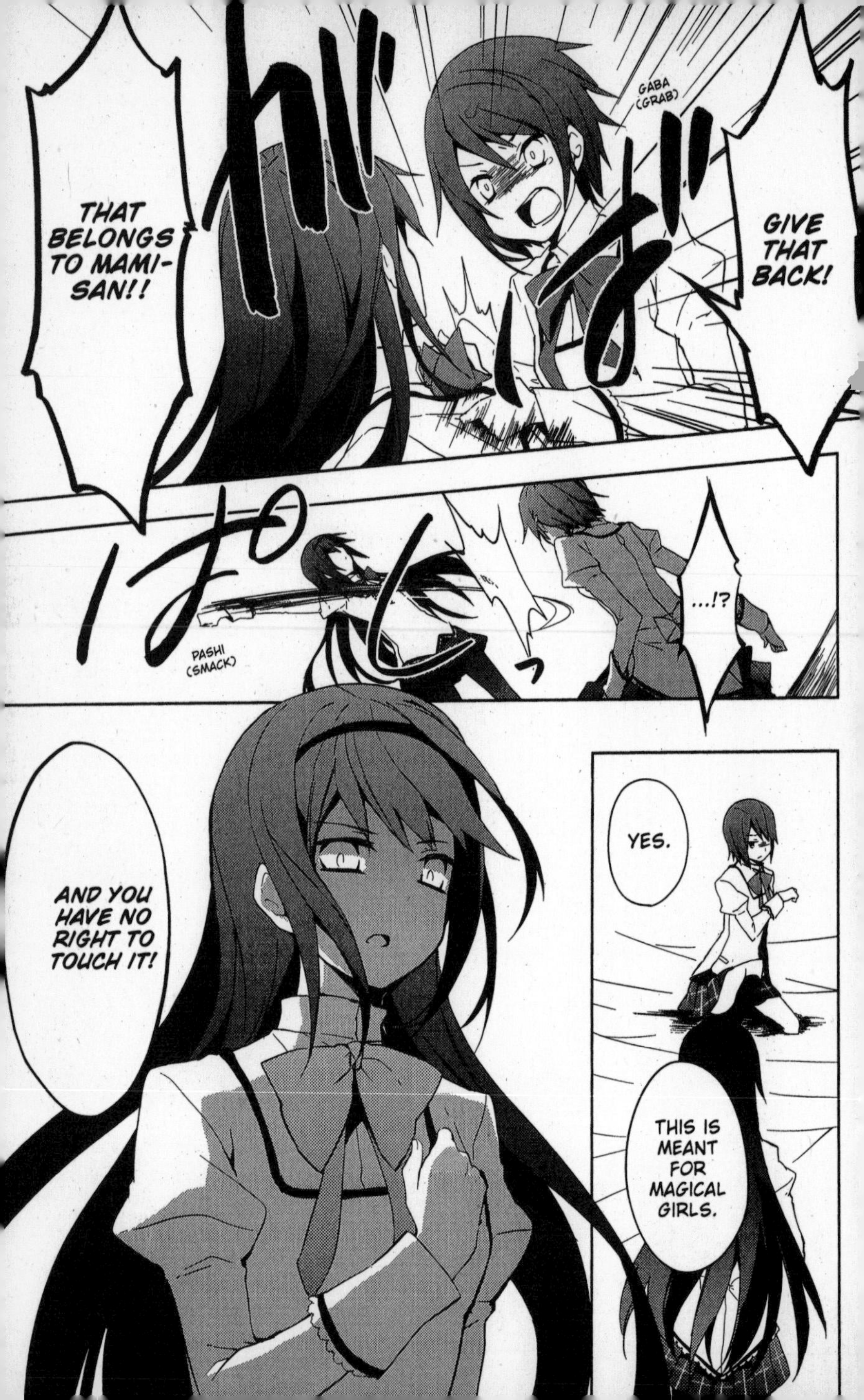
GABA (GRAB)
GIVE THAT BACK!
THAT BELONGS TO MAMI-SAN!!
...!?
PASHI (SMACK)
YES.
THIS IS MEANT FOR MAGICAL GIRLS.
AND YOU HAVE NO RIGHT TO TOUCH IT!

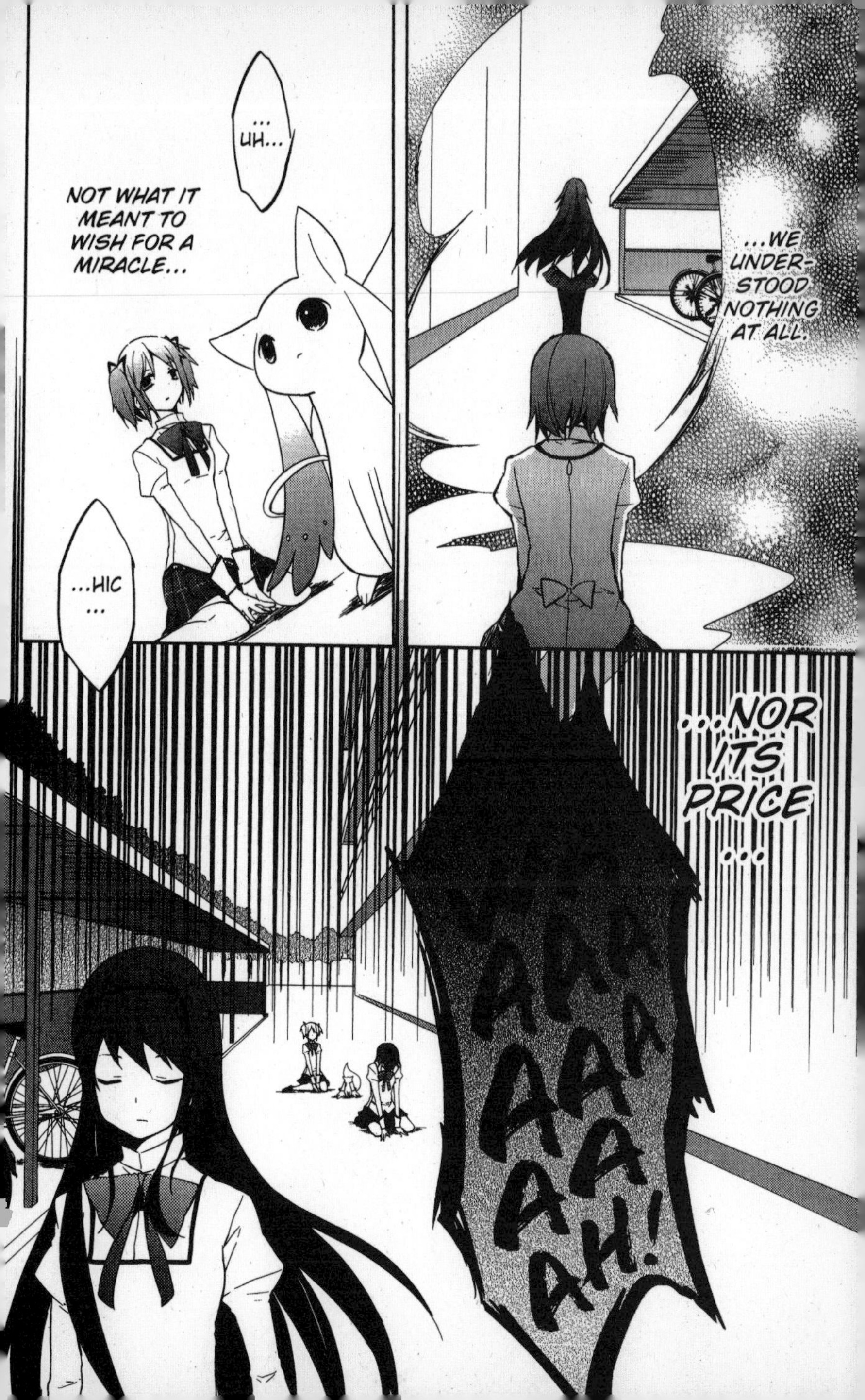
...WE UNDER-STOOD NOTHING AT ALL.
... UH...
NOT WHAT IT MEANT TO WISH FOR A MIRACLE...
...HIC ...
...NOR ITS PRICE ...
AAAAAAAAAAH!

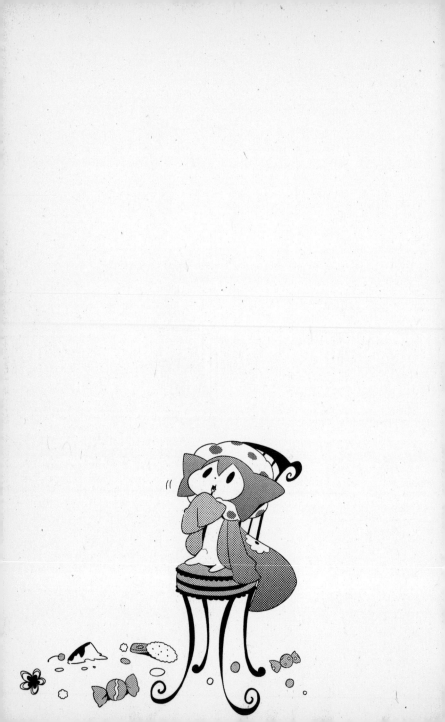

PUELLA MAGI
MADOKA★MAGICA

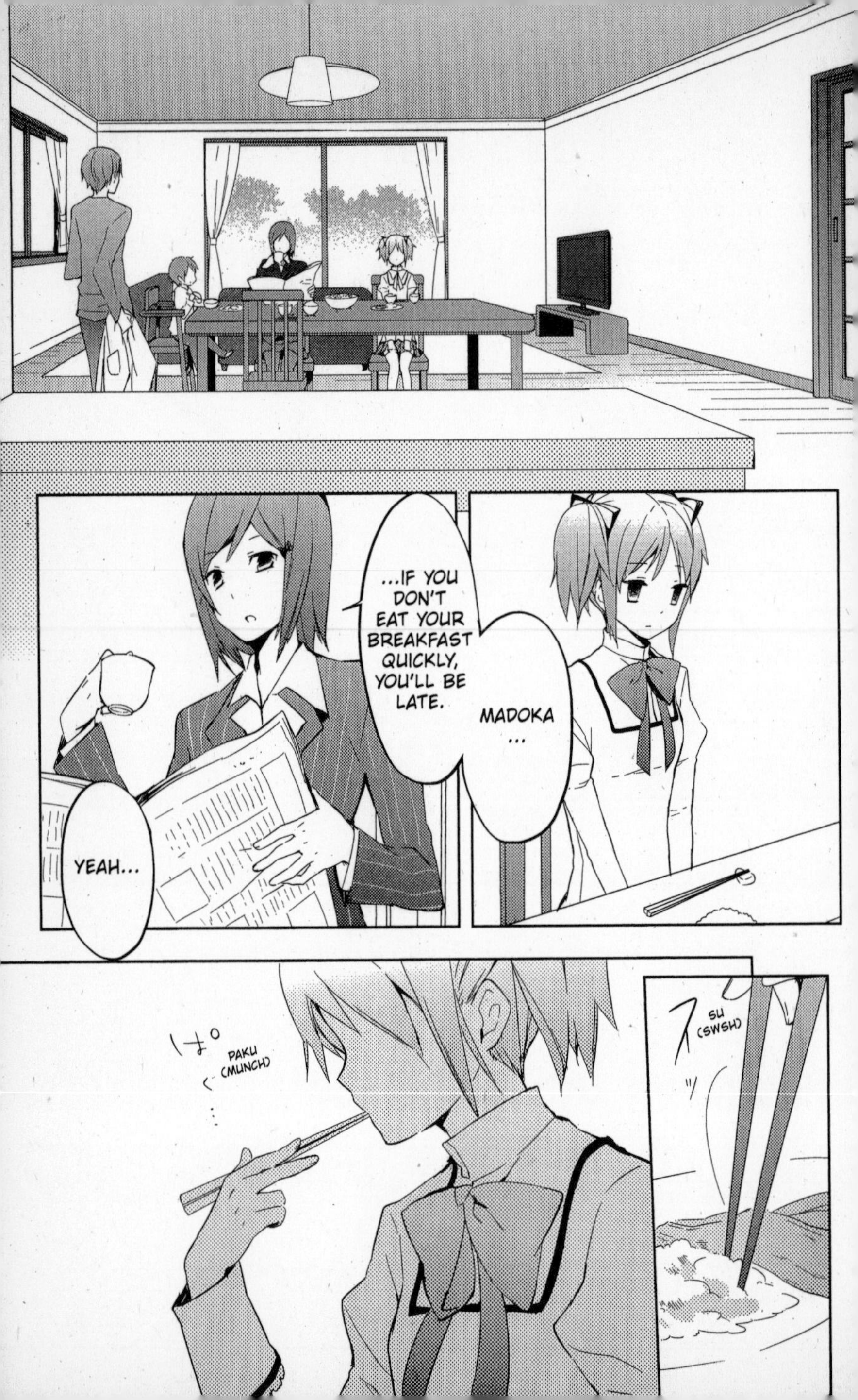
MADOKA...
...IF YOU DON'T EAT YOUR BREAKFAST QUICKLY, YOU'LL BE LATE.
YEAH...
SU (SWSH)
PAKU (MUNCH)

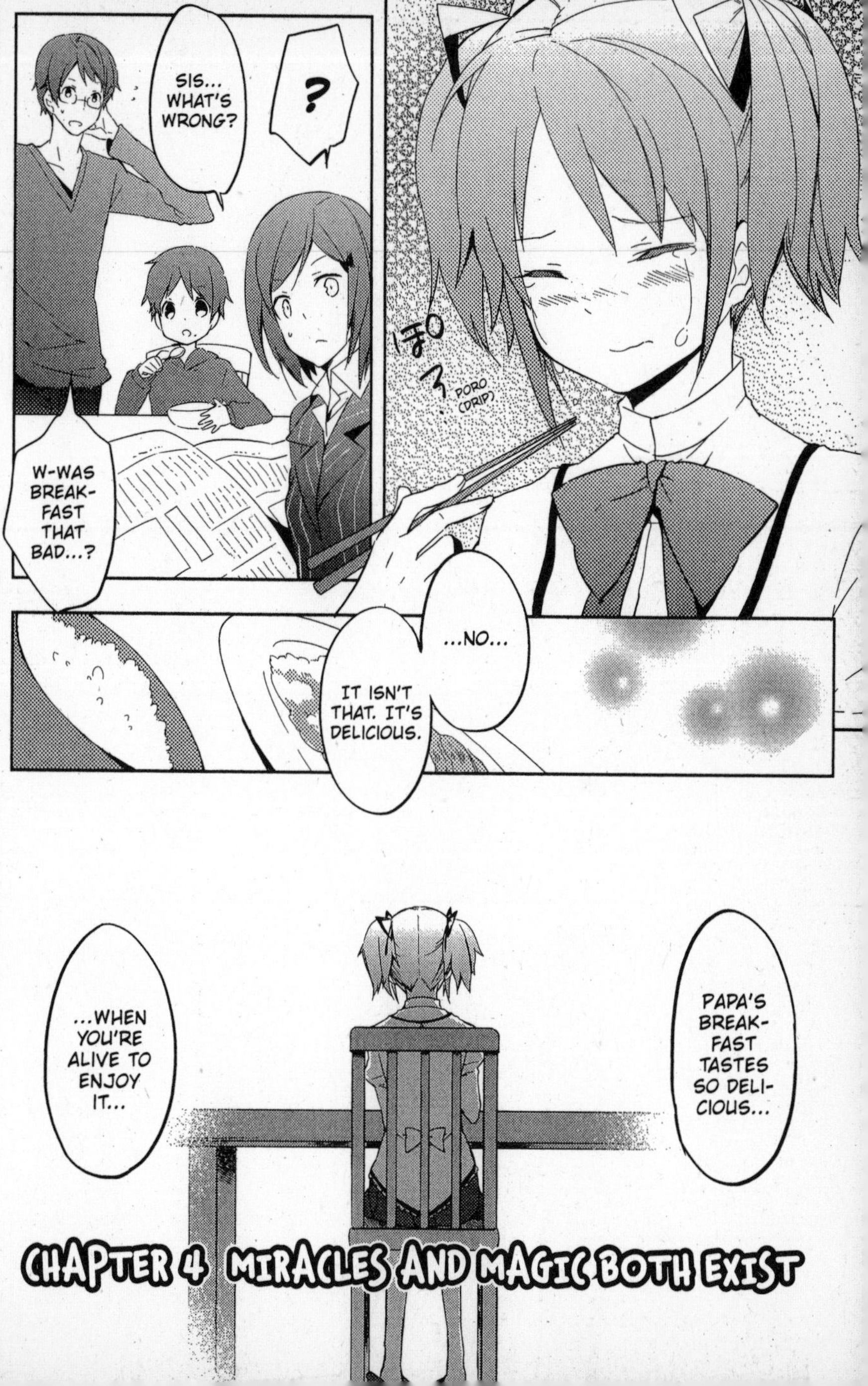
ぽろ
PORO (DRIP)
SIS... WHAT'S WRONG?
?
W-WAS BREAK-FAST THAT BAD...?
...NO...
IT ISN'T THAT. IT'S DELICIOUS.
PAPA'S BREAK-FAST TASTES SO DELI-CIOUS...
...WHEN YOU'RE ALIVE TO ENJOY IT...

CHAPTER 4 MIRACLES AND MAGIC BOTH EXIST

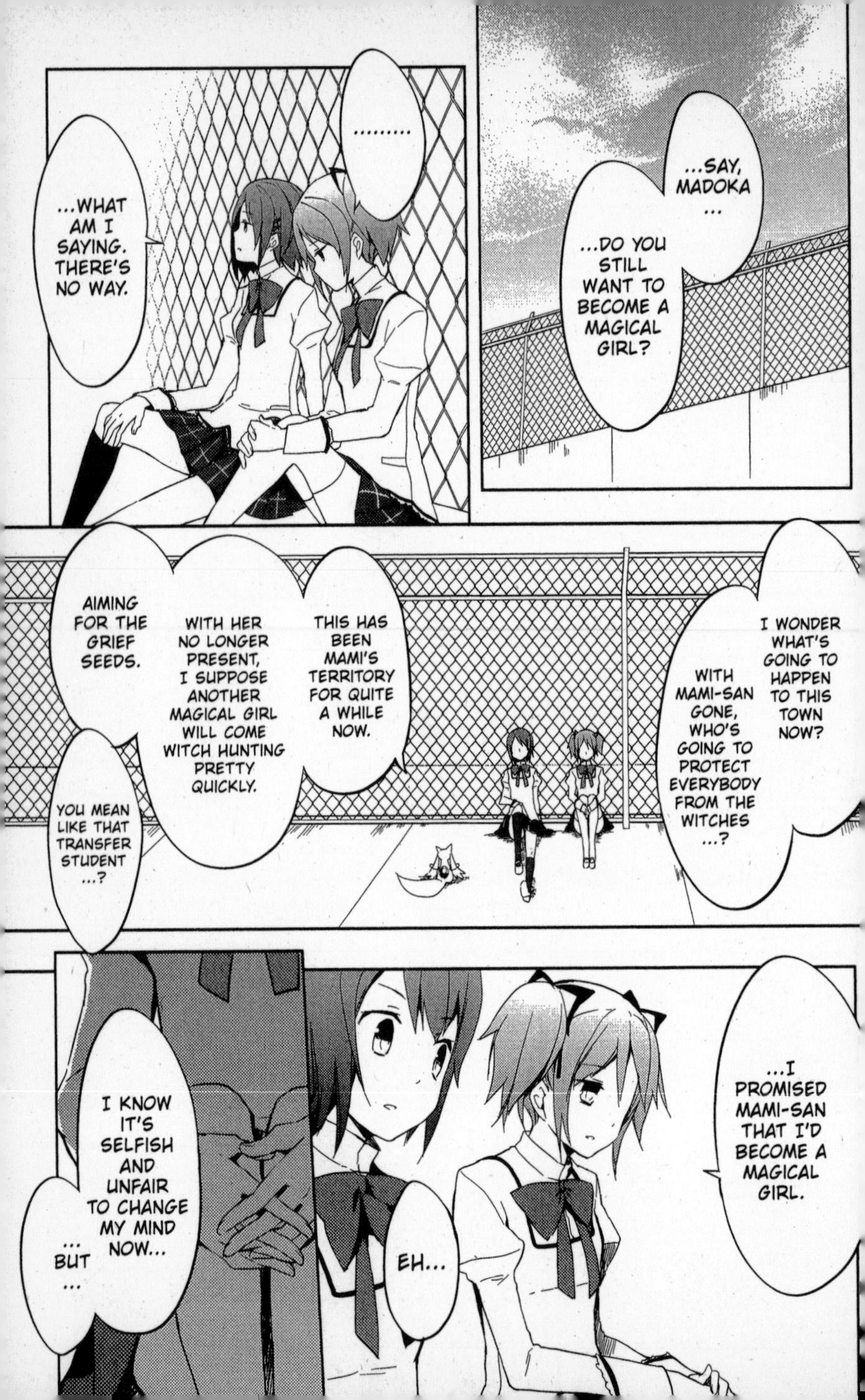
...SAY, MADOKA ...
...DO YOU STILL WANT TO BECOME A MAGICAL GIRL?
....
...WHAT AM I SAYING. THERE'S NO WAY.
I WONDER WHAT'S GOING TO HAPPEN TO THIS TOWN NOW?
WITH MAMI-SAN GONE, WHO'S GOING TO PROTECT EVERYBODY FROM THE WITCHES ...?
THIS HAS BEEN MAMI'S TERRITORY FOR QUITE A WHILE NOW.
WITH HER NO LONGER PRESENT, I SUPPOSE ANOTHER MAGICAL GIRL WILL COME WITCH HUNTING PRETTY QUICKLY.
AIMING FOR THE GRIEF SEEDS.
YOU MEAN LIKE THAT TRANSFER STUDENT ...?
...I PROMISED MAMI-SAN THAT I'D BECOME A MAGICAL GIRL.
EH...
I KNOW IT'S SELFISH AND UNFAIR TO CHANGE MY MIND NOW...
... BUT ...

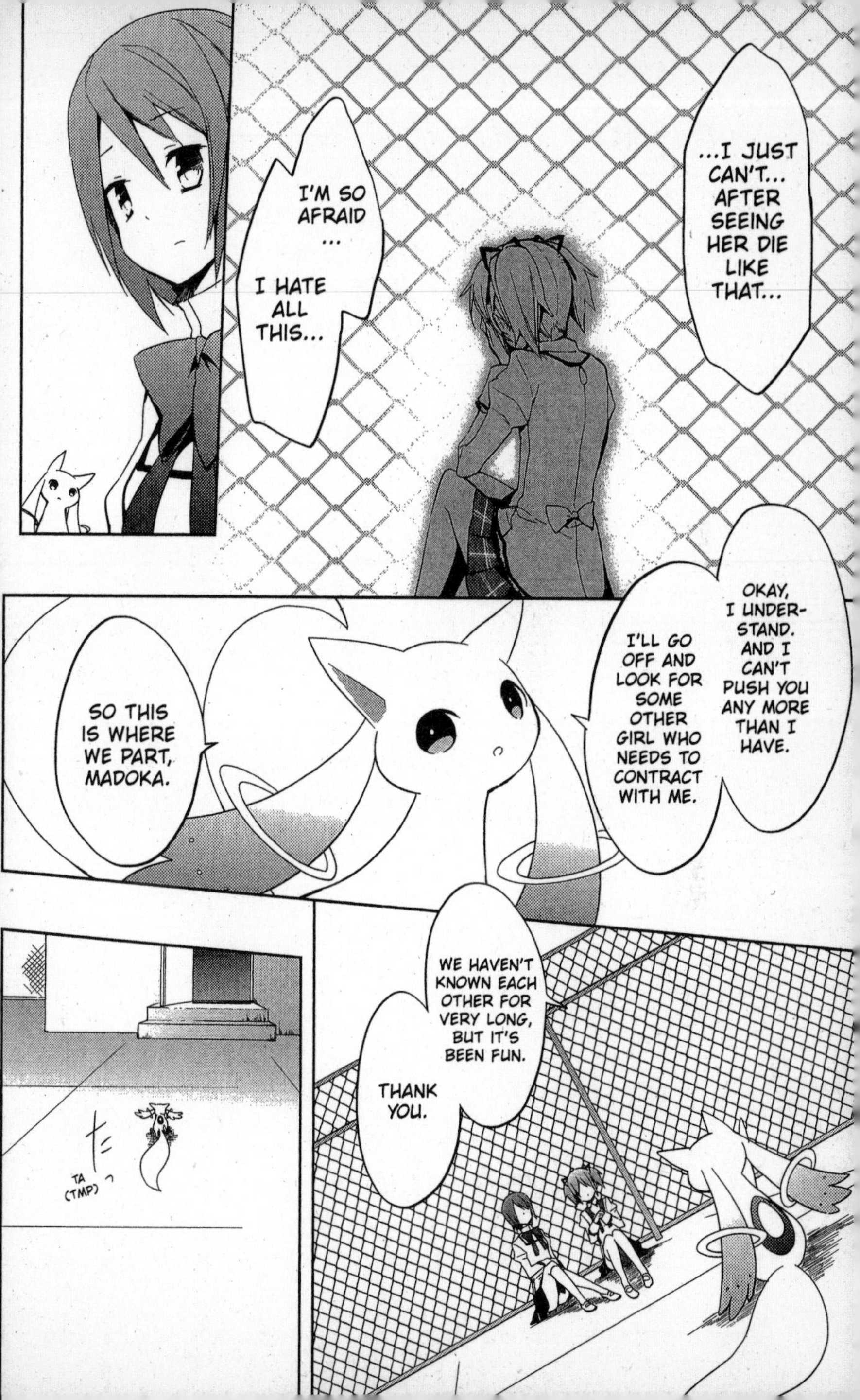
...I JUST CAN'T... AFTER SEEING HER DIE LIKE THAT...
I'M SO AFRAID ...
I HATE ALL THIS...
OKAY, I UNDER-STAND. AND I CAN'T PUSH YOU ANY MORE THAN I HAVE.
I'LL GO OFF AND LOOK FOR SOME OTHER GIRL WHO NEEDS TO CONTRACT WITH ME.
SO THIS IS WHERE WE PART, MADOKA.
WE HAVEN'T KNOWN EACH OTHER FOR VERY LONG, BUT IT'S BEEN FUN.
THANK YOU.
TA (TMP)

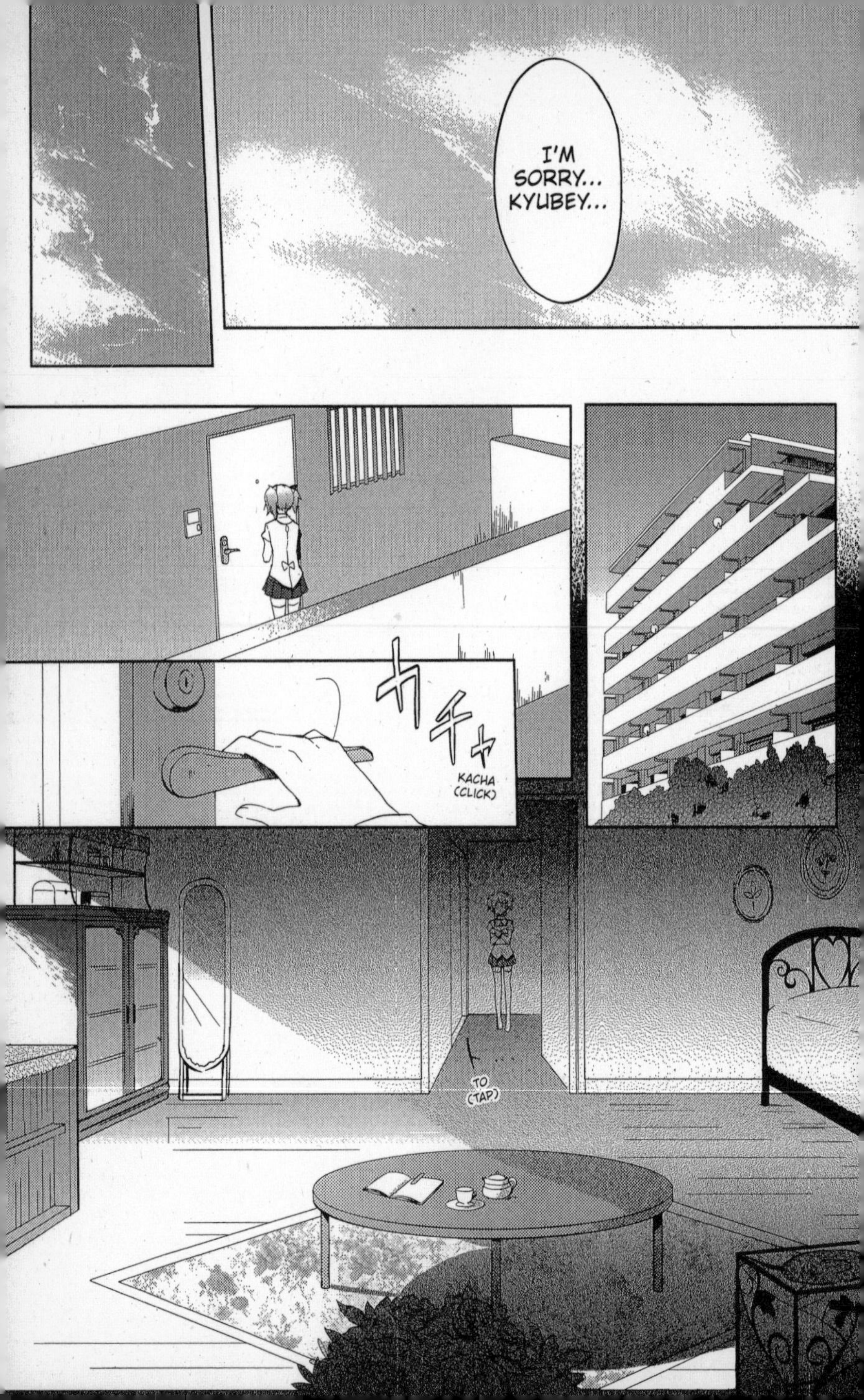
I'M SORRY... KYUBEY...
カチャ
KACHA (CLICK)
TO (TAP)

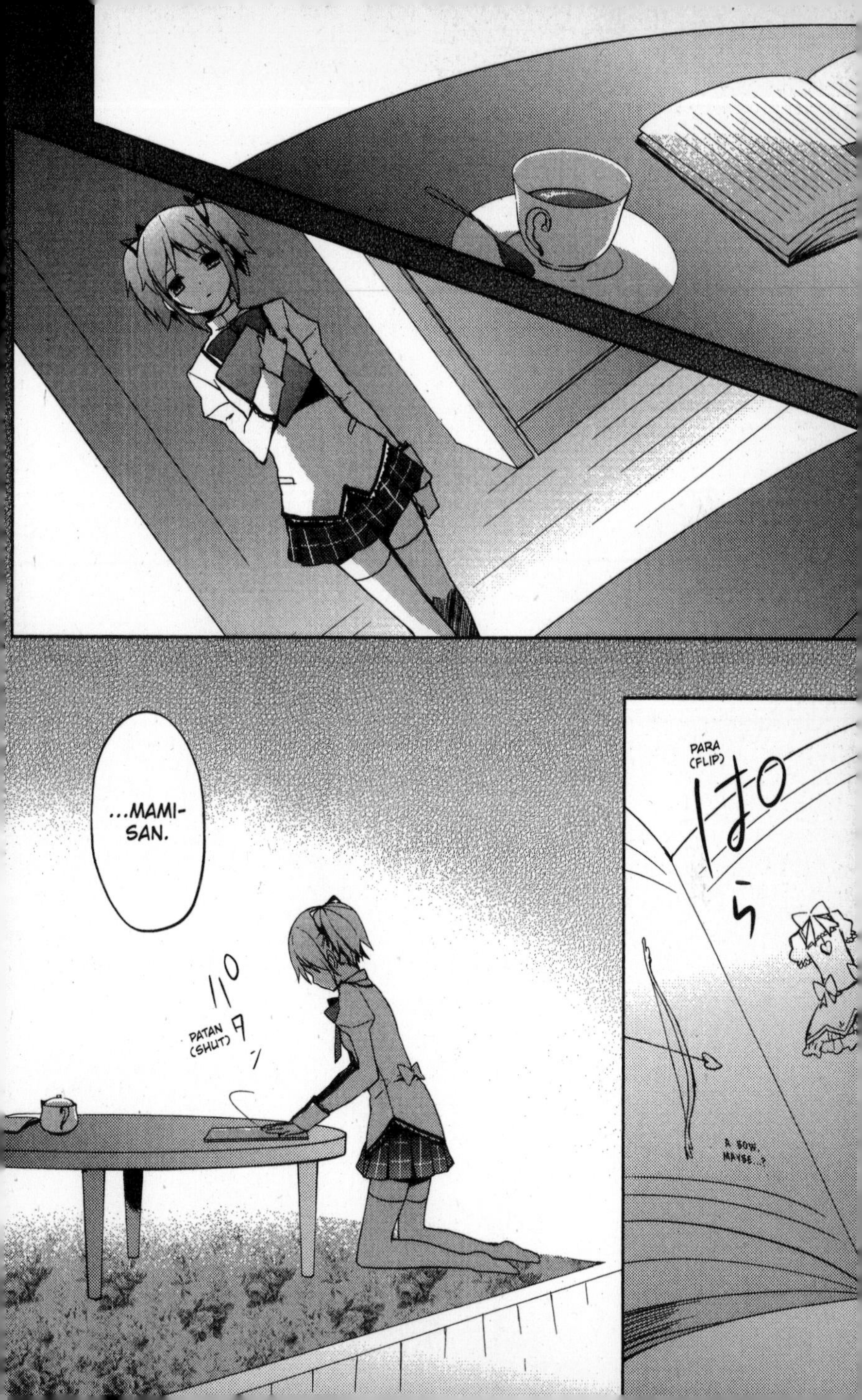
PARA (FLIP)
A BOW, MAYBE...?
...MAMI-SAN.
PATAN (SHUT)

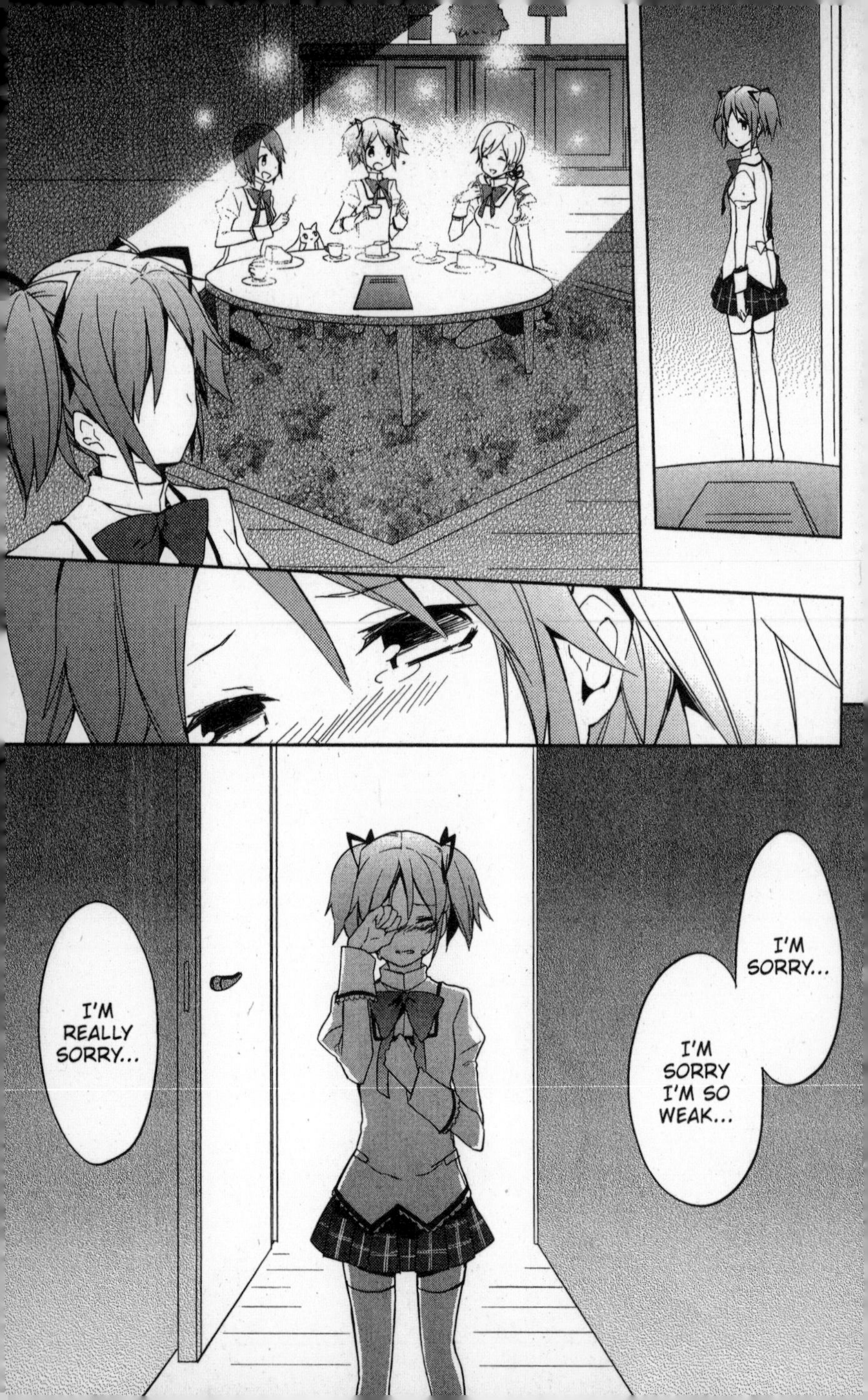
I'M SORRY...
I'M SORRY I'M SO WEAK...
I'M REALLY SORRY...

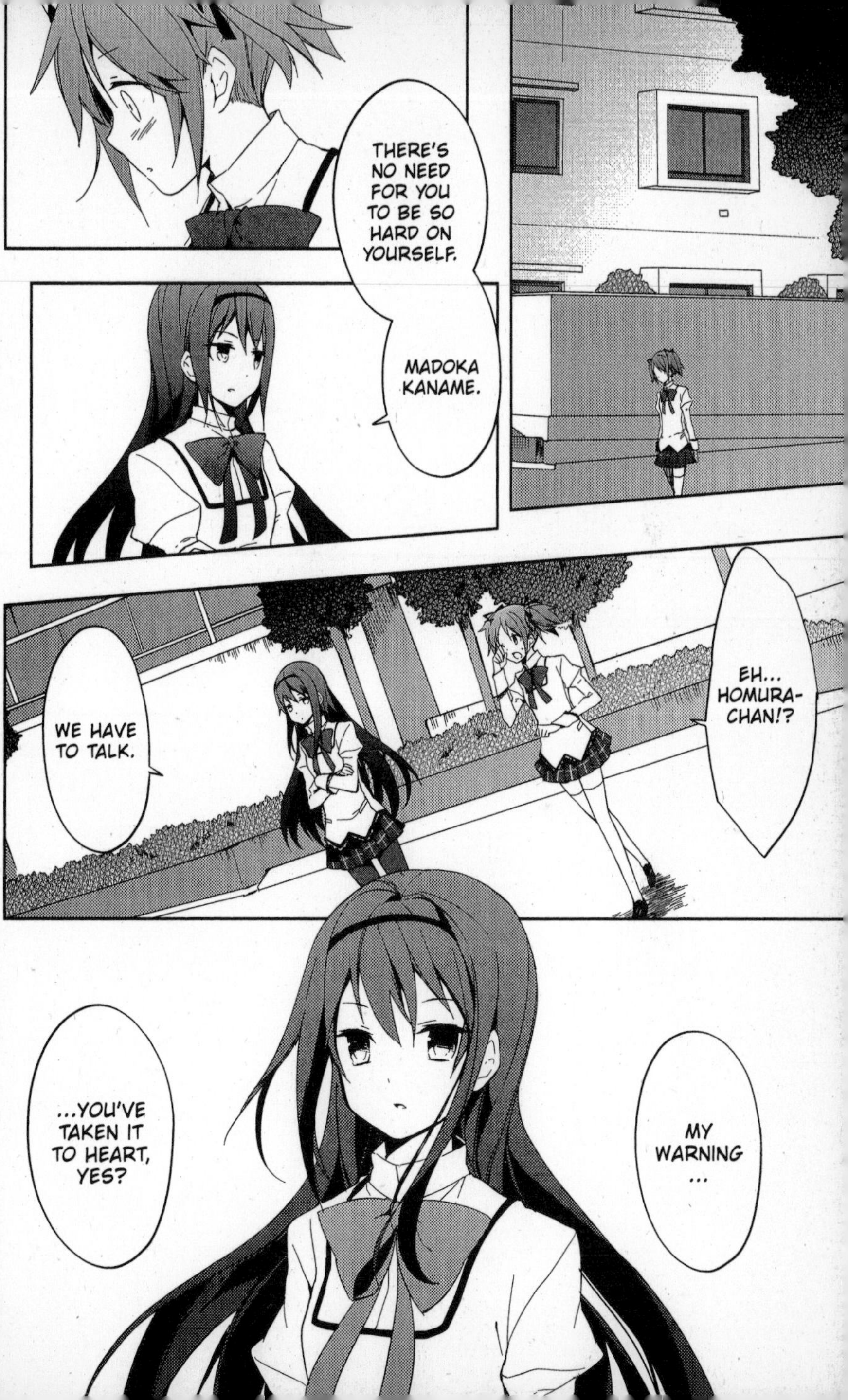
THERE'S NO NEED FOR YOU TO BE SO HARD ON YOURSELF.
MADOKA KANAME.
EH... HOMURA-CHAN!?
WE HAVE TO TALK.
MY WARNING...
...YOU'VE TAKEN IT TO HEART, YES?

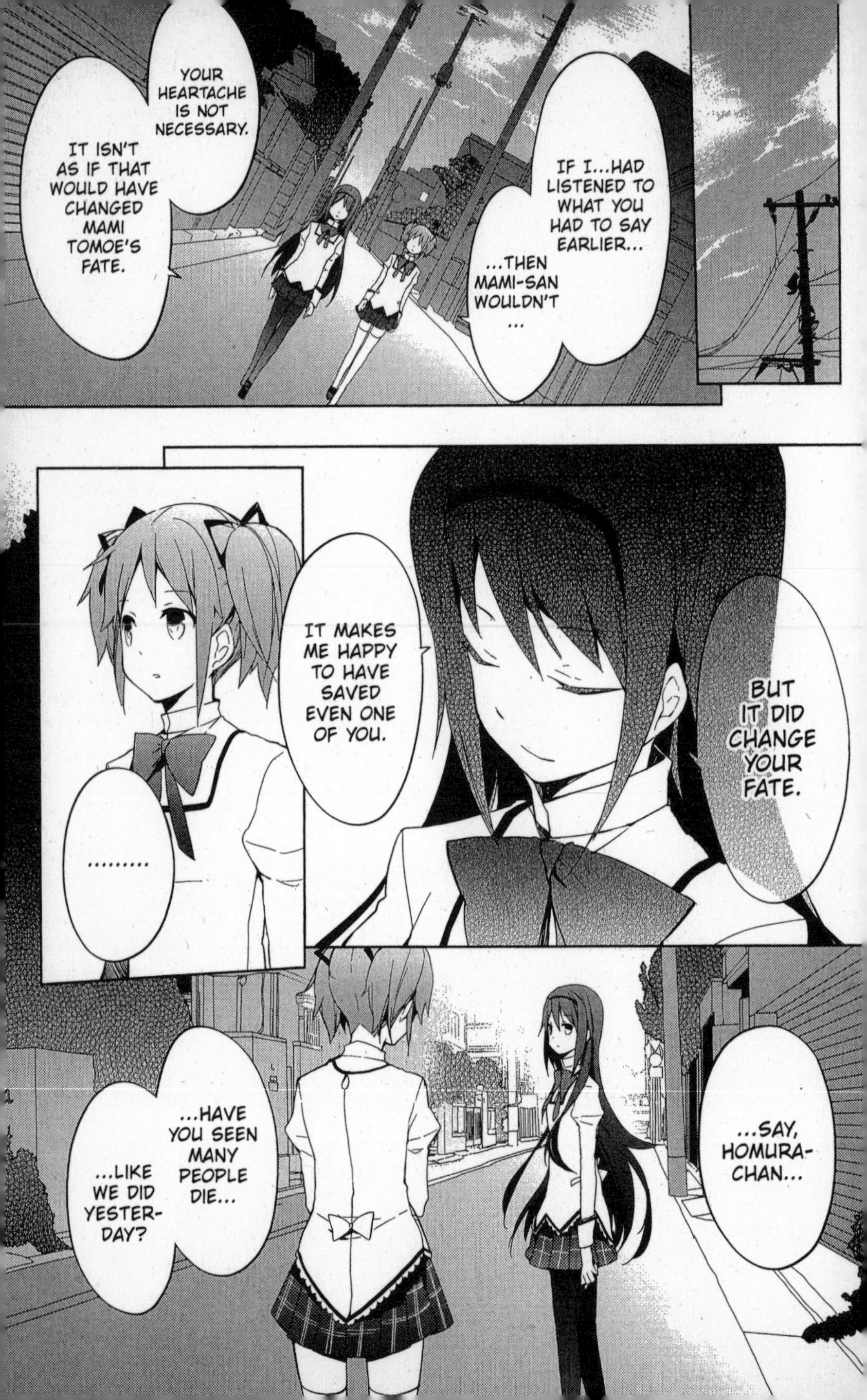
IF I...HAD LISTENED TO WHAT YOU HAD TO SAY EARLIER...
...THEN MAMI-SAN WOULDN'T ...
YOUR HEARTACHE IS NOT NECESSARY.
IT ISN'T AS IF THAT WOULD HAVE CHANGED MAMI TOMOE'S FATE.
BUT IT DID CHANGE YOUR FATE.
IT MAKES ME HAPPY TO HAVE SAVED EVEN ONE OF YOU.
....
...SAY, HOMURA-CHAN...
...HAVE YOU SEEN MANY PEOPLE DIE...
...LIKE WE DID YESTERDAY?

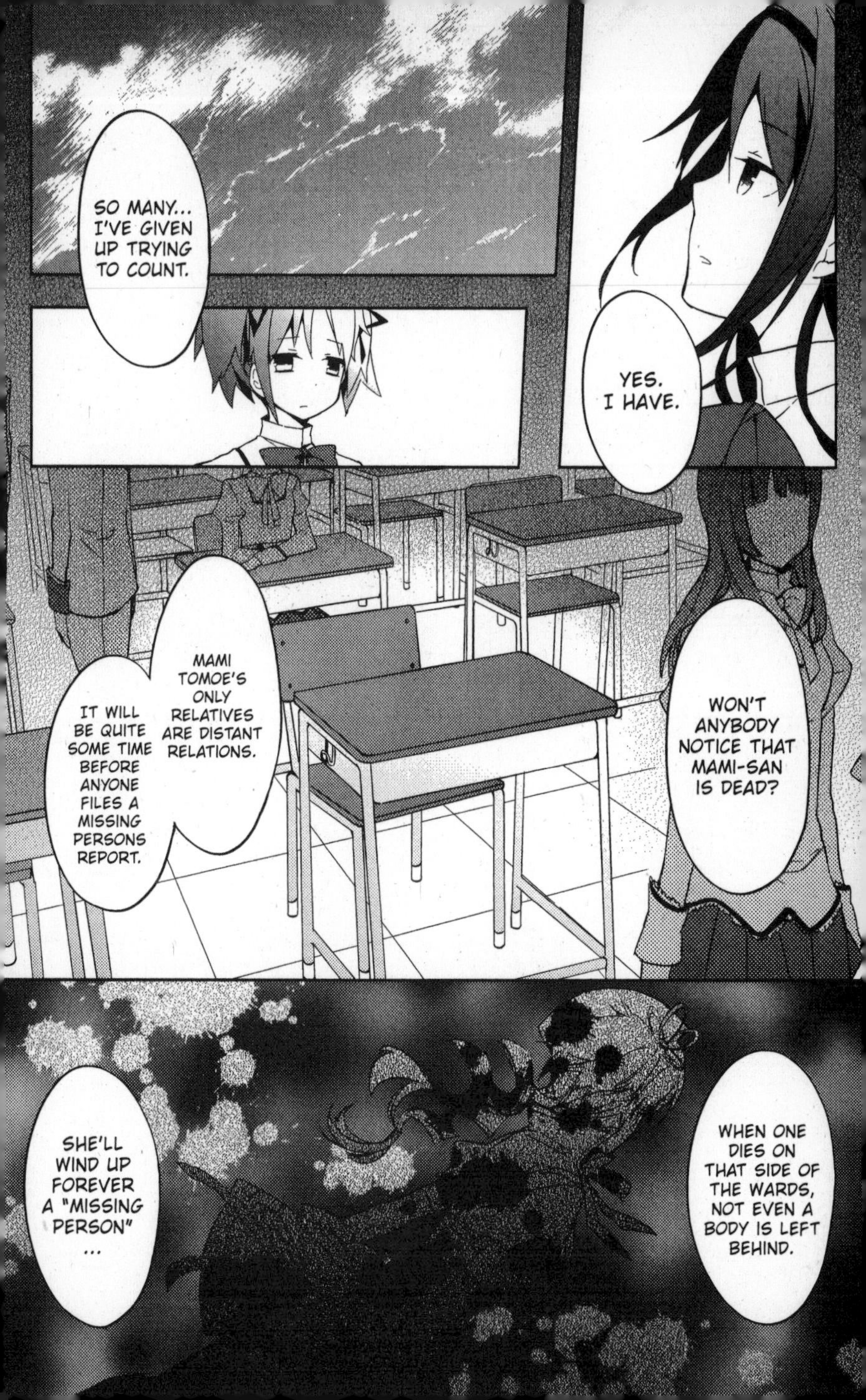
YES. I HAVE.
SO MANY... I'VE GIVEN UP TRYING TO COUNT.
WON'T ANYBODY NOTICE THAT MAMI-SAN IS DEAD?
MAMI TOMOE'S ONLY RELATIVES ARE DISTANT RELATIONS.
IT WILL BE QUITE SOME TIME BEFORE ANYONE FILES A MISSING PERSONS REPORT.
WHEN ONE DIES ON THAT SIDE OF THE WARDS, NOT EVEN A BODY IS LEFT BEHIND.
SHE'LL WIND UP FOREVER A "MISSING PERSON"...

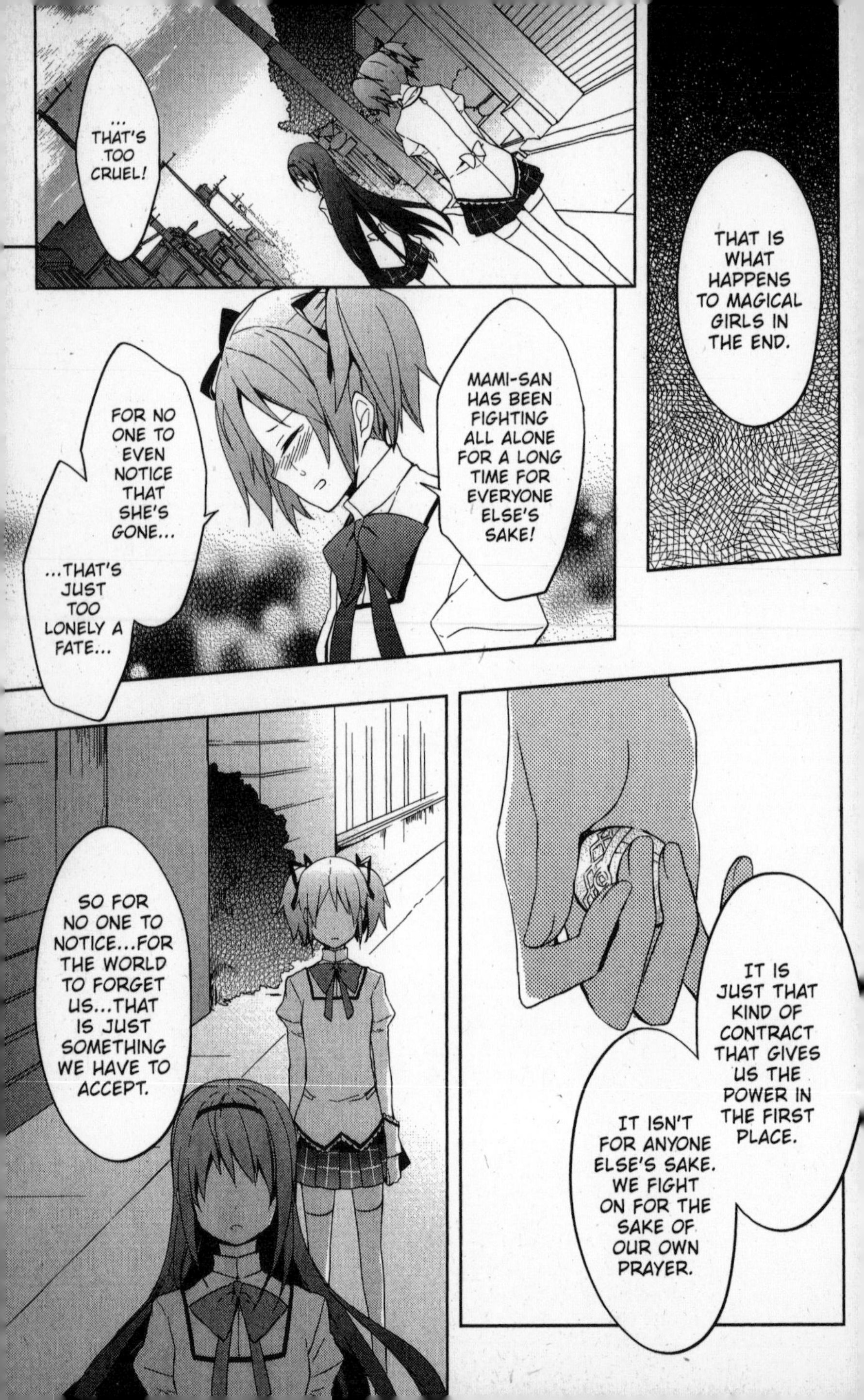
THAT IS WHAT HAPPENS TO MAGICAL GIRLS IN THE END.
...THAT'S TOO CRUEL!
MAMI-SAN HAS BEEN FIGHTING ALL ALONE FOR A LONG TIME FOR EVERYONE ELSE'S SAKE!
FOR NO ONE TO EVEN NOTICE THAT SHE'S GONE...
...THAT'S JUST TOO LONELY A FATE...
IT IS JUST THAT KIND OF CONTRACT THAT GIVES US THE POWER IN THE FIRST PLACE.
IT ISN'T FOR ANYONE ELSE'S SAKE. WE FIGHT ON FOR THE SAKE OF OUR OWN PRAYER.
SO FOR NO ONE TO NOTICE...FOR THE WORLD TO FORGET US...THAT IS JUST SOMETHING WE HAVE TO ACCEPT.

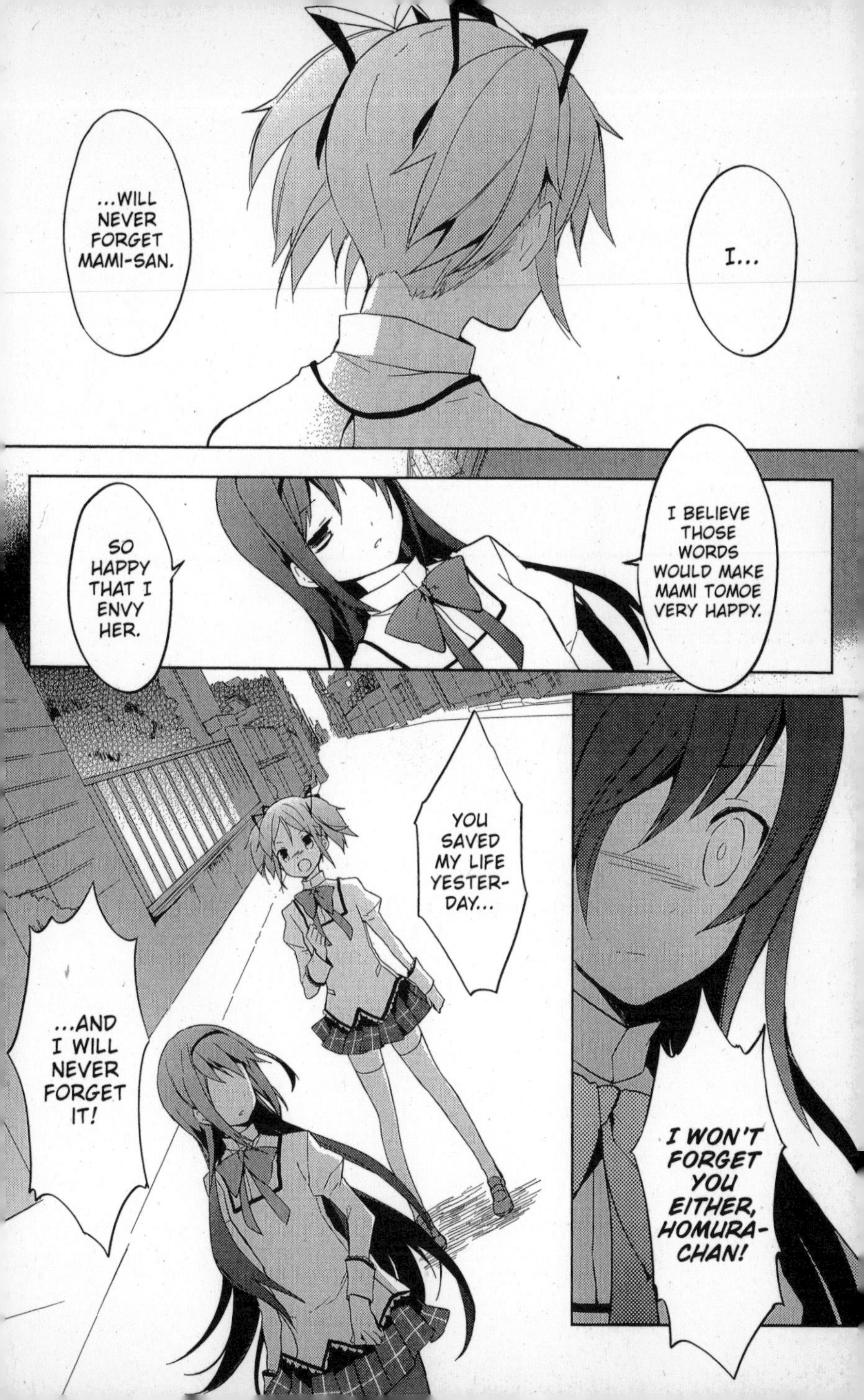
I...
...WILL NEVER FORGET MAMI-SAN.
I BELIEVE THOSE WORDS WOULD MAKE MAMI TOMOE VERY HAPPY.
SO HAPPY THAT I ENVY HER.
I WON'T FORGET YOU EITHER, HOMURA-CHAN!
YOU SAVED MY LIFE YESTER-DAY...
...AND I WILL NEVER FORGET IT!

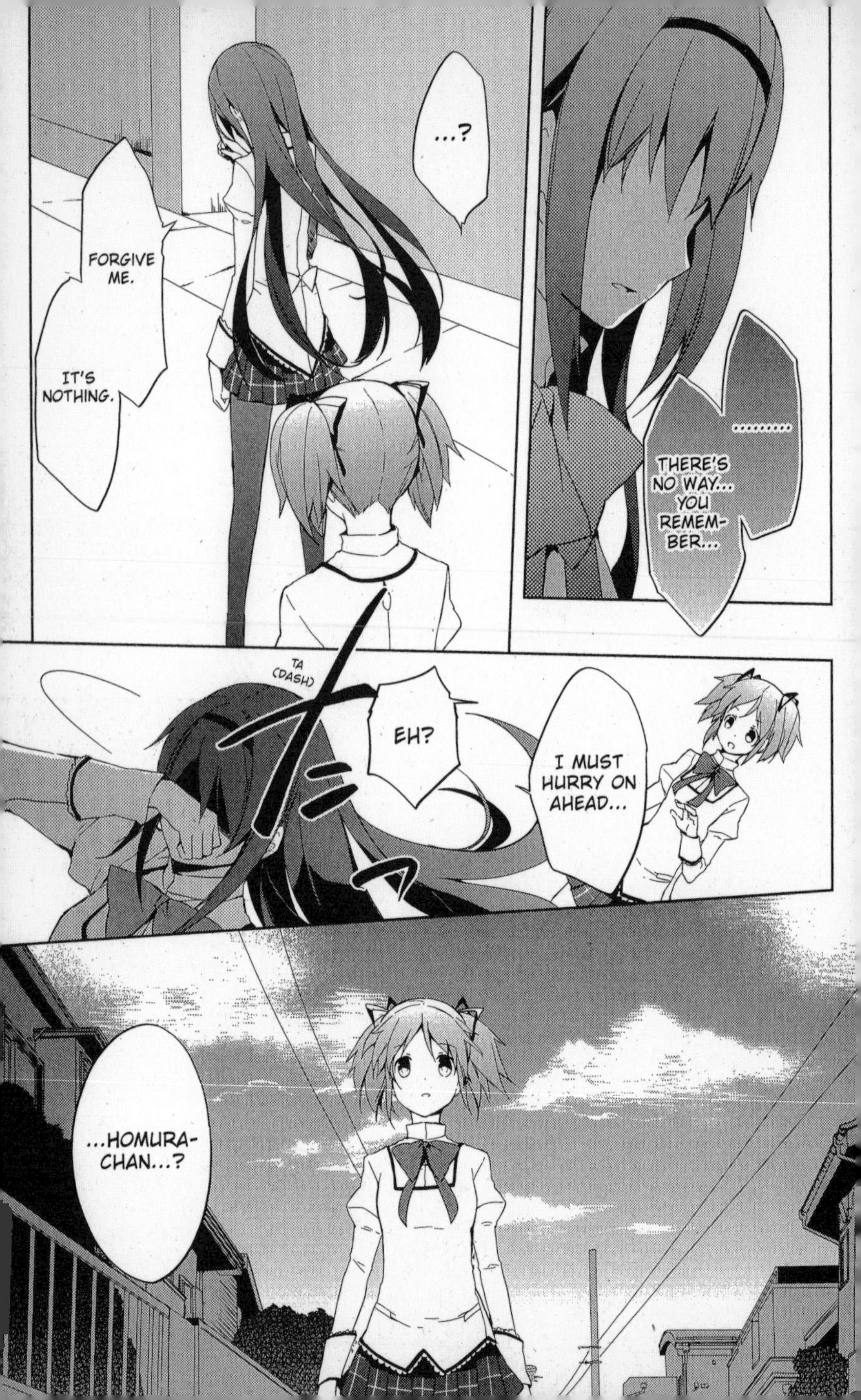
....
THERE'S NO WAY... YOU REMEMBER...
...?
FORGIVE ME.
IT'S NOTHING.
I MUST HURRY ON AHEAD...
EH?
TA (DASH)
...HOMURA-CHAN...?

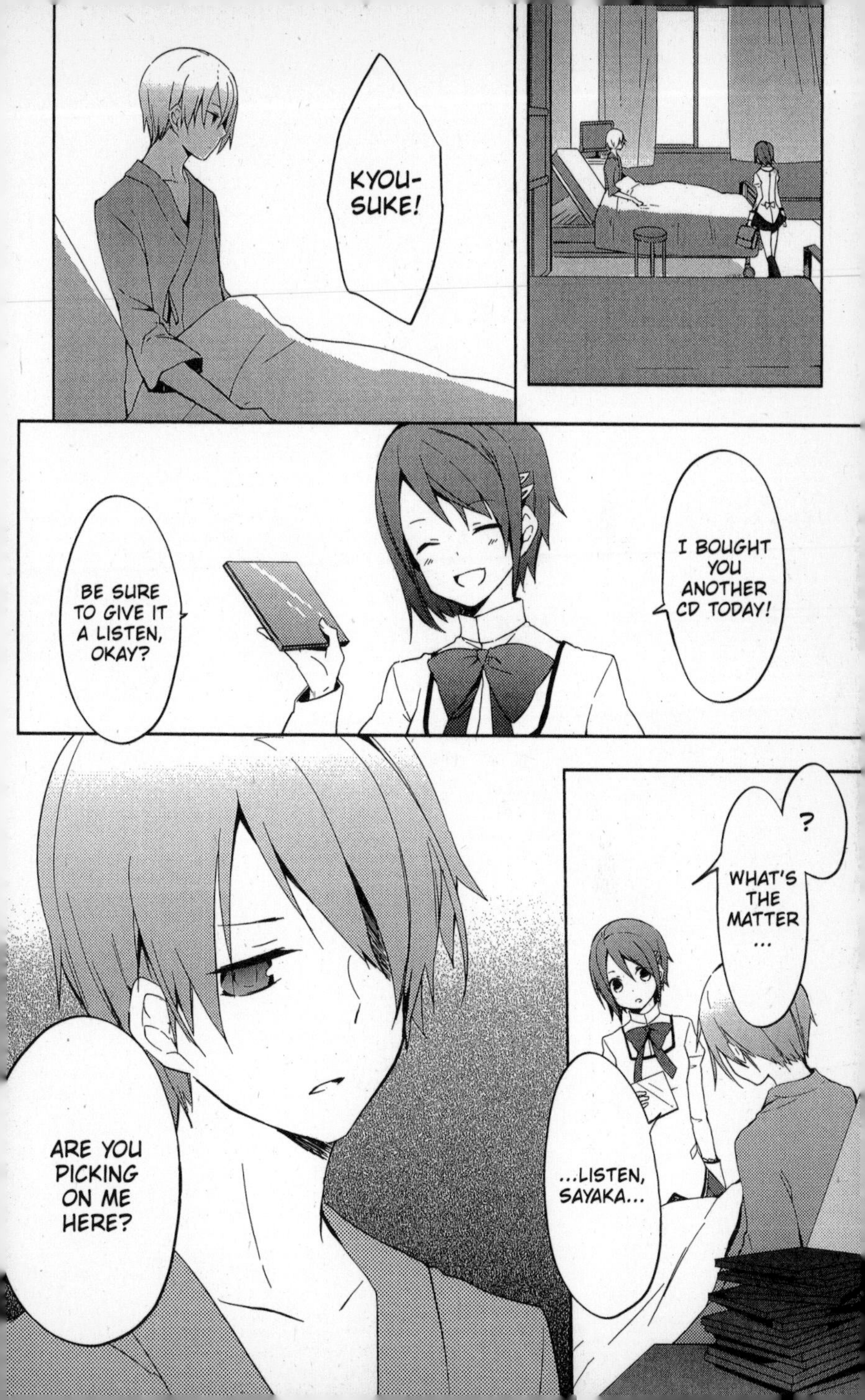
KYOU-SUKE!
I BOUGHT YOU ANOTHER CD TODAY!
BE SURE TO GIVE IT A LISTEN, OKAY?
? WHAT'S THE MATTER ...
...LISTEN, SAYAKA...
ARE YOU PICKING ON ME HERE?

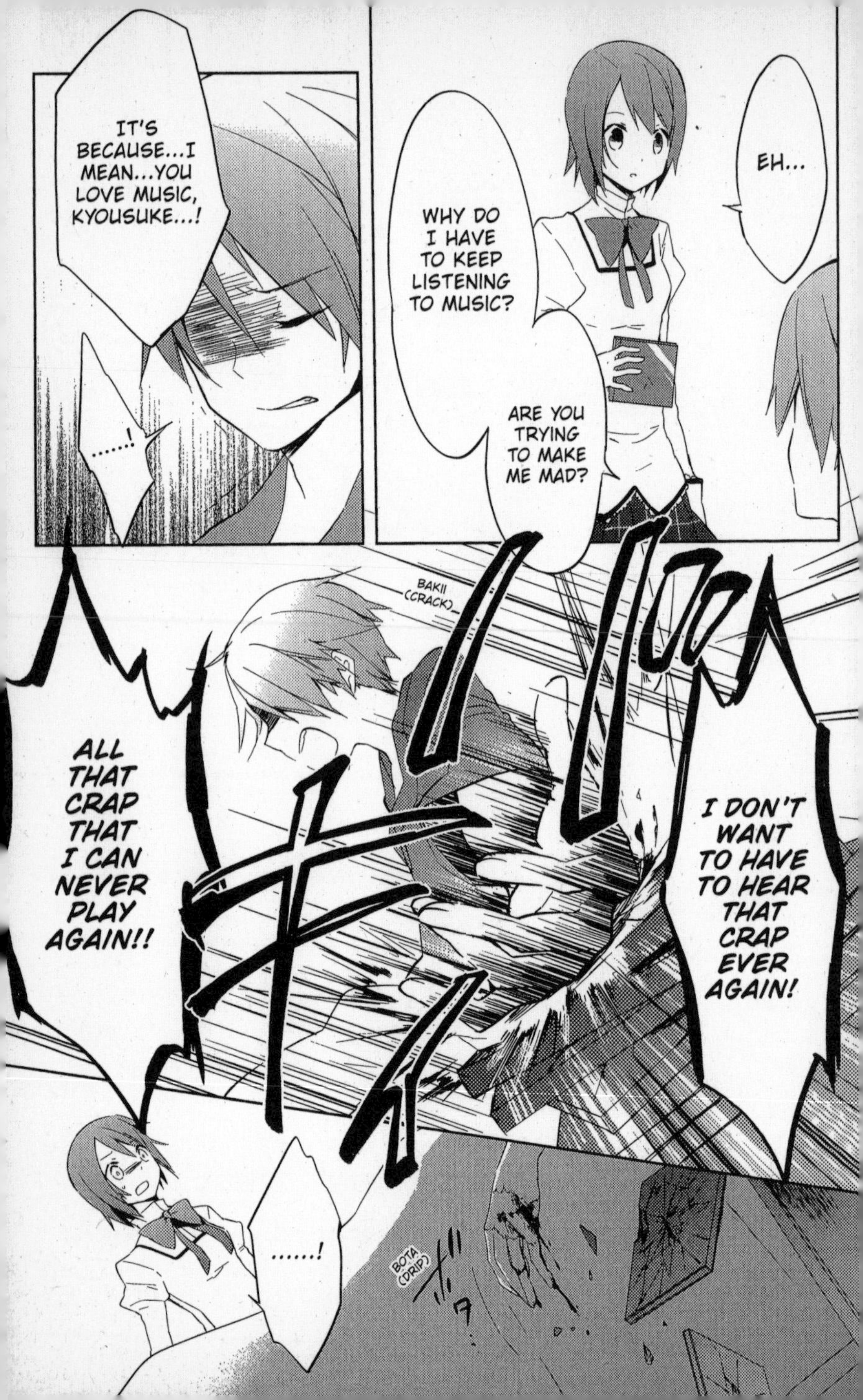
EH...
WHY DO I HAVE TO KEEP LISTENING TO MUSIC?
ARE YOU TRYING TO MAKE ME MAD?
IT'S BECAUSE...I MEAN...YOU LOVE MUSIC, KYOUSUKE...!
......!
I DON'T WANT TO HAVE TO HEAR THAT CRAP EVER AGAIN!
BAKII (CRACK)
ALL THAT CRAP THAT I CAN NEVER PLAY AGAIN!!
BOTA (DRIP)
......!

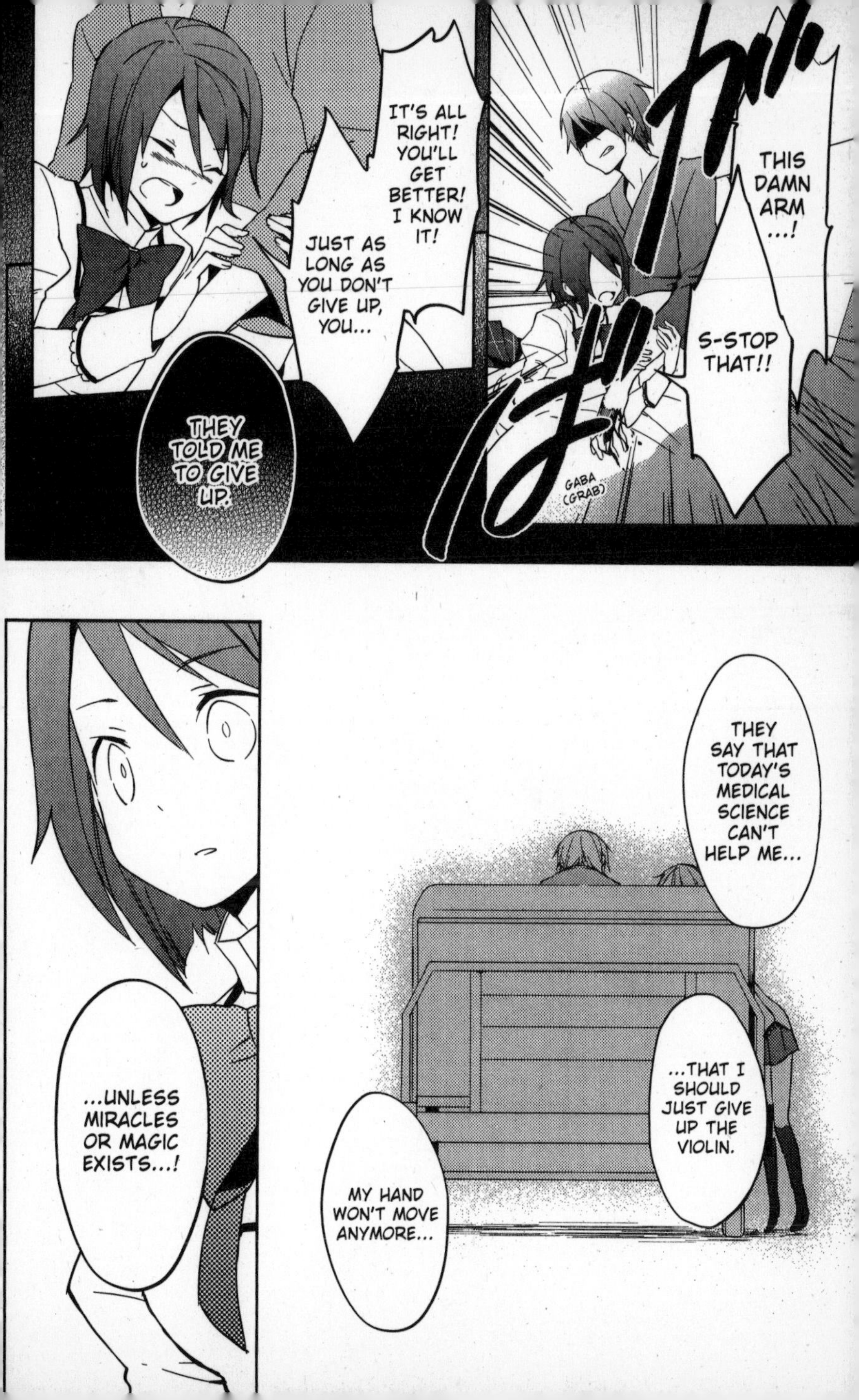
THIS DAMN ARM ...!
S-STOP THAT!!
GABA (GRAB)
IT'S ALL RIGHT! YOU'LL GET BETTER! I KNOW IT!
JUST AS LONG AS YOU DON'T GIVE UP, YOU...
THEY TOLD ME TO GIVE UP.
THEY SAY THAT TODAY'S MEDICAL SCIENCE CAN'T HELP ME...
...THAT I SHOULD JUST GIVE UP THE VIOLIN.
MY HAND WON'T MOVE ANYMORE...
...UNLESS MIRACLES OR MAGIC EXISTS...!

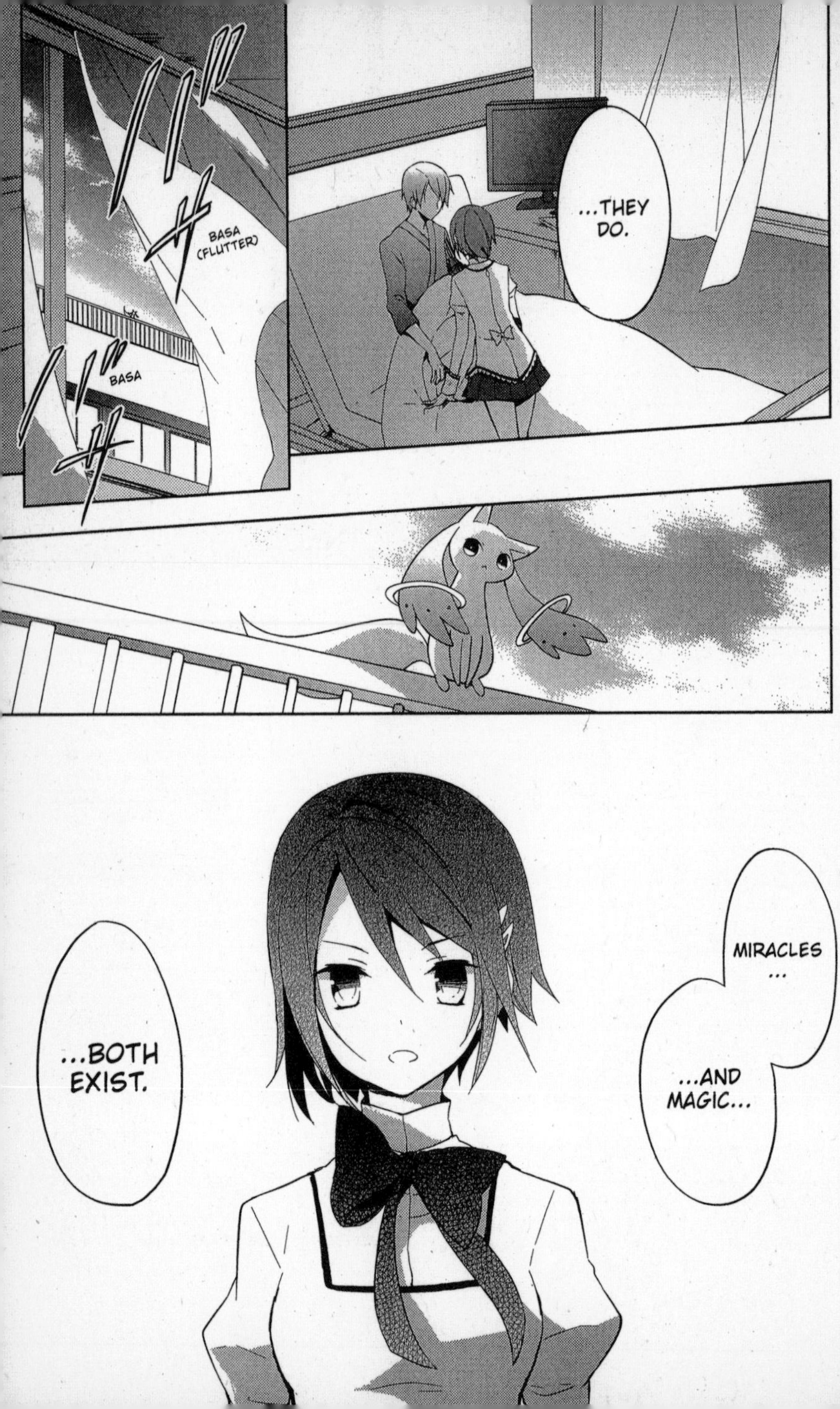
...THEY DO.
BASA (FLUTTER)
BASA
MIRACLES ...
...AND MAGIC...
...BOTH EXIST.

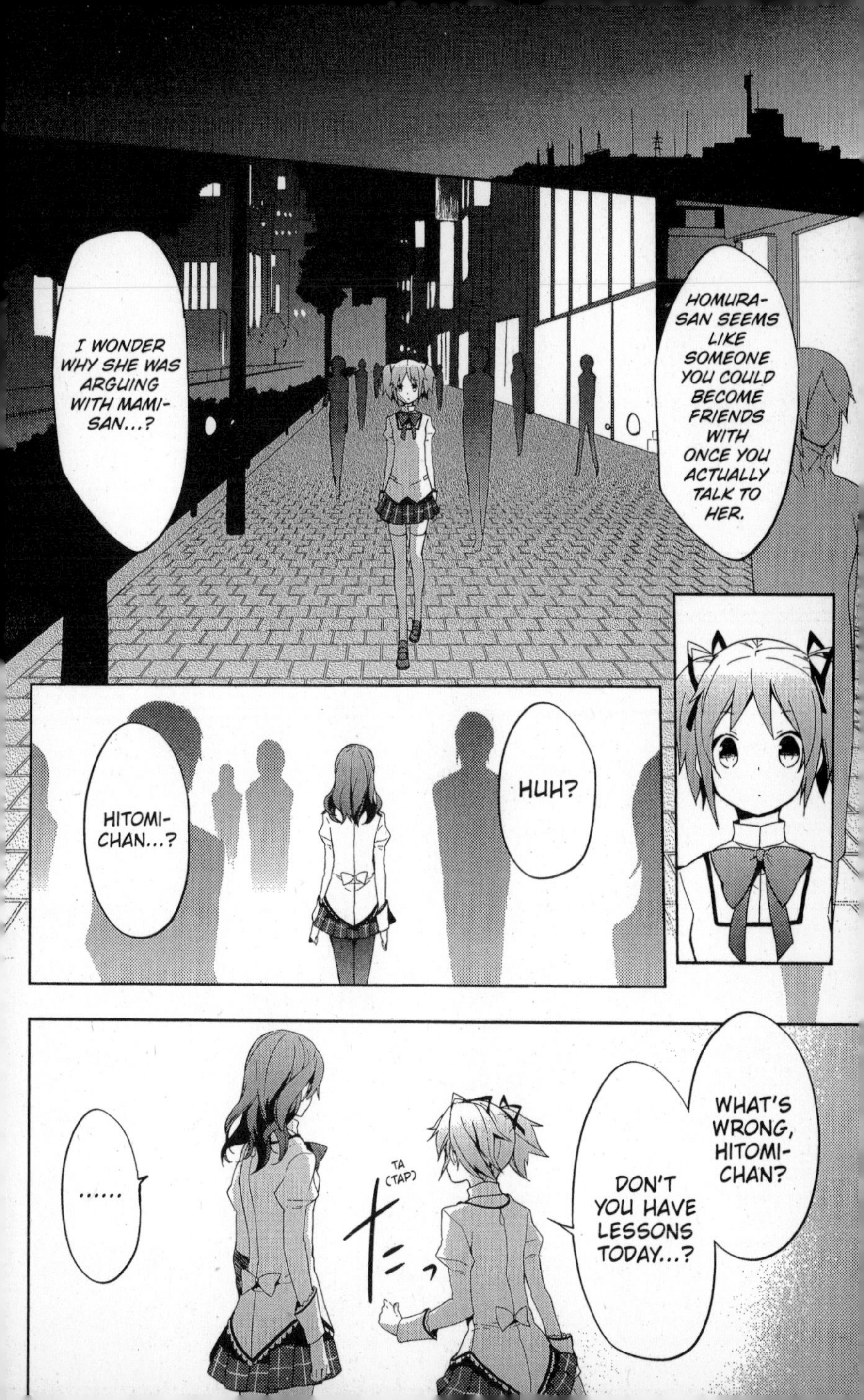
HOMURA-SAN SEEMS LIKE SOMEONE YOU COULD BECOME FRIENDS WITH ONCE YOU ACTUALLY TALK TO HER.
I WONDER WHY SHE WAS ARGUING WITH MAMI-SAN...?
HUH?
HITOMI-CHAN...?
WHAT'S WRONG, HITOMI-CHAN?
DON'T YOU HAVE LESSONS TODAY...?
TA (TAP)
......

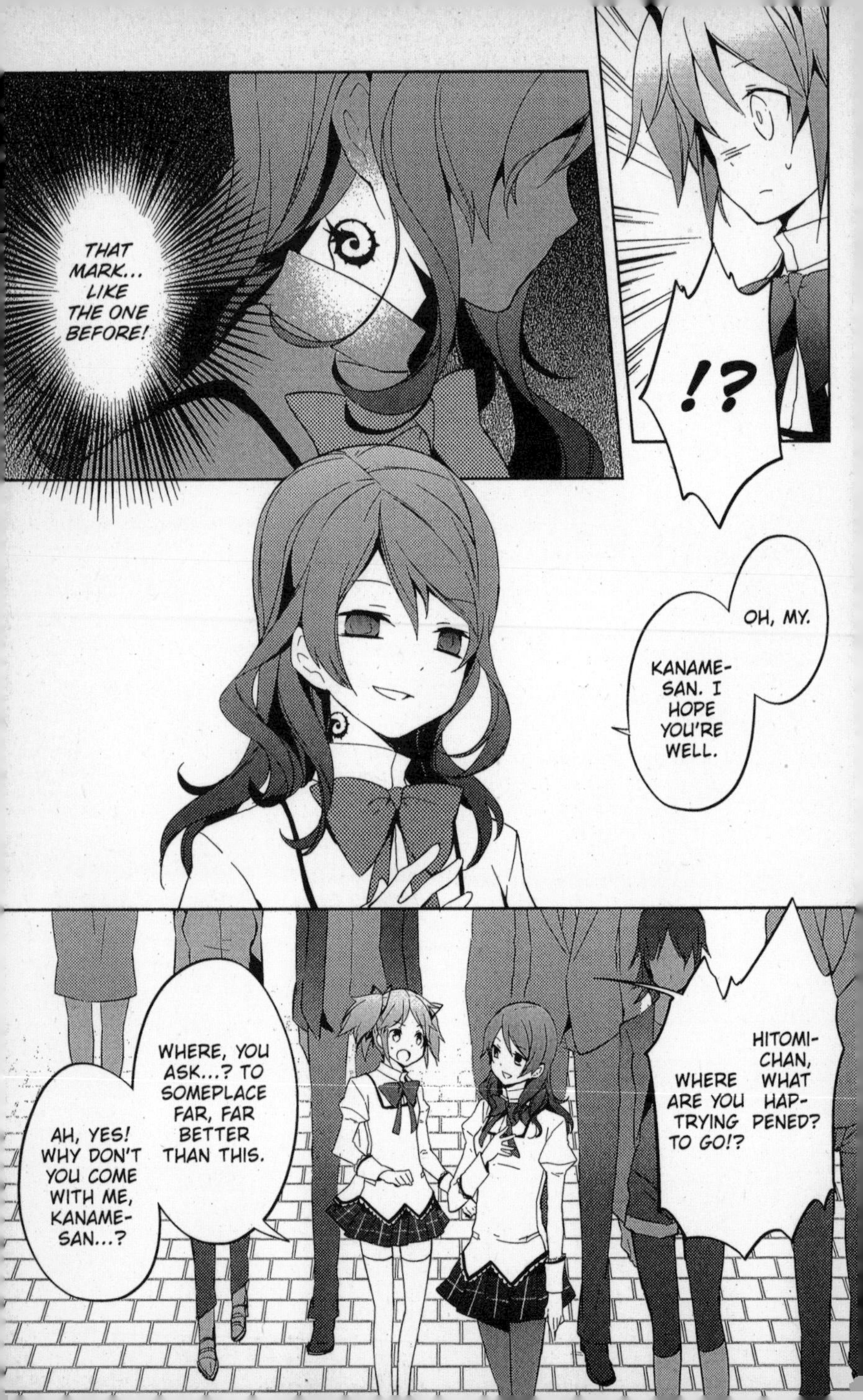
!?
THAT MARK... LIKE THE ONE BEFORE!
OH, MY.
KANAME-SAN. I HOPE YOU'RE WELL.
HITOMI-CHAN, WHAT HAP-PENED?
WHERE ARE YOU TRYING TO GO!?
WHERE, YOU ASK...? TO SOMEPLACE FAR, FAR BETTER THAN THIS.
AH, YES! WHY DON'T YOU COME WITH ME, KANAME-SAN...?

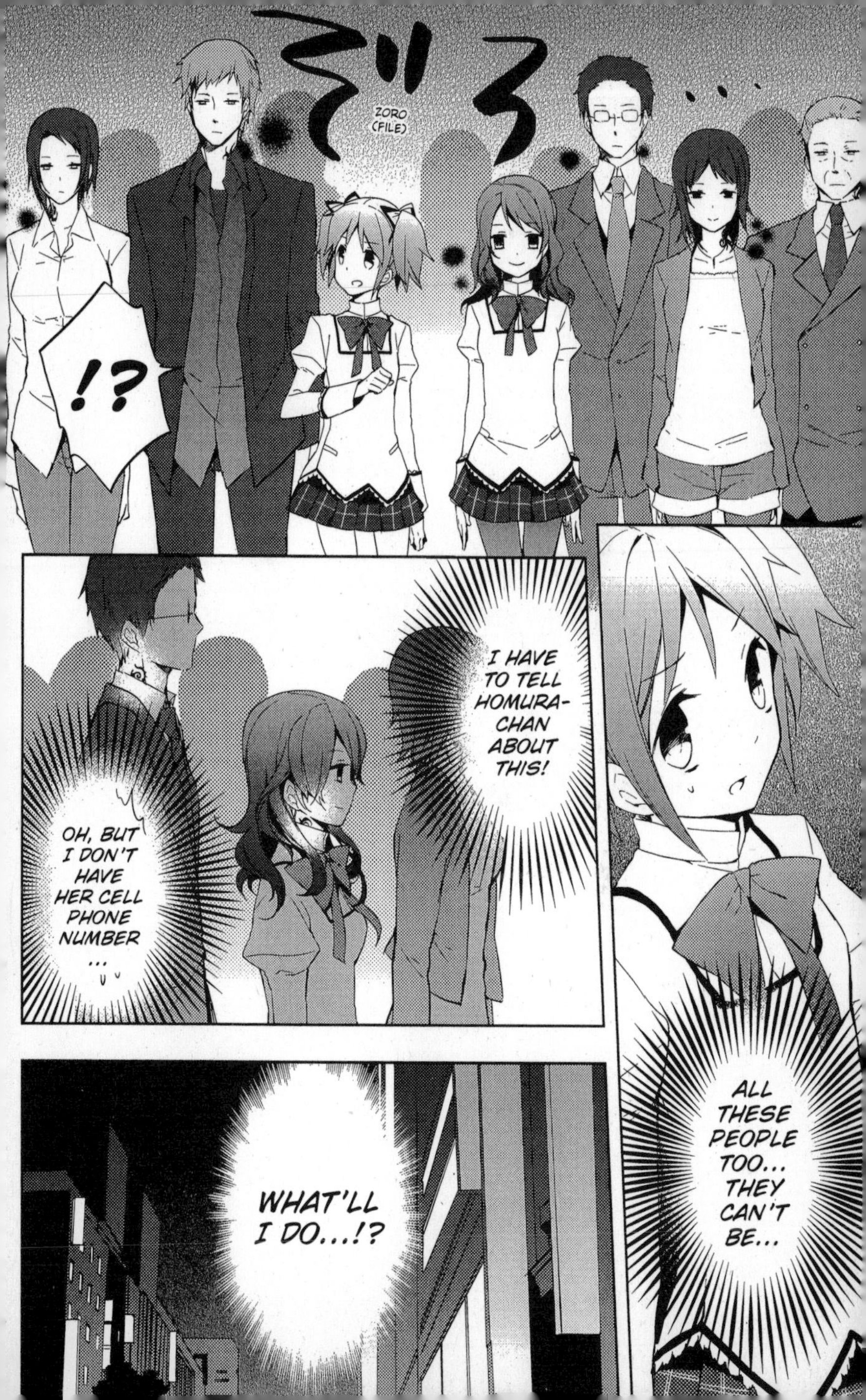
...
ぞろ
ZORO (FILE)
!?
ALL THESE PEOPLE TOO... THEY CAN'T BE...
I HAVE TO TELL HOMURA-CHAN ABOUT THIS!
OH, BUT I DON'T HAVE HER CELL PHONE NUMBER...
WHAT'LL I DO...!?

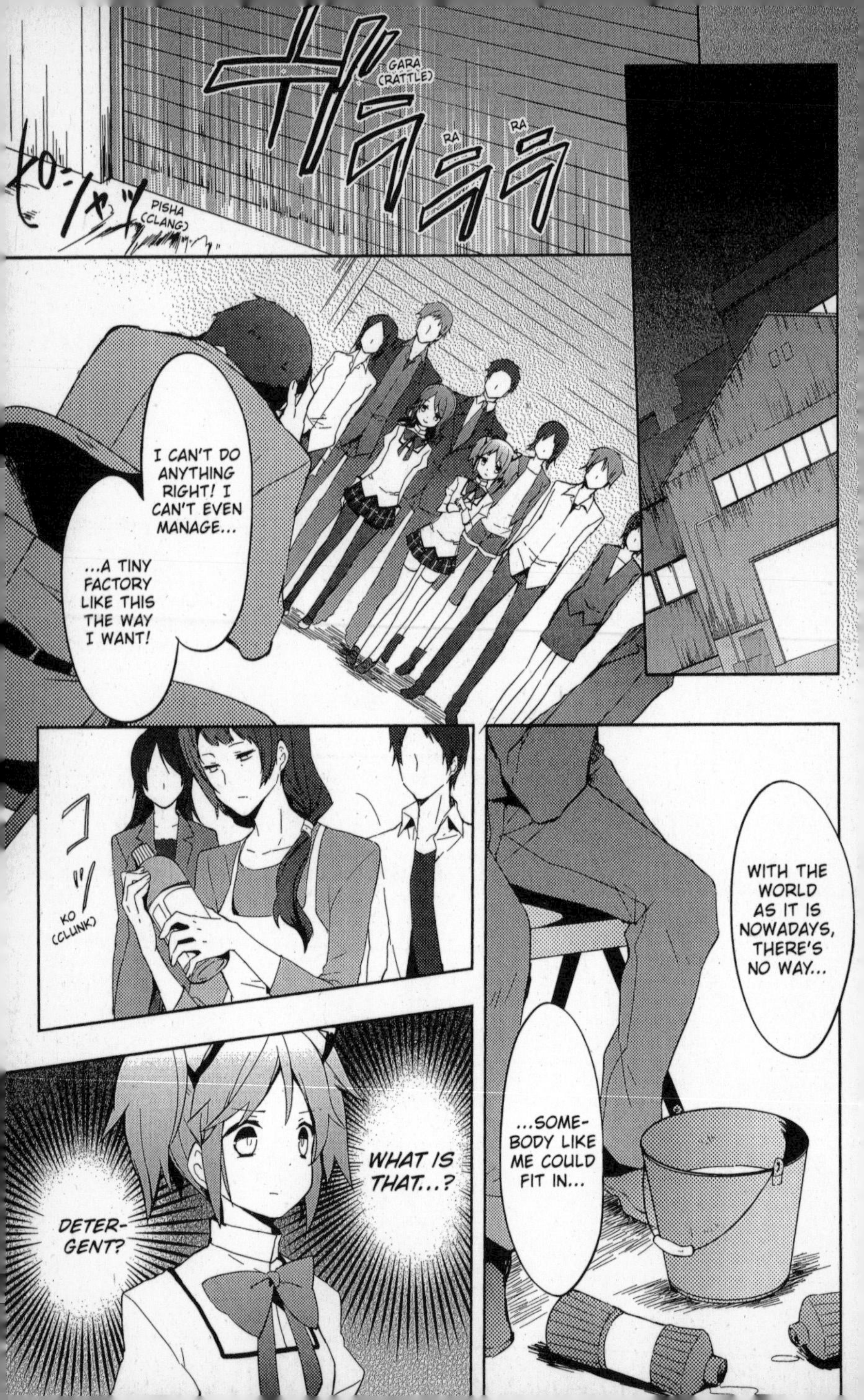
GARA (RATTLE)
RA
RA
PISHA (CLANG)
I CAN'T DO ANYTHING RIGHT! I CAN'T EVEN MANAGE...
...A TINY FACTORY LIKE THIS THE WAY I WANT!
WITH THE WORLD AS IT IS NOWADAYS, THERE'S NO WAY...
...SOME-BODY LIKE ME COULD FIT IN...
KO (CLUNK)
WHAT IS THAT...?
DETER-GENT?

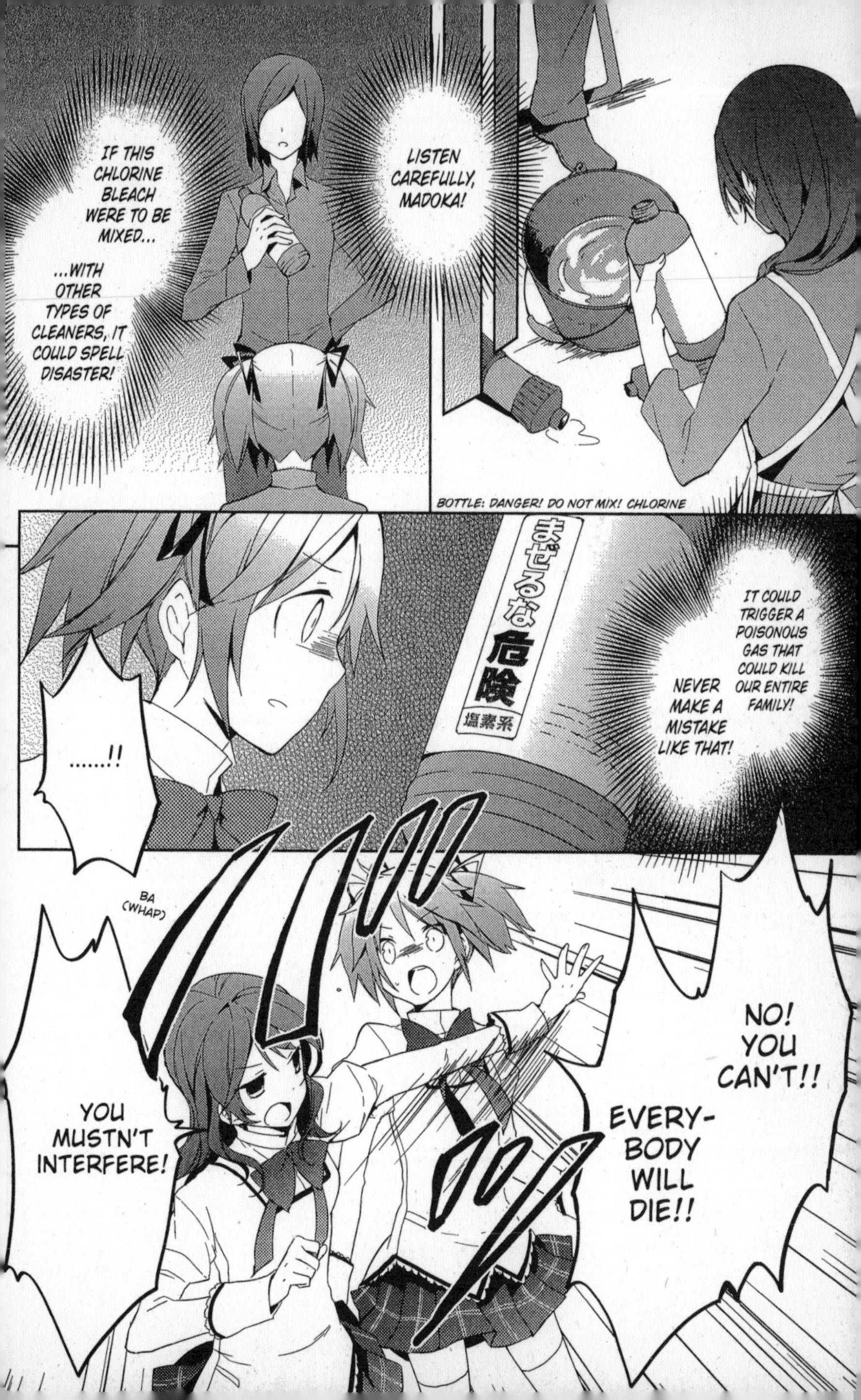
BOTTLE: DANGER! DO NOT MIX! CHLORINE
LISTEN CAREFULLY, MADOKA!
IF THIS CHLORINE BLEACH WERE TO BE MIXED...
...WITH OTHER TYPES OF CLEANERS, IT COULD SPELL DISASTER!
まぜるな 危険
塩素系
IT COULD TRIGGER A POISONOUS GAS THAT COULD KILL OUR ENTIRE FAMILY!
NEVER MAKE A MISTAKE LIKE THAT!
......!!
NO! YOU CAN'T!!
EVERY-BODY WILL DIE!!
BA (WHAP)
YOU MUSTN'T INTERFERE!

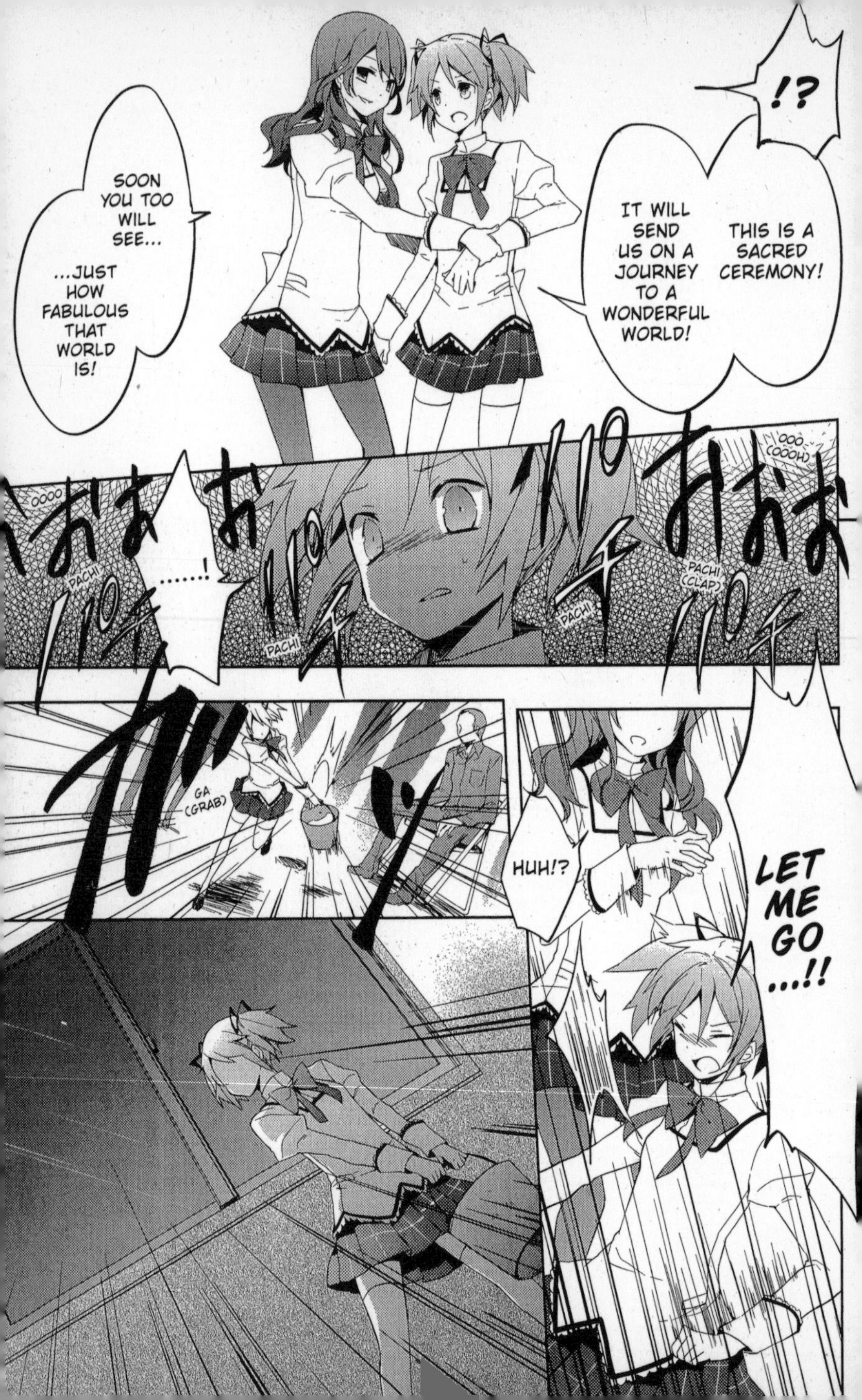
!?
THIS IS A SACRED CEREMONY!
IT WILL SEND US ON A JOURNEY TO A WONDERFUL WORLD!
SOON YOU TOO WILL SEE...
...JUST HOW FABULOUS THAT WORLD IS!
OOO- (OOOH)
PACHI (CLAP)
PACHI
PACHI
PACHI
OOOO
......!
LET ME GO ...!!
HUH!?
GA (GRAB)

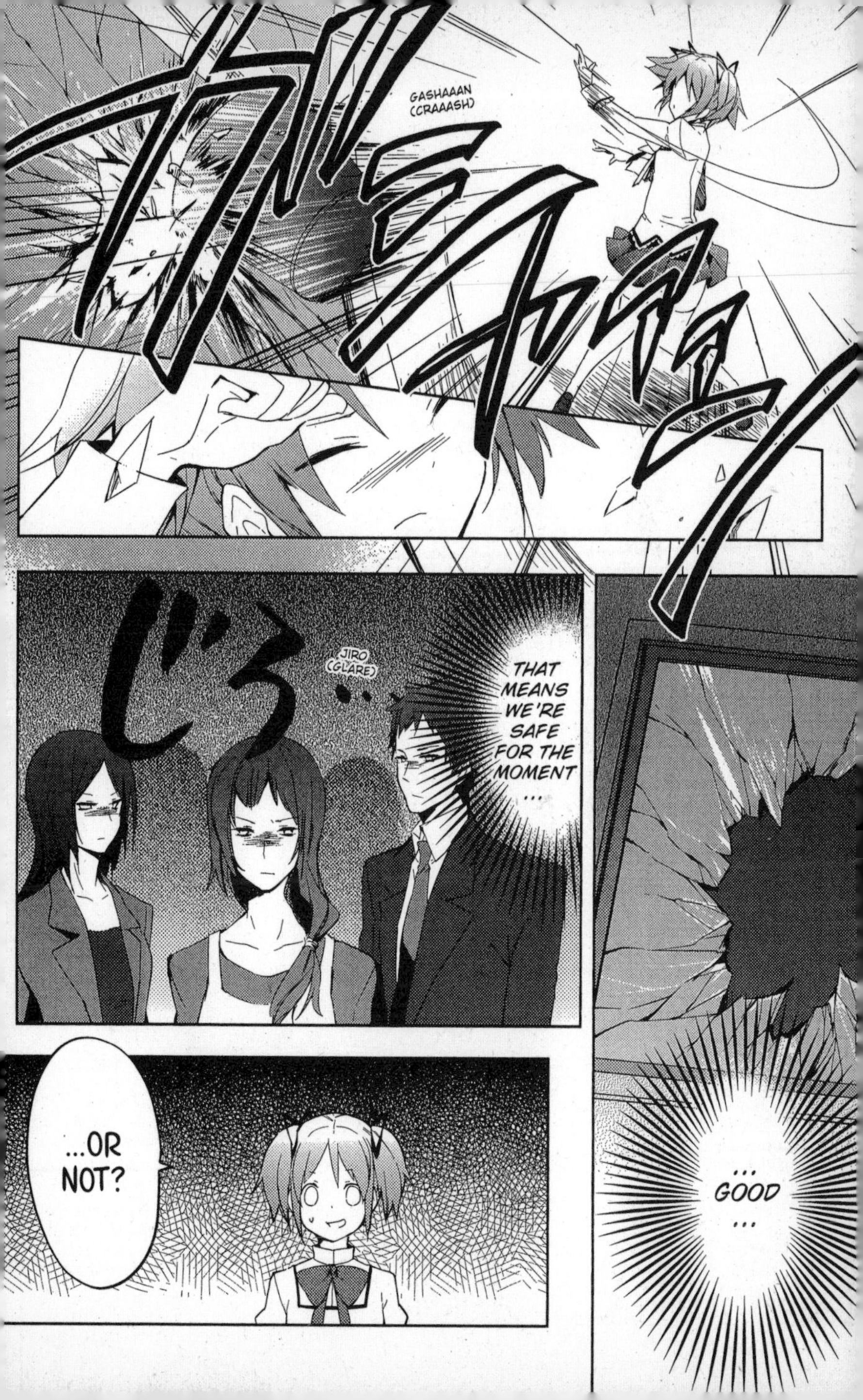
GASHAAAN (CRAAASH)
...GOOD...
JIRO (GLARE)
THAT MEANS WE'RE SAFE FOR THE MOMENT...
...OR NOT?

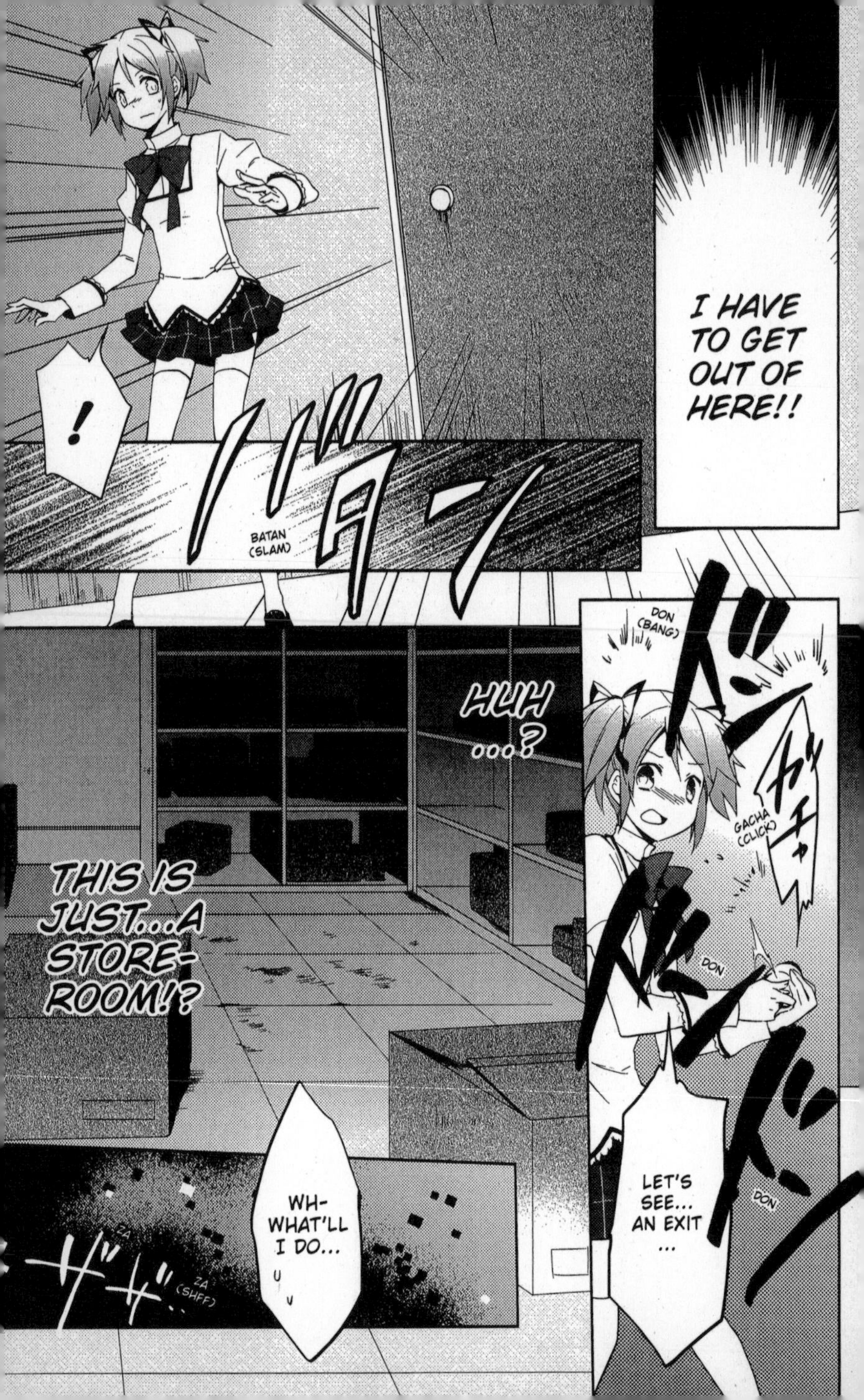
I HAVE TO GET OUT OF HERE!!
!
BATAN (SLAM)
DON (BANG)
GACHA (CLICK)
DON
DON
LET'S SEE... AN EXIT ...
HUH ...?
THIS IS JUST...A STORE-ROOM!?
WH-WHAT'LL I DO...
ZA
ZA (SHFF)

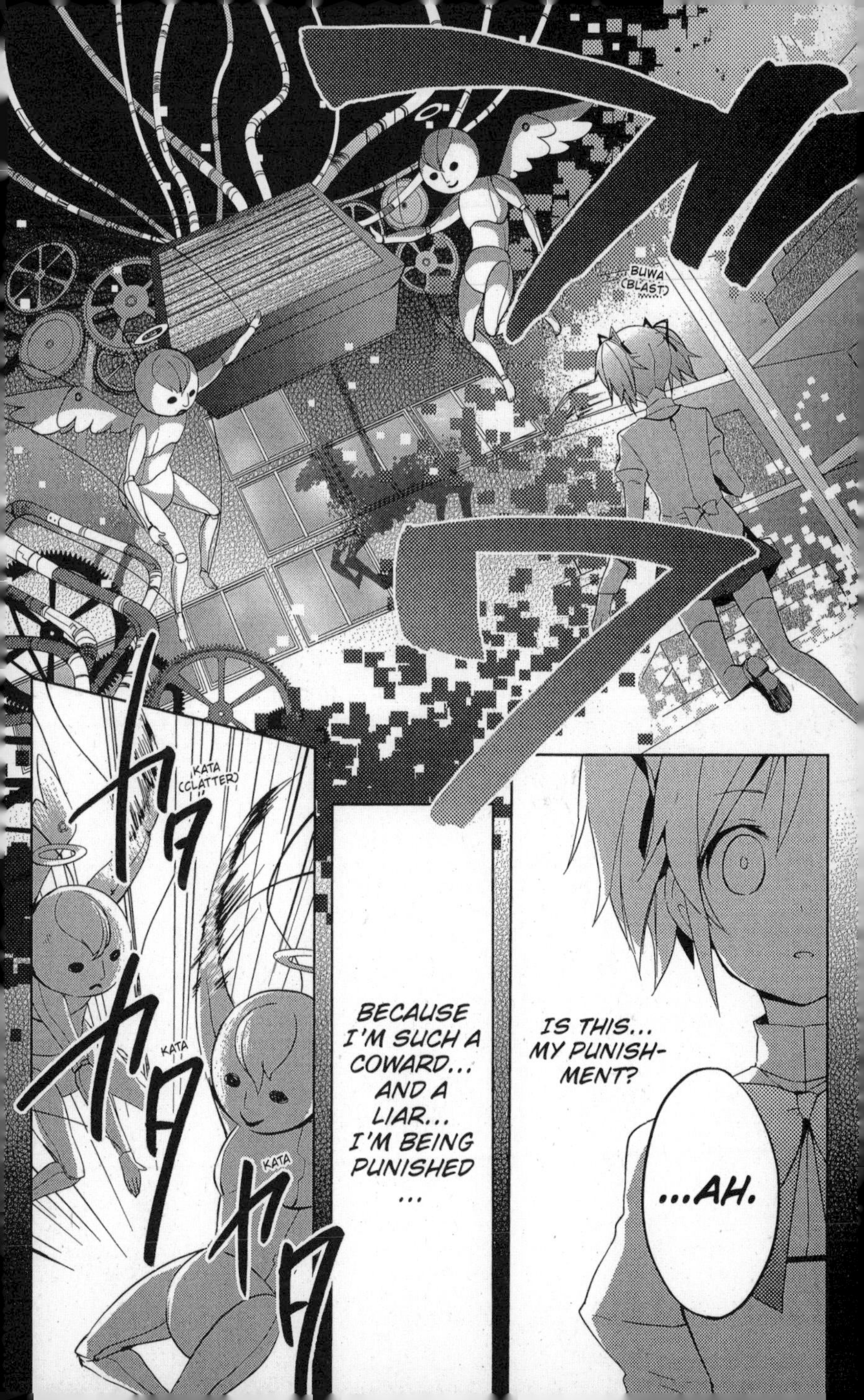
BUWA (BLAST)
IS THIS... MY PUNISHMENT?
...AH.
BECAUSE I'M SUCH A COWARD... AND A LIAR... I'M BEING PUNISHED ...
KATA (CLATTER)
KATA
KATA

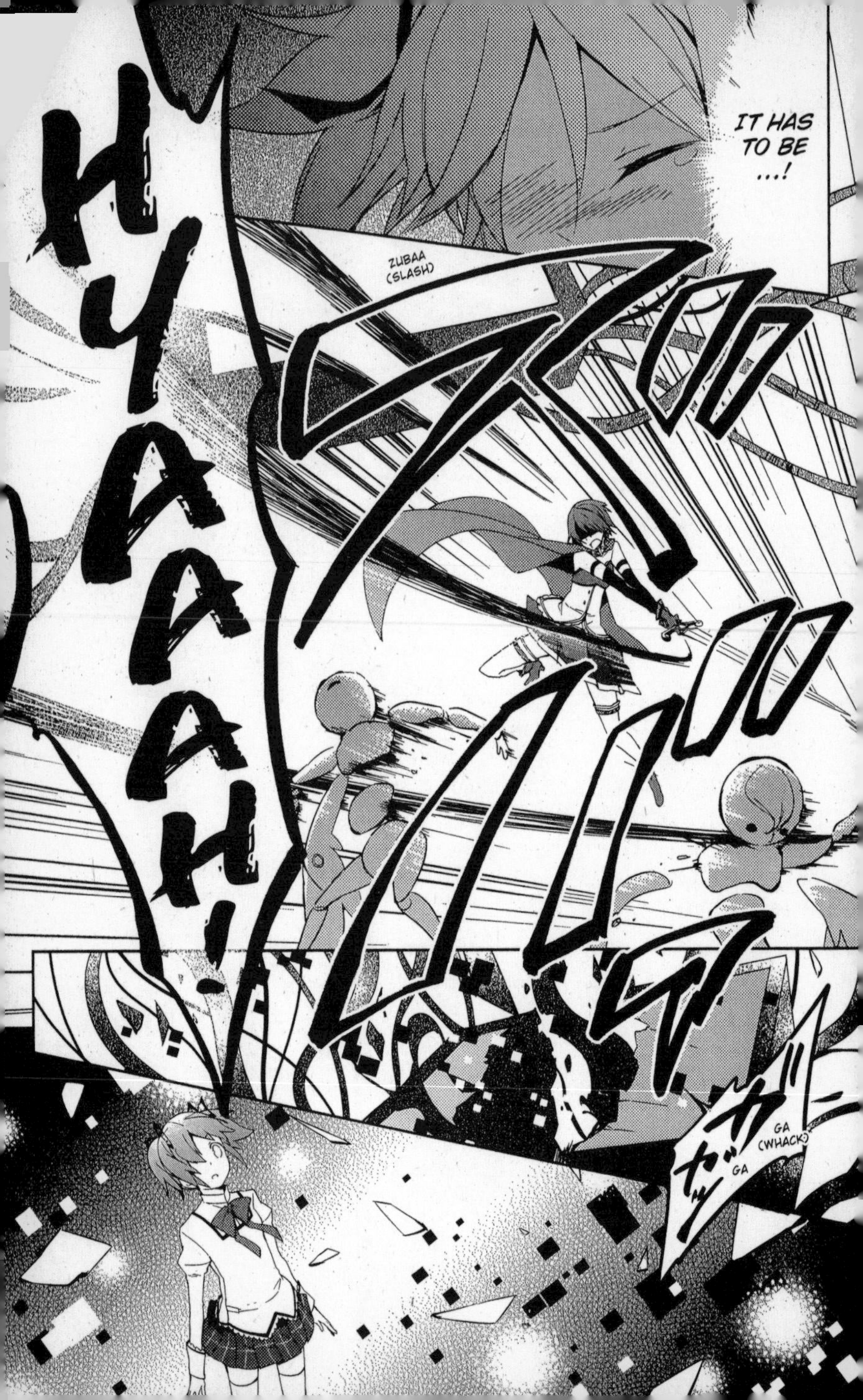
IT HAS TO BE ...!
ZUBAA (SLASH)
HYAAAH!
GA (WHACK)
GA

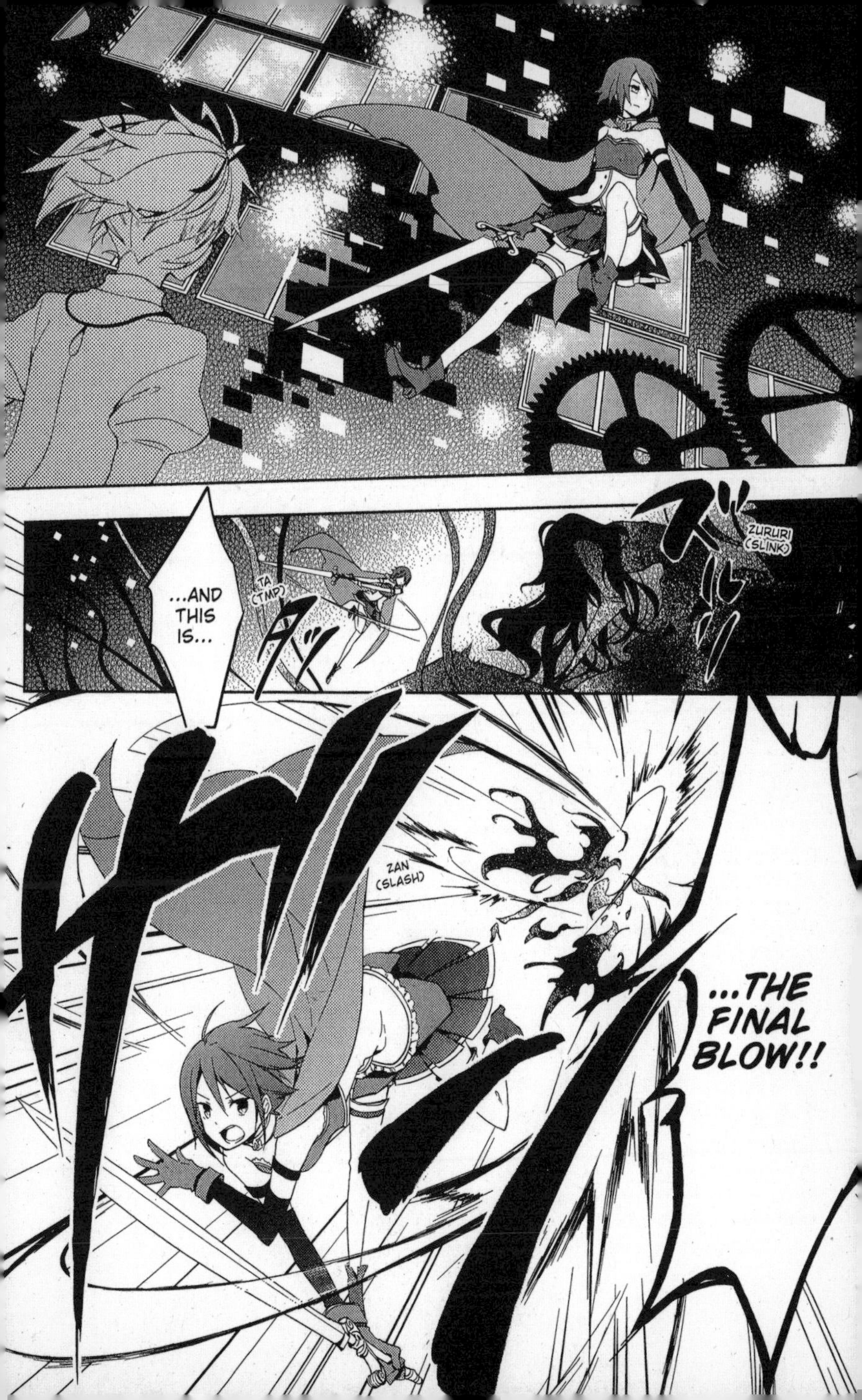
ZURURI (SLINK)
TA (TMP)
...AND THIS IS...
ZAN (SLASH)
...THE FINAL BLOW!!

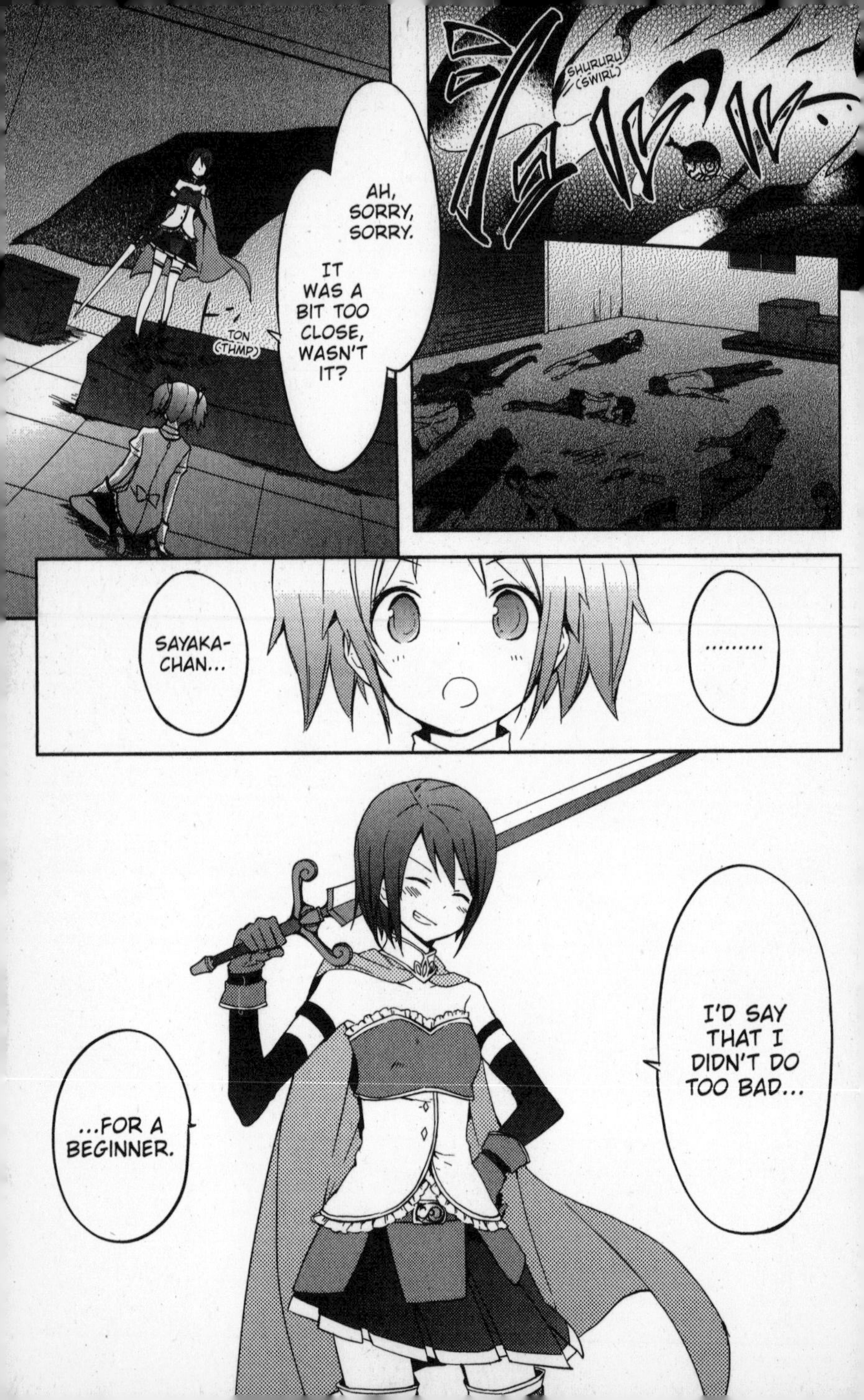
SHURURU (SWIRL)
AH, SORRY, SORRY.
IT WAS A BIT TOO CLOSE, WASN'T IT?
TON (THMP)
....
SAYAKA-CHAN...
I'D SAY THAT I DIDN'T DO TOO BAD...
...FOR A BEGINNER.

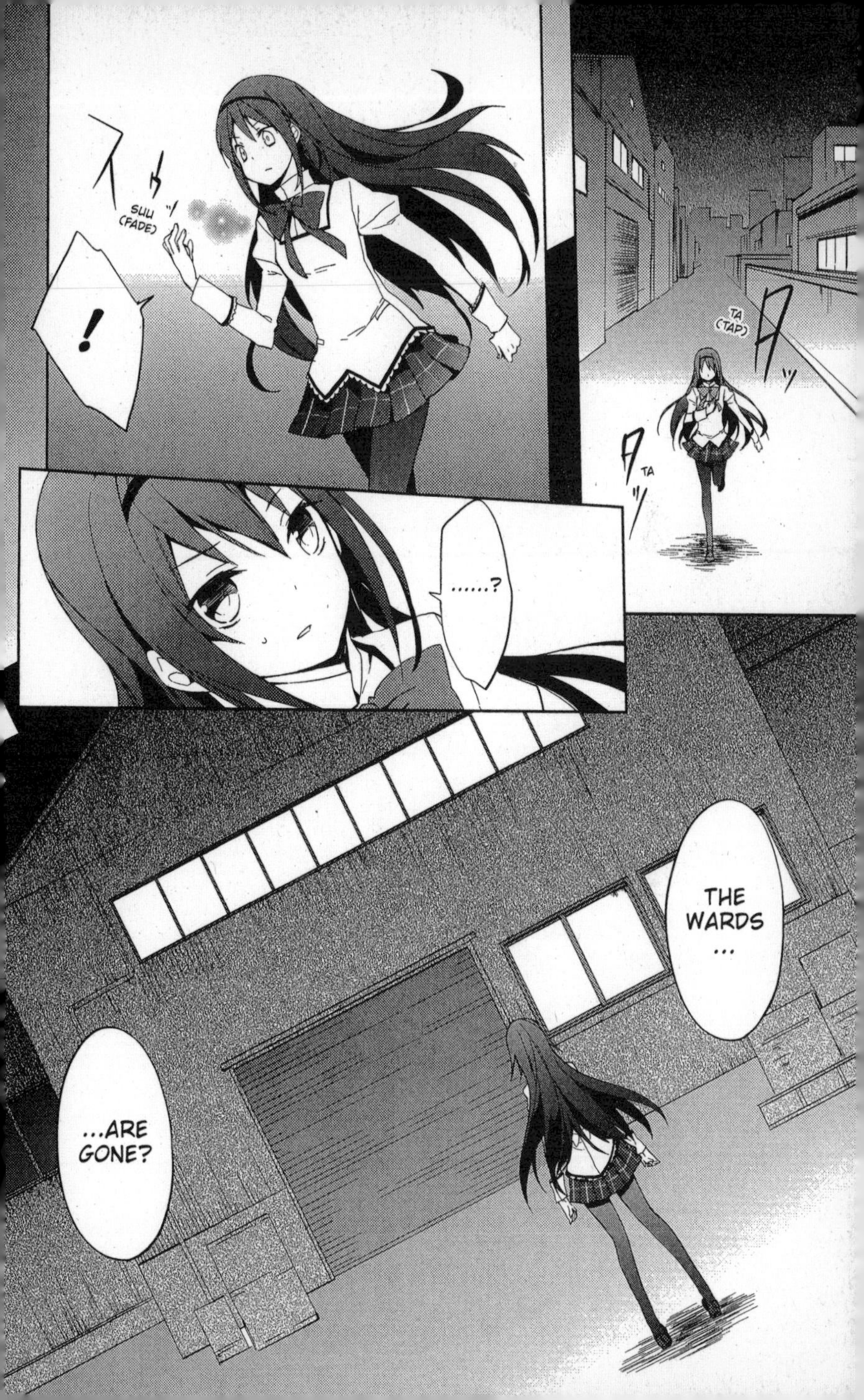
TA (TAP)
TA
SUU (FADE)
!
......?
THE WARDS ...
...ARE GONE?

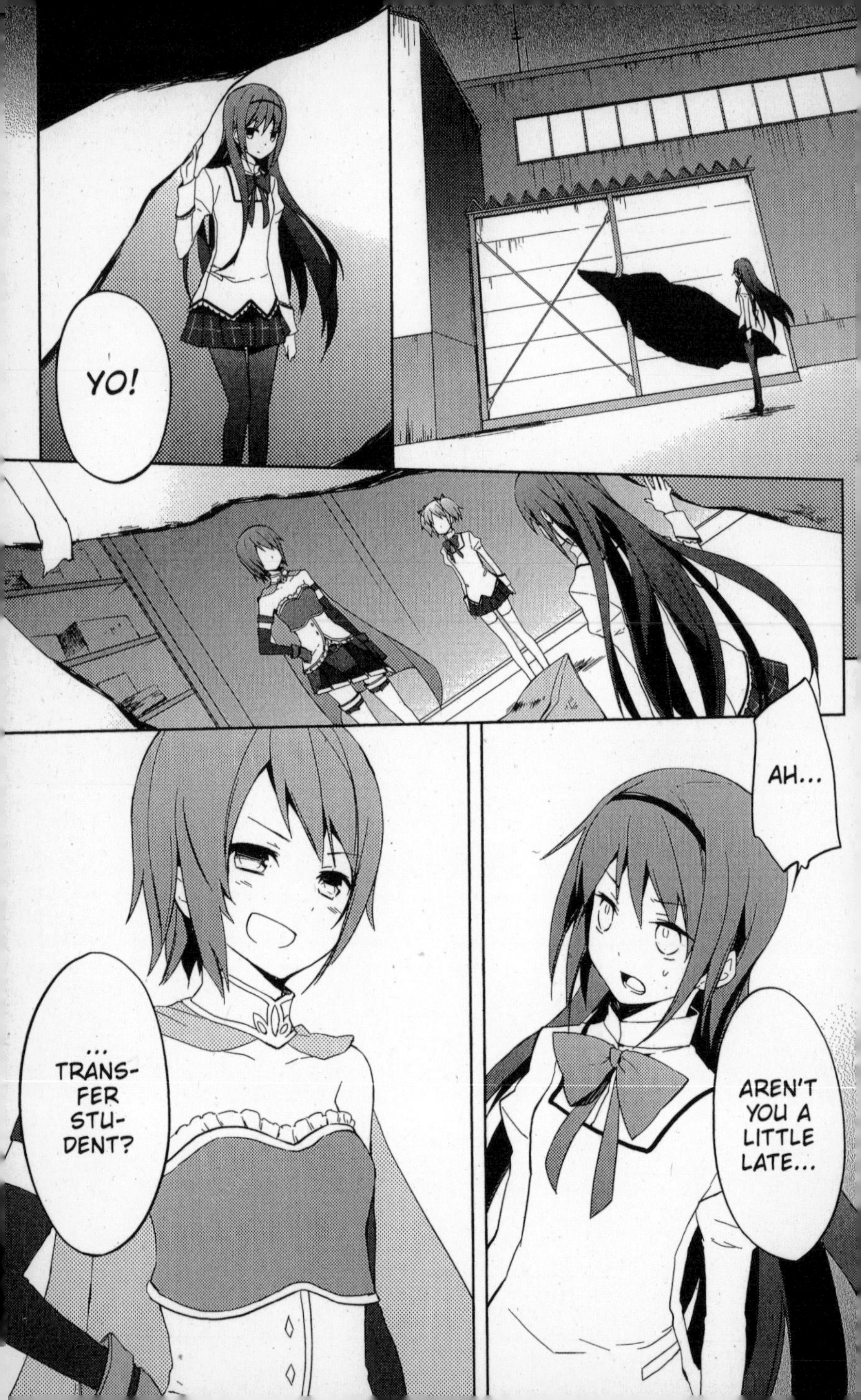
YO!
AH...
AREN'T YOU A LITTLE LATE...
... TRANS-FER STU-DENT?

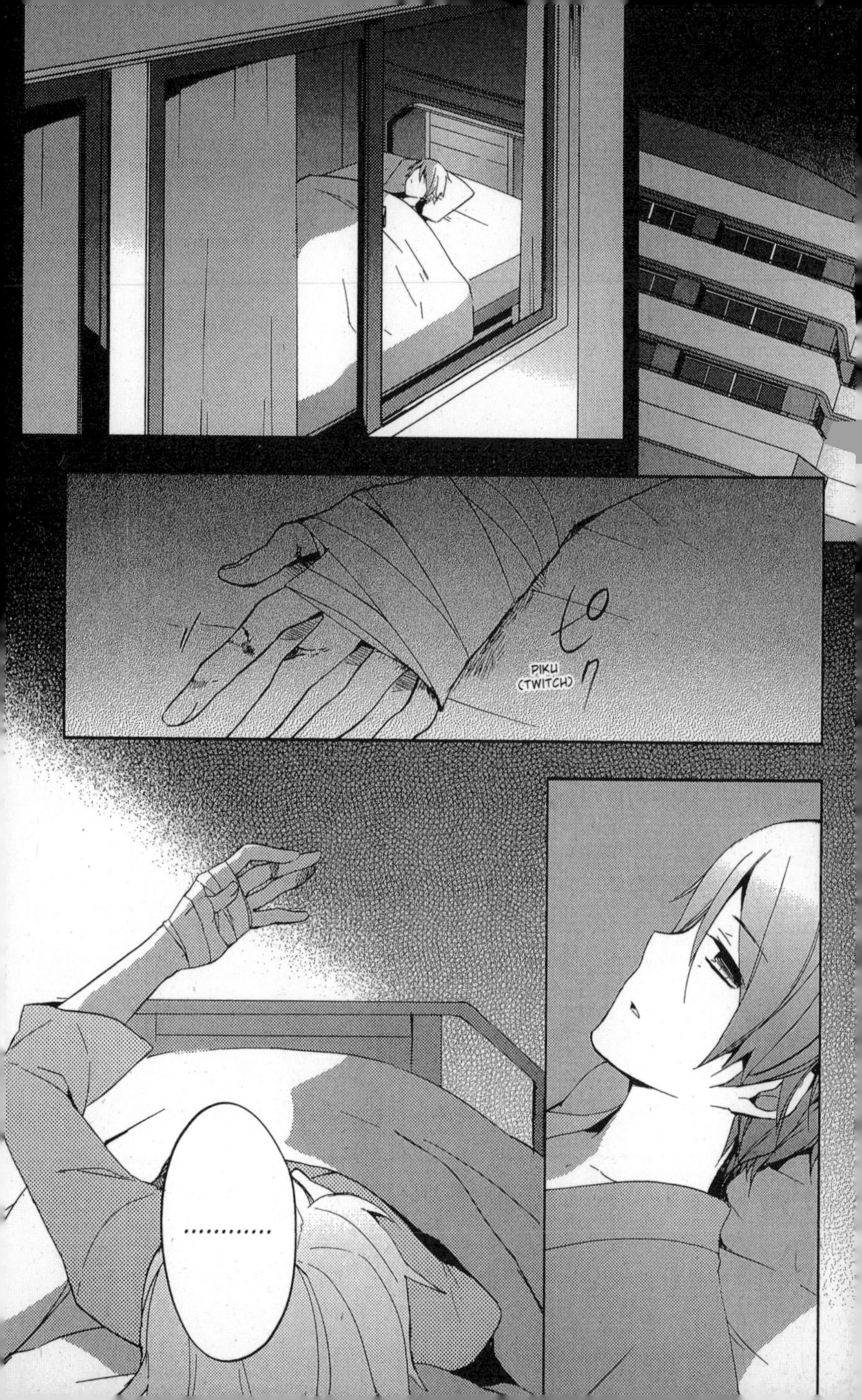
PIKU (TWITCH)
....

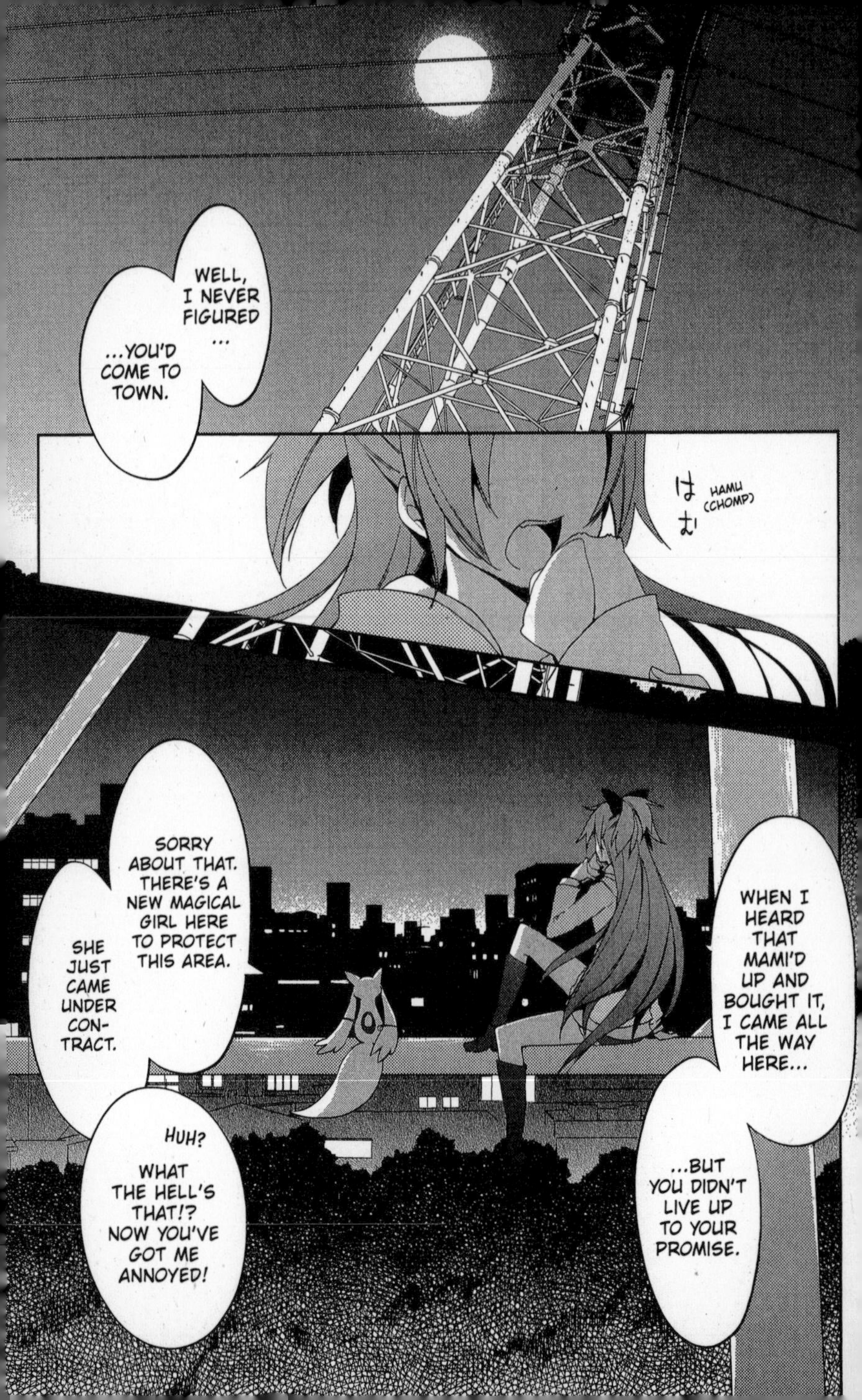
WELL, I NEVER FIGURED...
...YOU'D COME TO TOWN.
はむ
HAMU (CHOMP)
WHEN I HEARD THAT MAMI'D UP AND BOUGHT IT, I CAME ALL THE WAY HERE...
...BUT YOU DIDN'T LIVE UP TO YOUR PROMISE.
SORRY ABOUT THAT. THERE'S A NEW MAGICAL GIRL HERE TO PROTECT THIS AREA.
SHE JUST CAME UNDER CON-TRACT.
HUH?
WHAT THE HELL'S THAT!? NOW YOU'VE GOT ME ANNOYED!

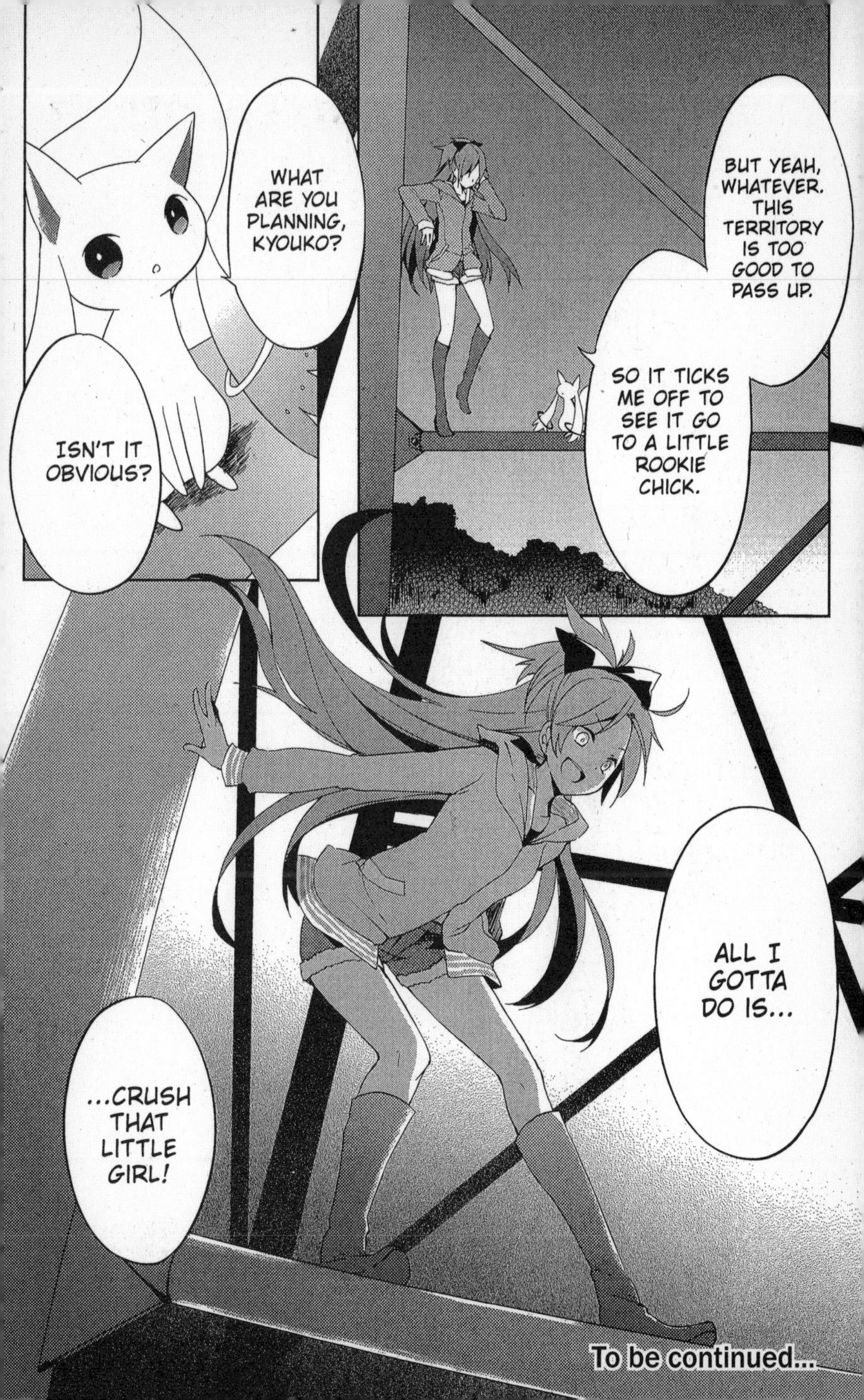
BUT YEAH, WHATEVER. THIS TERRITORY IS TOO GOOD TO PASS UP.
SO IT TICKS ME OFF TO SEE IT GO TO A LITTLE ROOKIE CHICK.
WHAT ARE YOU PLANNING, KYOUKO?
ISN'T IT OBVIOUS?
ALL I GOTTA DO IS...
...CRUSH THAT LITTLE GIRL!
To be continued...

☆ AFTERWORD ☆

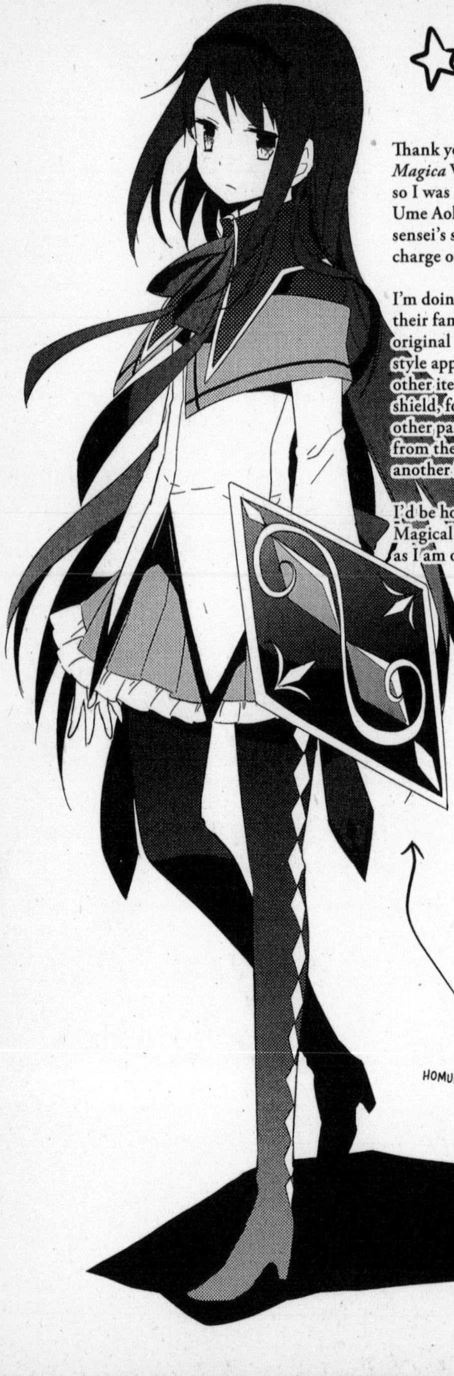

Thank you so much for picking up *Puella Magi Madoka Magica* Volume 1! This is the first book I've ever done, so I was so excited and nervous about it. It combines Ume Aoki-sensei's cute characters with Gen Urobuchi-sensei's solid writing, so when I was told that I'd be in charge of making the manga, I was so incredibly happy.

I'm doing my best to base my portrayal of the Witches, their familiars, and the world within the wards on the original work by Gekidan Inu Curry and draw it in a style appropriate for manga. There are some weapons and other items that I was the designer on. (Such as Homura's shield, for example...) Not just the designs—there are other parts of the manga that will be a little different from the anime too, but if you simply think of this as another form of "Madoka," then it'll make me happy.

I'd be honored if you'd welcome the new Magical Girl, Kyouko, and get as excited as I am over the events in Volume 2!

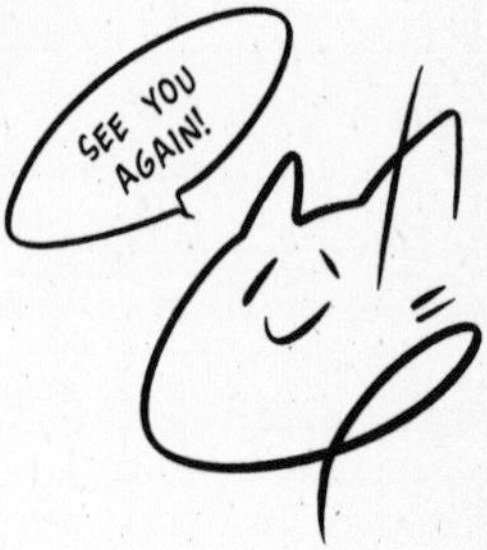
SEE YOU AGAIN!

THIS IS THE FULL VIEW OF THE SHIELD THAT HARDLY EVEN MADE AN APPEARANCE IN THE MANGA PAGES. (SORRY!)

HOMURA-CHAN IS SO CUTE. I WANT TO BE PICKED ON BY HER!

PUELLA MAGI
MADOKA☆MAGICA ❶

MAGICA QUARTET
HANOKAGE

Translation: William Flanagan • Lettering: Alexis Eckerman

MAHO SHOJO MADOKA ☆ MAGICA vol.1
© 2011 Magica Quartet / Aniplex · Madoka Partners · MBS. All rights reserved. First published in Japan in 2011 by HOUBUNSHA CO., LTD, Tokyo. English translation rights in United States, Canada and United Kingdom arranged with HOUBUNSHA CO., LTD. through Tuttle-Mori Agency, Inc., Tokyo.

Translation © 2012 by Hachette Book Group, Inc.

Yen Press
Hachette Book Group
237 Park Avenue, New York, NY 10017

www.HachetteBookGroup.com
www.YenPress.com

Yen Press is an imprint of Hachette Book Group, Inc. The Yen Press name and logo are trademarks of Hachette Book Group, Inc.

First Yen Press Edition: May 2012

ISBN: 978-0-316-21387-5

10 9 8 7 6

BVG

Printed in the United States of America